DATE DUE

Demco, Inc. 38-293

Out of the Present Crisis

Rediscovering Improvement in the New Economy

improving hospital operations based on a deep understanding of the present dilemmas facing our healthcare environment. The author's practical guidance about how to implement major improvement initiatives successfully is the rudder needed to change the course of this colossal industry, preventing it from running aground."

James (Jay) Varrone MBA
Director of Materials
Norwalk Hospital

"This book contains a wealth of common sense and practical advice about improvement backed up by decades of real world experiences about what truly makes a difference in your business. It also provides an instructive and provocative analysis of how globalization, innovation, and technology are all reshaping the urgent need to discover new approaches and sources of improvement in all industries."

Michael Anthony
Executive Vice President
Cambridge Semantics

"Every now and then an author gets it right, hitting the right target at the right time with the firepower to actually get the job done. I found this book to be a refreshing, optimistic look at an old, festering, solution-resisting problem, and the author presents a feasible solution, Lean Six Sigma, and continuous improvement in general, in a comprehensive and succinct call for action. This book provides an abundance of proven knowledge about how progress and improvement can actually be made, and that is remarkable in our time of rhetoric and paralyzed decision-making. Burton's book shows a new path, and it is well worth walking down it to find good answers. Those are hard to find today."

Alexis N. Sommers, Ph.D.
Professor of Industrial Engineering
University of New Haven

…'Out of the Present Crisis: Rediscovering Improvement in the New Economy' *is a perfect title for Burton's new book. Reading the book was like eating dinner at a five-star restaurant. After consuming the Preface as my appetizer, I then feasted on the next few chapters. I was blown away with how this book has correctly and succinctly described what I and others have also observed and experienced regarding the state of continuous improvement in the Western World's business and leadership ranks. The author has created a practical and realistic line of scenarios, approaches, and deployment methods to help a business stabilize, reestablish, and then accelerate improvement across the enterprise. The dessert course of* his new book is the author's next generation of improvement, improving how we improve, and how to avoid the stages of insanity and hyperinsanity through the continuous leadership development process of reckoning, renewal, and enlightenment. Like Chinese food for many people, I was hungry for more after about an hour."

Don A. Blake
Director of Quality and Site Services
North Carolina Business Unit
Spirit AeroSystems, Inc.

"Having spent a career focusing on process improvement, this book provides a wealth of proven and poignant advice as well as real world examples of what works in helping organizations continually improve all aspects of their business. Continuous improvement is one of the major strategic enablers for any company to achieve sustainable success, and this book helps provide solid, practical guidance . . . especially in this challenging economy and beyond."

Eric Lussier, P.E.
Vice President, Operational Excellence
Handy & Harman Ltd.

"Hospitals today have to be as focused on the business of operational improvement as on the business of saving lives. With so many resources devoted to protecting the bottom line, an organizationwide, systematic approach to improvement is imperative. This book outlines an adaptable, executive-led approach to imbedding Lean Six Sigma throughout all organizations for sustainable, silo-free improvement."

LeeMichael McLean
Six Sigma Green Belt
Director, Business Development and Networks
VHA New England

"In this timely guidebook for all industries, Burton emphatically reminds us that the need for improvement never goes away, and he spotlights the importance of enlightened leadership and behavioral alignment in achieving real cultural change. Read it, and benefit from a profusion of real world advice."

Joseph F. Geary
Executive Vice President
Sciessent

"Having spent years in manufacturing I understand all too well the transformations that need to take place in America. The author's discussions about the *higher moral purpose of improvement make one realize that everyone has a large stake in improving our organizations, the quality of society in general, America's competitive global position, and the quality of life for future generations."*

Wayne Pearson
Supply Chain Manager
GT Solar, Inc.

"Full of practical advice, experiences, and real world examples, this book presents a great understanding of sustainable business improvement. It also provides an enlightening analysis of how globalization, technology, and market forces across different industries are driving the need to adapt a different focus and approach to strategic improvement. The Improvement Excellence™ framework and other directions presented in the book provide a comprehensive roadmap for responding to those trends and ensuring the ongoing delivery of stakeholder value."

K. Joanne Kalp
Vice President, Product Management
Draeger Monitoring Systems and IT Solutions

"Mr. Burton's latest book updates Deming's famous 1982 book, Out of the Crisis, *for the 21st century business leader by integrating Lean Six Sigma innovation, enabling technologies, and a healthy dose of common sense with Deming's back-to-basics approach. Those readers seeking to rediscover improvement as an integral part of a successful business strategy will find that* Out of the Present Crisis: Rediscovering Improvement in the New Economy *provides an easy-to-follow roadmap that ensures their improvement efforts translate into operational and strategic achievement."*

Hermann Miskelly
Vice President of Quality
Matheson Tri-Gas, Inc.

"I am inspired by Terry's passion and unswerving commitment to advancing the art and science of sustainable performance improvement. His new book convincingly describes how Lean Six Sigma methods can achieve breakthrough process and cultural transformations in healthcare delivery. Terry 'gets it right' regarding the importance of strategically aligning improvement work, the critical role of hospital leadership in improvement, and the all-important engagement of physicians and healthcare employees."

Dave Gronewold, MS, MBA
Certified Master Black Belt
Global Director, Customer Excellence
Covidien

"The competitive landscape has changed significantly within the medical device industry. Emerging markets and technologies have brought increased pricing pressures on Hospitals, OEMs, and Healthcare providers. The author provides a practical and concise approach in utilizing Lean Six Sigma tools and methodologies in transforming business leaders to be more competitive in the global healthcare industry marketplace."

David Delmonico
Director, Global Sourcing
Smiths Medical, Inc.

"Full of practical advice, experiences, and real world examples, this book presents a great understanding of business improvement. While grounded in experience the advice is geared to the dynamics of today's economy, and includes a valuable discussion of the enabling capability of new technologies on strategic improvement initiatives."

Tim Andreae
Senior Vice President, Global Marketing
MCA Solutions

"Spreading the skills necessary to drive strategic improvement will be the most important component of a new, more value-oriented healthcare system. This book gives healthcare leaders the insight into this most critical role."

Robert G. Norton
President
Partners–North Shore Medical Center

"The rapid deployment and rapid results approaches of improvement resonate well with executives faced with the challenges of global uncertainty and not interested in another corporate train-the-masses program. This is exactly the approach SAP is taking with Rapid Deployment Solutions packages that contain preconfigured applications and productized services for accelerated time to value."

Martin Mrugal
Senior Vice President
Manufacturing Industries & Solutions
SAP AG

"The role of the CIO in organizations today is a critical, complex, and dynamic role. The chapter on the role of technology provides a significant perspective on how companies can really leverage the role and overall IT function in creating

breakthroughs in improvement and value that will in turn provide a strategic differentiation in the marketplace. This book is a must read for all levels within an organization."

Peter Girgis
Vice President, Information Technology
Visio, Inc.

"Having worked with the author on many Lean Six Sigma projects within our business, his passion for continuous improvement is infectious and flows throughout this book, becoming quite hard hitting and direct at times, and reinforcing the view that a continuous improvement culture should not be considered a mere 'option.' As business leaders, our world is changing more than ever before and we are facing tougher challenges. This book provides an up-to-date set of tools to help us become better leaders, improve the way we improve our businesses, and to ultimately not just survive—but excel and win."

Andy Trott
Vice President and General Manager
Mixing, Microphones and Headset (MM&H) SBU
Harman International Industries, Inc.

"Terry's passion shines through in his emphasis on the higher moral purpose of improvement. It creates a sense of personal ownership in improving organizations, the broader quality of society in general, America's role as a global leader, and the quality of life for our future generations."

Jeff Sams
Vice President, Quality & Lean Systems
Sequa Automotive Group

"This book will serve as a map during the adventurous quest for 'best in class.' I couldn't recommend a more effective partner than the author—and this book— as a supremely effective guide for the successful 'change warrior' to compete in this 21st century."

Michael L. Goldman, CPC
President & Founder, Strategic Associates, Inc.
Past President and Lifetime Honorary Member, The Pinnacle Society

"This book provides the inspiration and direction for rediscovering improvement while integrating technology as a major enabler to strategic and operating

success. Follow the step-by-step advice in this book and your organization will put the word continuous back into continuous improvement."

Phil Pegg
Vice President, Business Management Office
North America Marketing
SAP

"This book provides a simplified process of implementing continuous improvement for real, which is much needed in this economy. The author demonstrates the importance of laser targeting the larger global improvement opportunities, and how rapid improvement is essential to building a nimble culture and staying on track with continuous improvement."

Jim Hardiman
Vice President, Engineering
The AVC Group

"I enjoyed this book . . it provides a fresh look at improvement in the new economy, and thoroughly addresses the leadership, strategy, sustainable infrastructure, and other critical success factors that actually create the cultural standard of excellence, and the solid foundation for successful continuous improvement. An outstanding reference on improvement!"

Stephen A. McCusker
Sr. Director, Global Supply Chain & Consumables Engineering
Gen-Probe, Inc.

"The author provides a thoughtful and reasonable approach to applying improvement techniques to federal, state, and local governments, and other not-for-profit organizations. In addition to its social and political components, government also possesses economic and process components that are too often overlooked but that must be improved by applying sound business techniques."

Erik M. Filipiak, PhD
Theodore J. Eismeier Fellow in Political Science
The Alexander Hamilton Institute

"Improving business processes and practices is no longer just for the associates on the manufacturing floor. Terry Burton's new book, Out of the Present Crisis: Rediscovering Improvement in the New Economy, *provides a compelling treasure trove of actionable ideas for and real-life examples of applying practical, proven approaches to improve all kinds of organizations such as manufacturing, hospitals, service corporations, and government, and corporate functions not always included in improvement initiatives such as strategic planning, sales and*

marketing, engineering, financial management, and other professional, knowledge-based transactional processes. Not only does his book make a compelling case for becoming expert at improvement itself (his concept of Improvement Excellence™), but it provides numerous examples and a multimillion-dollar list of ideas about how organizations can improve competitiveness to overcome challenges and succeed in the global economy."

Sherry R. Gordon
President
Value Chain Group LLC

"Terry's pragmatic approach has a way of turning the complicated into the simple. The guidance offered throughout his book has helped us to lower our functional costs, improve quality, and continue to keep us at the front of the pack as we speed along the world class track. I am confident that any organization that vigorously applies the principles in this book will see dramatic results in their bottom line, and a renewed culture of continuous improvement."

Rob Urry
VP and General Manager
Signal Processing and Amplifier Business Units
Chief Technical Leader Harman Pro Division
Harman International Industries

"A truly remarkable work . . . I endorse the idea of Improvement Excellence™ – The last thing our organization and others need is another fad, train-the-masses improvement program. The future is about organizations adapting to constant challenges and improving how they improve."

Jim Foster
Vice President of Sales North America
Philips Consumer Lifestyle

"The author presents the next generation of improvement based on the fusion of technology and process innovation to 'improve the way we improve.' It is refreshing to finally find a practical guide for rediscovering improvement success!"

Jennifer Ellis
Technology, Operations and Information Management Faculty
Babson College

Out of the Present Crisis

Rediscovering Improvement in the New Economy

Terence T. Burton

CRC Press
Taylor & Francis Group
Boca Raton   London   New York

CRC Press is an imprint of the
Taylor & Francis Group, an **informa** business

A PRODUCTIVITY PRESS BOOK

CRC Press
Taylor & Francis Group
6000 Broken Sound Parkway NW, Suite 300
Boca Raton, FL 33487-2742

© 2012 by Taylor & Francis Group, LLC
CRC Press is an imprint of Taylor & Francis Group, an Informa business

No claim to original U.S. Government works

Printed in the United States of America on acid-free paper
Version Date: 20111215

International Standard Book Number: 978-1-4665-0442-4 (Hardback)

Library of Congress Cataloging-in-Publication Data

Burton, Terence T., 1950-
　　Out of the present crisis : rediscovering improvement in the new economy / Terence T. Burton.
　　　　p. cm.
　　Includes bibliographical references and index.
　　ISBN 978-1-4665-0442-4 (alk. paper)
　　1. Total quality management. 2. Organizational effectiveness. 3. Continuous improvement process. 4. Strategic planning. I. Title.

HD62.15.B8672 2012
658.4'013--dc23   2011050375

Visit the Taylor & Francis Web site at
http://www.taylorandfrancis.com

and the CRC Press Web site at
http://www.crcpress.com

Contents

Preface

There is certainly no question about the current state of the U.S. economy. Every organization is facing many new challenges brought on by the 2008 meltdown and slow recovery as they crawl out of the economic rubble. The rate of change is exploding and overwhelming. Instability, chaos, turmoil, and uncertainty have brought with it new opportunities for those organizations that approach it the right way. The best response to these new challenges is rapid and large-scale improvement via a different kind of leadership, a rediscovered process of implementation, and totally engaged organizations.

Unfortunately, the meltdown has also brought with it an unintentional change for the worse in leadership behaviors. In times of crisis, it is the norm for executives to take their organizations on a temporary course of reactionary leadership, spending freezes, downsizing, and a collection of other survival tactics. Although many may argue that this is improvement, the fact is that it is not. It is buying time because nothing has changed in terms of process. Buying time is not an improvement strategy. Organizations in this mode replace improvement with temporary firefighting and other sandbags and shovels approaches to stop the bleeding. Usually, the crisis is a short, finite period of buying time, and then executives begin pursuing the important, longer-term needs of their organizations.

Executives can only do so much on their own before the process of leadership breaks down. The problem with the slow recovery is that the crisis window is turning into years, keeping executives and their organizations in this "whack-a-mole" mode of leadership. This is the opposite of improvement with structured disciplines and deliberate actions. The current economy has locked many leaders into this crisis mode long enough for it to become the new organizational norm. When one thinks about it, it is the equivalent of being locked in stage one (the wrecking ball stage) of a typical turnaround. These leadership behaviors, decisions, and actions change the rules of perceived success and run counterintuitive with improvement. In essence, many executives have a freeze on formal improvement when their organizations need it the most.

Organizations can never expect to be successful unless they embrace a simple fundamental: The only way to get better is to improve the current state. As you will learn throughout this book, the continued leadership stages of *insanity* and *hyperinsanity* drive culture backward and suck the oxygen out of any formal improvement initiatives focused on root cause problem solving. The longer organizations remain in these stages, the less successful they become with any formal improvement. This is the case now; over 80% of Lean Six Sigma deployments have failed based on several different benchmarking studies. This is also the case over the past three decades with the familiar birth-death cycles of many other continuous improvement initiatives. Many executives have once again lost interest in their Lean Six Sigma programs, but they and their organizations are missing out on the most incredible opportunities in this new economy if they lose interest in improvement. The need for improvement never goes away, and the need for improvement today is now more urgent than any other time in history.

Out of the Present Crisis: Rediscovering Improvement in the New Economy is a contemporary reference guide for all organizations interested in implementing Lean Six Sigma and other strategic improvement initiatives with incredible and lasting success. This book provides a rediscovered but practical view of improvement in the new economy for people from a diverse range of industries: all chief executive officers (CEOs) and their executive teams, middle managers, physicians, nurses, lending officers, claims managers, government agency directors and managers, politicians, union leadership, not-for-profit executives, and everyone else with the desire to learn how to implement improvement successfully. The book provides a proven roadmap for success in the new economy based on rapid and large-scale change, and the combined strategy of Deming back-to-basics, innovation, enabling technology, and adaptive improvement. The next generation of improvement is not another buzzword program; it is a nimble, systematic execution of this combined strategy that creates the continuous cultural standard of excellence. The future is a well integrated *system* of improvement similar to the Toyota Production System (TPS) but a more dynamic system that leverages technology and harvests the larger enterprise and extended enterprise opportunities.

When one peels back the onion of continuous improvement for the past three decades, the differences between success and failure are predictable, explainable, and manageable. As Chapters 1–3 suggest with a great deal of evidence, root cause analysis is the prerequisite of improvement:

- First, it is important to better understand the true root causes of failure with improvement initiatives of the past. History demonstrates that there is a repeatable pattern, which is revealed in detail in the book. Improvement programs have been highly training and tools intensive. Many programs have also been structured as knockoff improvement successes at GE, Honeywell, Motorola, or the Toyota Production System (TPS). Some begin by drinking the magic Kool-Aid followed by the mass spreading of tools and buzzwords across the organization. These improvement initiatives quickly turn into beautification exercises, symbolic storyboards, labeling, and signage—but few results. Leadership has justifiably abandoned some of these improvement programs. The *process* of improvement (top down, executive mandated, train the masses, flavor of the month, wavering commitment) has remained fixed for decades. Blaming leadership has been a convenient cop-out and not the true root causes of failure. Leadership is definitely a major factor, but we need to understand the why-why-why-why-why (Five Whys) behind this empty blanket statement. When one understands the root causes and their relative influence and interactions on success or failure, putting improvement on the continuous track becomes a logical and straightforward endeavor.

- Next, one must step back and look at the current conditions in many organizations. Executives in good faith and working with the best of intentions have their organizations on a treadmill of non-value-adding activities. Although things may appear speedy on the surface and the numbers look good, there is a significant amount of hidden waste being generated in the background. Many people are so busy and overloaded solving the same issues repeatedly that they do not have the time or the support to improve. Something is needed to break this vicious separation disorder of improvement, and it is not magic. It is not more of the same leadership but *enlightened leadership*—the powerful force that breaks the insanity and hyperinsanity cycles and creates a new vision of success.

- Finally, one must forecast the future of work. Technology is increasing the ability for individuals to multiprocess to a point at which they are becoming less effective at everything. Technology is evolving at a faster rate than most organizations can assimilate it. However, technology is not a replacement for improvement and root cause problem solving. Improvement is not as easy as buying the latest device or apps. We used to talk about management by walking around and going to the Gemba. Now the Gemba is walking around with us 100% of the time in our personal handheld devices. People are increasingly communicating in cyberspace; walking to the next cubicle to talk with another associate is outmoded. There is so much knowledge and information available within a few clicks. Also, the tolerable problem-solving windows are shrinking because people expect answers to their questions in the time it takes to answer an e-mail or text. Generation Y and Z kids can text more words per minute blindfolded than most baby boomers can type on a conventional keyboard. It is truly amazing to observe and be a part of all of this unfolding. All of this adds up to the need to *improve how we improve.*

In summary, the requirements of strategic and sustainable improvement in the future must incorporate the characteristics of velocity, laser targeting of highest-impact opportunities, a simplified and technology-enabled process of improvement, rapid talent development, and an accelerated rate of improvement. Some of the basics of improvement still apply; the newer requirements require adaptive measures when implemented across different industries and creativity and innovation in the new economy.

Strategic improvement is a legitimate core competency that has been, and continues to be, missing in the majority of organizations. The tools look simple, but the larger process of implementing improvement successfully with a demonstrated and sustainable return on investment (ROI) is much more difficult. We have openly discussed many of the delicate behavioral and human detractors of successful and sustainable improvement. As you will read many times throughout the book, the intent is not to personally belittle or criticize anyone, but to candidly expose the ugly facts of failure and increase the recognition of the need to change course. We have a saying that "the answer is usually obvious," but it is the human drama of change that makes or breaks a strategic improvement initiative. Taking continuous and sustainable improvement to the level of internalization and cultural transformation (and keeping it there) is the ultimate state of strategic improvement and superior industry performance.

A major challenge of Lean Six Sigma and other strategic improvement initiatives is its introduction and implementation in industries that have been alienated from the need to improve. Many financial services have difficulty connecting the dots between improvement and their transactional environments. Hospitals, government agencies, and other not-for-profit organizations have always found the additional revenue through various means to cover their costs. To complicate matters, the employees in these organizations have been rewarded and promoted for doing what an improvement practitioner might classify as waste and non-value-added work. The methodologies and tools of improvement are very adaptable to these organizations. The regulatory, compliance, and legalese activities in these organizations present additional challenges to improvement, but they are not showstoppers by any means. Preparing these organizations for the acceptance and commitment to improvement is a delicate matter that requires deep leadership and mentoring experience.

Strategic improvement is both complex and logical and must be approached as an investment with an entitled ROI, not another risky fad program or limited set of tools and jargon. Strategic improvement also requires a bold approach that is backed up by thinking big and acting even bigger. Bad news for the laggards and copycats: casual improvement activities that begin on a note of low expectations and getting one's feet wet will never make it in the new economy. This is the exciting future of strategic improvement: a cultural standard of excellence and a mission-critical enabler of strategic and operating success.

IMPROVEMENT EXCELLENCE™: AN ACCELERATED IMPROVEMENT MODEL FOR THE NEW ECONOMY

The book strongly promotes the notion that it is time to turn things around and get continuous improvement right. Chapters 4–6 provide an updated framework and step-by-step tour of strategic and sustainable improvement in the new economy called Improvement Excellence™—the mastery of developing and implementing successful strategic and continuous business improvement initiatives, transforming culture, and enabling organizations to "improve how they improve." Improvement Excellence™ is a legitimate core competency based on four critical components:

1. The Formal Sustaining Infrastructure of Strategic Leadership and Vision, Deployment Planning, and Execution. This is the new process of improvement: the strategy, structure, processes, and metrics to

keep strategic improvement such as Lean Six Sigma on a continuous track. The book presents a detailed discussion of the Ten Accelerators of Lean Six Sigma, which are embedded within the three elements of infrastructure.

2. Integration of Improvement Methodologies. No single-point improvement activity or tool within Kaizen, Lean, Six Sigma, enabling information technology (IT), or other improvement methodologies is all inclusive and all encompassing. The wide spectrum of improvement opportunities (particularly professional, knowledge, and transactional processes) in the new economy requires a blended approach in the methodologies. Many of these opportunities are comprised of clusters of smaller opportunities requiring different improvement tools to harvest the benefits.

3. Scalable Lean Six Sigma™, a rapid deployment and rapid results improvement model that includes within it the best practices of laser targeting, leveraged mentoring, controlled execution, and risk mitigation. The focal points of Scalable Lean Six Sigma™ are highest-impact opportunities, making every effort count, and establishing a rate of improvement that enables the attainment of strategic and operating objectives.

4. Enlightened leadership, by which executives work their way through the stages of insanity, hyperinsanity, reckoning, renewal, and finally the enlightened state in which they discover a new business model and higher moral purpose of improvement. The true greatness in leadership arises when organizational success depends on innovation and doing something that has not been done before. Enlightenment requires cycles of renewal. This state can never be sustained in an individual, an organization, or society in general unless improvement is internalized as a universal philosophy and the core competency of continuously *improving how we improve* is developed as the underpinning of this philosophy. This is the future of leadership: talented executives who use complexity and challenging situations to their advantage and recognize the need to improve much earlier in the game.

Every organization must learn how to continuously improve how they improve at a rate that is comparable to the chaos, turmoil, and shifts in the economy. Believe me, this is an invigorating and energizing process for organizations when it is approached and executed the right way.

INTERNALIZATION AND CULTURAL TRANSFORMATION

Improvement Excellence™ is the core competency of improvement that leads to a higher level of organizational performance called internalization and the transformation of culture. This is where the philosophy of improvement and its corresponding behaviors, decisions, and actions become woven into the norms of how people think and work every day. This is improvement on autopilot; organizations develop the ability to identify changing conditions and improve current conditions repeatedly. Only Toyota and a handful of other organizations operate in this benchmark level of strategic and continuous improvement. Their journeys are not luck but the right sustaining behaviors, choices, and actions. Chapter 7 provides the dynamics of culture change, the subprocesses of internalization, and metrics for measuring the ongoing success of strategic and continuous improvement initiatives.

INTEGRATING TECHNOLOGY AND IMPROVEMENT

Chapter 8 discusses the key role of technology in the next generation of strategic improvement. In the new economy, technology is enabling the warp speed transformation of organizations into global, multilevel networks of transactional enterprises. Unlike manufacturing improvement, transactional improvement is transparent and comprised of key business processes, information flows, knowledge, and decisions. Further, there are literally hundreds of professional and knowledge resources managing thousands of dynamic process touch points, a continuous churn in changing requirements, specific country needs, time constraints, communications issues, and exponentially greater opportunities for waste, variation, human risk, and bad decisions. Chapter 8 provides guidance about how to get the most out of existing technology and integrated enterprise architectures and assimilating emerging technologies such as mobility, real-time enterprises, cloud computing, and other capabilities as a strategic weapon of global competitiveness. Emerging technology is a major enabler of the next generations of strategic and continuous improvement.

MULTIMILLION-DOLLAR LIST OF TRANSACTIONAL IMPROVEMENT OPPORTUNITIES

The largest opportunities for improvement in the new economy are in the interconnected network of professional, technical, knowledge, and transactional processes. Based on our experiences, many organizations are shifting their improvement focus and saving millions of dollars annually in the transactional process space. Chapter 9 provides a multimillion-dollar list of improvement opportunities for manufacturing and service organizations. The reader will find dozens of improvement examples in the areas of strategic management, new product and services development, global supply chain management, quality and compliance, sales and marketing, financial management, facilities management, information technology, human resources, organizational development, and performance management. This chapter represents but a partial list of significant transactional improvement opportunities.

STRATEGIC IMPROVEMENT IN HEALTHCARE

Hospitals have reached their own tipping point in terms of shrinking revenues and escalating costs. Although there is a real sense of urgency to change, hospital leadership remains perplexed with how to solve their business dilemma. Lean Six Sigma has made its initial inroads in many healthcare institutions. This is a positive trend because the power of Lean Six Sigma is just what the doctor ordered. Hundreds of hospitals are either evaluating or have begun their Lean Six Sigma journey in hopes of adapting the methodologies to improve their financial challenges. Chapter 10 is dedicated to implementing Lean Six Sigma and strategic improvement successfully in hospitals. The reader will find informative discussions about the uniqueness and complexities of hospitals, transforming leadership thinking and cultural norms, and how to innovate and adapt Lean Six Sigma to these specific industry requirements. This chapter also includes a detailed implementation plan for deploying Lean Six Sigma successfully in hospitals. Healthcare and other not-for-profit organizations need to reinvent their business models because the endless stream of funding is drying up in the new economy.

STRATEGIC IMPROVEMENT IN GOVERNMENT

Finally, our federal, state, and local governments represent the largest improvement opportunity pool on the planet. These opportunities represent trillions of dollars. Chapter 11 provides a nonpartisan root cause analysis of government waste in general and some of the cultural barriers to improvement. Government is the most difficult environment to implement improvement not because of process complexity, but because of deeply rooted cultural norms and barriers. Much of this complexity is self-imposed by decades of accepted government practices and norms. The problem with acceptance is that improvement is a nonnegotiable process based on facts, metrics, and accountability. The reader will become aware of the massive wastes, redundancies, and politically motivated self-interest processes in government. A more detailed root cause analysis of the 2008 meltdown demonstrates how many horrible decisions could have been avoided with fact-based improvement. It is no secret that the American people are literally "fed up" with waste in government. Neither the present Administration nor the Republican candidates for the Presidency are stepping up with a plan that is bold enough to address the large-scale changes required to turn the current economic situation around. The chapter suggests the industrialization of government through the infusion of basic leadership, accountability, and controls from private industry, followed by an aggressive injection of Lean Six Sigma and other strategic improvement initiatives. The chapter also provides a nonpartisan, high-impact government turnaround plan based on the author's research findings. This plan provides a "beyond-the-box" view of government and is intended to be a starting point for reinventing government.

THE LARGER MORAL PURPOSE OF IMPROVEMENT

The Epilogue ties everything from the previous chapters together. The book provides all of the proven best practices for success with Lean Six Sigma and other strategic improvement initiatives. My intent in the book was not to promote Lean Six Sigma by itself as the cure-all and end-all for every challenge in every organization. The discussions about leadership, improvement strategy, and the formal sustaining infrastructure provide new insights about rapid, technology-enabled improvement in the new economy. I provide specific examples and the applicability of strategic improvement across all industries and provide better direction about how to begin or jumpstart a new improvement journey successfully, especially in nonmanufacturing environments. Success is a choice, and that choice is up to you.

The objective of this book is to present the facts and influence others about rediscovering improvement—in the self, the workplace, the quality of life, and the future for generations to follow. There is a higher moral purpose for writing this book, and it goes way beyond improving the profit-and-loss (P&L) statement. America finds itself in another historical pickle of losing ground on the world stage, and the quality of life as we have known it is at stake in the new economy. The U.S. manufacturing base has been exported to China and other third-world countries in the interest of short-term profits. A closer analysis reveals that many of these decisions are justified based on homeland cost structures, and many are loaded with new inefficiencies and waste. Much of what used to be domestic manufacturing investments are now disproportionate executive compensation. Our government is gambling with bankruptcy and an even larger meltdown, and the levels of waste and inefficiencies are sickening. Unemployment is at an all-time high. It will take years to recover from the Dodd-Frank mortgage fiasco, and private industry executives would have been incarcerated for these irresponsible actions. Healthcare providers are looking at implosion if their leadership does not act quickly on their industry dilemma. Banks are faced with new lending regulations and revenues from mortgage interest are down. They are trying to make up the difference by "feeing" their customers to death—and their customers are moving to more efficient community institutions. Medical, home, automobile, and life insurance are reaching a point of being unaffordable to a large segment of the population. I could go on and on, but I think everyone gets the point.

Without continuous improvement, an individual, an organization, or a society can never sustain the same standard of basic survival, security, and safety needs—or improve their quality of life. It becomes increasingly difficult for employees or citizens to develop a true sense of family, friendship, loyalty, commitment, and intimacy in what people are doing when they are running around at work unappreciated with their hair on fire. Following the logic, it is even more difficult for organizations to provide an environment where people can satisfy their self-esteem needs and feel self-validated for their contributions. Most important, it is difficult to remain a global leader and build the right success infrastructure for our generations to follow. It is time to turn things around on a grand scale; balance all federal, state, and local government budgets through radical changes in their operating models; rebuild America's manufacturing base and global competitiveness; improve the quality of education based on global standards; make healthcare more affordable for everyone; and regain our superior quality of life. This is not ideology, and I am not running for political office. But I do have strong convictions and knowledge about strategic improvement as a powerful enabler to turn many of these bad situations around. The great American humorist Will Rogers once said, "I never met a man I didn't like." I have a twist on Mr. Rogers's quotation backed by nearly four decades of experience: "I never met an organization that could not improve significantly." Improvement is like Jell-O®: There is always room for it.

Executives and their people have been pummeled long enough by the recovery. It is time to shift gears from recovery to rediscovery, pick up the improvement flag, and regain a superior competitive position in the global economy. This book provides direction for this renewed journey of improvement to a brighter future. Rediscovery through improvement is the fast lane out of the slow recovery because it brings out the best in people, organizations, societies, and economies. When one cuts through the surface level gloom and doom, there is an improvement renaissance emerging for public and private corporations, hospitals, financial services, and government (federal, state, local). The meltdown and slow recovery have also brought more opportunities for improvement in every organization than ever before in history. Waste is not a product of doing something wrong; it is the result of a changing world and rising expectations. The only thing wrong with waste is allowing it to grow while choosing to do nothing about it. The risks of doing nothing are much higher than taking action, and doing nothing has far reaching consequences on others in the organization. All organizations have the opportunity to choose whether they are the emerging industry leaders and champions of improvement, or casualties of the improvements of competitors. Look around . . . some organizations will miss the renaissance train and may not be around in a few years. All executives have the moral obligation to make sure it is not their organization. It is time to place the *continuous* back in continuous improvement. The larger philosophy of Improvement Excellence™ and *improving how we improve* (by all and every means) will make a dramatic difference in our places of work, our lives, and the futures of generations to follow. Please join me, and encourage others around you to join in with the greatest improvement renaissance in history.

Terence T. Burton, President
The Center for Excellence in Operations (CEO)
Bedford, New Hampshire
http://www.ceobreakthrough.com

Acknowledgments

As I reach the prelegacy stage of my career, I feel a strong need to share the experience, knowledge, and wisdom I have accumulated in the field of continuous improvement. *Out of the Present Crisis: Rediscovering Improvement in the New Economy* is a contemporary compilation of nearly four decades of learning, knowledge, and experiences implementing the spectrum of successful strategic improvement initiatives in a wide variety of organizations and countries. The inspiration of this book comes not only from these experiences but also from the urgent need to retrofit improvement across many different industry sectors and the rapid evolution of technology that is reinventing conventional business models.

If I attempted to thank everyone who has influenced my career journey and ability to create this book, the Acknowledgment section would be larger than the book itself. I have consciously decided not to acknowledge individuals because it is inevitable that I would unintentionally fail to mention the names of many people. The reason is because the number of people who have challenged, influenced, and contributed to my journey are in the thousands. I wish to acknowledge all of these great people by not mentioning just a few dozen people like other authors. I am grateful to all my former employers and hundreds of clients who have developed my talent and passion for continuous improvement.

First, I thank my family and friends who tolerated the Zen-like dedication and passion that it takes to create a respectable book. Writing a book is a huge professional commitment and a bold personal contract to provide new value to the world. Although one attempts to write as much as possible during hotel stays, limo rides, room service dinners, and airline flights, most of the time and effort eats into one's personal life. Authors write when their ideas and thoughts flow, and that causes many disruptions in personal life. In retrospect, writing is very much like improvement: It works best when one executes and asks for forgiveness instead of hanging around waiting for permission. In the latter case, the work of writing and improvement never gets done. I am blessed to be surrounded by family and friends who appreciate my career commitment to improvement and the relentless need to share my experiences and positively influence others.

Next, I thank every client and every individual in these organizations who has directly participated in our consulting assignments. I lost count a long time ago, but I know my combined experiences represent hundreds of diverse industry environments, cultures, and international locations; thousands of executives with their own leadership styles; and tens of thousands of people working on different improvement initiatives in their respective teams. Until one makes the time to reflect, they do not realize how blessed they are for these valued opportunities, experiences, and wisdom of improvement. I sincerely thank clients with whom I have worked on their strategic improvement journeys. I thank each person from the bottom of my heart for the dedicated efforts, the mindsets to never give up, the emotional experiences and realization of mutual success, and the many lasting friendships that have resulted over the years. The successes that we have shared are the best successes possible because:

- Our successes occurred through multidirectional learning: learning, developing, and growing from each other's knowledge and expertise;
- Our successes created renewed, winning attitudes. Together we made a big difference on strategic and operating performance and achieved sustainable and quantifiable results—in the majority of cases, beyond what was thought to be unreachable or impossible; and
- Our successes positively affected a large base of people's professional and personal lives.

You have helped me to grow an incredible knowledge base of improvement and implementation experiences. Together, we shared the rewarding challenges, fun, and benefits of improvement when organizations and individuals give it their all. Over the years, it also gives me great pleasure and satisfaction to help and observe many of our client colleagues grow and benefit professionally and personally from continuous improvement. Writing this book has been a challenge, but it has also been reminiscent of our adventures together with large-scale strategic improvement.

Next, I thank the thousands of universities, professional societies, industry and trade associations and their associated publications, and other knowledge sources for the opportunity to learn and benefit from talent development. We are all so fortunate to have access to this great learning and talent development infrastructure, and technology continues to make this access easier, faster, and more widespread. Today, the ability to learn is a few clicks away thanks to things like Google, Apple, Amazon, Microsoft, Yahoo!, Time Warner, Barnes and Noble, and many others. This book is another addition to this great learning infrastructure and an opportunity to give back and share the collected experiences and wisdom that has been bestowed on me.

Finally, a special thanks to Kristine Mednansky, Laurie Schlags, and Judith Simon, and others who touched this book from concept to the bookshelf. Taylor & Francis is a great publishing organization that understands how to put continuous improvement, excellence, and technology into action. I enjoyed working with this organization with their lean, nimble, superior quality, and velocity-conscious best practices. Thanks to Taylor & Francis, bringing this new book to market has been a pleasurable customer experience.

About the Author

Terence T. Burton is president and chief executive officer of The Center for Excellence in Operations, Incorporated (CEO), a management consulting firm headquartered in Bedford, New Hampshire, with offices in Munich, Germany. Terry's background includes extensive leadership and executive operations experience with Atlantic Richfield, Polaroid Corporation, and Wang Laboratories. Previously, he also held senior practice leadership positions with two large international consulting firms, KPMG and Pittiglio, Rabin, Todd, & McGrath (PRTM).

Since founding his own management consultancy in 1991, Terry has led international management consulting assignments with over 300 manufacturing, healthcare, and service clients, implementing thousands of strategic improvement initiatives in the Americas and Europe. In the firm's 20 years of existence, CEO's clients have accumulated billions of dollars in documented benefits through various strategic improvement initiatives, such as Lean Six Sigma. He is an industry-recognized thought leader, implementation expert, keynote speaker, and author of seven previous books and hundreds of articles on improvement and industrial engineering topics such as Kaizen, Lean, Six Sigma, outsourcing, acquisitions, global quality, supply chain management, new product and services development, change management, and other strategic improvement initiatives.

Terry holds an MBA from Boston University and a BSIE and an MSIE/OR from the University of New Haven and is a certified Lean Six Sigma Black Belt. Terry is best known for his "hands-on" approach to consulting, his personable and approachable style, and his executive leadership savvy in transforming organizations.

1 The Seeds of Continuous Improvement

INTRODUCTION

Today, most organizations are still dealing with the repercussions from the largest recession since the Great Depression. The recent meltdown and tortoise-speed recovery have created a disturbing trend in which leaders have their organizations stuck in short-term survival mode. Granted, many of these immediate survival tactics were necessary as the financial crisis unfolded before our very eyes. However, too many executives are continuing to drive their businesses in this short-term, reactionary survival mode as the new cultural norm. These respective inconsistent leadership behaviors are a major contributor to recent benchmarking data indicating that over 80% of Lean Six Sigma and other formal improvement initiatives are derailed and repeating the same familiar birth-death cycle of continuous improvement programs since the 1980s. At the beginning of each of these life cycles, the early successes have a hundred fathers, but when improvement fails, it becomes an orphan. With each of these cycles, the word *continuous* keeps falling out of continuous improvement. Today, many organizations could add more to their financial statements through successful continuous improvement initiatives than they will add via their wavering and reactionary hot lists of actions.

Continuous improvement is not always the most enticing topic for executives because it reveals waste and root causes and establishes accountability and metrics for progress. On the one hand, the concept is decades old, and people have talked a good game about continuous improvement under a variety of different banners and buzzwords. On the other hand, the concept is relevant because, like it or not, the need for continuous improvement never goes away. Yet there are always excuses to postpone continuous improvement that, when one thinks about this statement, it is a silly choice. Authentic excuses such as the ones that follow are easier than performance:

- "There's no money in the budget for improvement until 2012."
- "The time is not quite right for improvement."
- "Improvement is not in my goals and objectives."
- "We finished our continuous improvement program years ago."
- "We eliminated our Six Sigma program. … It did not work for us; we're different."

- "We don't have the time and resources to improve and do our regular jobs."
- "If I had more time, I would have found a better way."

Move over Sophocles! Are these comments inspirational or tragic? Today, many organizations may not openly admit it, but they have traded in their true commitment to Lean Six Sigma for many *improvement-dysfunctional* behaviors that are driving culture backward, all in the interest of illusive short-term results.

In the midst of our present anemic recovery, one of the greatest challenges of every organization is strategic and sustainable improvement. Whether your organization is a Fortune 500 corporation, a rapidly growing software start-up, an established small or midsize manufacturing company, a financial services organization, a pharmaceutical or biotech company, an aerospace and defense contractor, a services supplier to the automotive industry, a large construction company, a large healthcare institution, or part of the federal, state, and local government infrastructure—the urgency and magnitude for continuous improvement grows proportionally and often exponentially to the emerging global economic, social, and political challenges of the postmeltdown economy. Even federal, state, and local government agencies are under significant voter pressure to follow improvement practices of private industry and figure out how to do more with less. Unfortunately, government does not get it yet. After decades of existence, continuous improvement is the fast lane out of our slow economic recovery—and the fast lane of success in good times, bad times, and everything else between these two extremes.

CONTINUOUS IMPROVEMENT: A BRIEF HISTORY FOR THE UNINITIATED

Lean Six Sigma and most other improvement initiatives have their roots in the formal discipline of industrial and systems engineering. Within the typical industrial and systems engineering curriculum is a wide variety of courses on topics such as methods analysis and process improvement, management science, statistical engineering, financial engineering, engineering management, maintenance and equipment management, supply chain management, facilities planning and design, production planning and scheduling, inventory management, process engineering and development, operations research and process optimization, systems engineering, knowledge-based systems design, performance and measurement systems design, human factors and ergonomics, team-based problem solving, value engineering, and quality engineering. The details and body of knowledge presented in these courses are almost identical to what has been packaged in the various improvement programs of the past three decades. Industrial and systems engineering is the foundation for most of the analytical and human factors content of Lean Six Sigma.

The discipline of industrial and systems engineering is accredited to Frederick Taylor, father of scientific management, and Frank Gilbreth, a pioneer in motion study and creator of the 17 basic motions or *therbligs* (Gilbreth spelled backward with the *th* transposed). Shortly thereafter, there was Henry Ford, who wrote the first book about Lean in his 1926 classic, *Today and Tomorrow*. Taiichi Ohno, father of the Toyota Production System (TPS), was inspired by Henry Ford's discussions about standardization, waste, and continuous flow production. Around the same time, Walter Shewhart, the father of statistical process control, was developing the discipline at Western Electric and later at Bell Labs, where he was introduced to William Edwards Deming.

During the era after World War II, Japan recognized that its recovery was highly dependent on these improvement topics. Dr. Deming and his expertise on statistical quality improvement and Taiichi Ohno with his industrial and systems engineering background and visionary thinking from Toyota took center stage in business improvement. Some level of complacency set in for America after winning the war. Rather than listening to the wisdom of Deming and others, we exported it to Japan, which was faced with postwar reconstruction issues related to manufacturing. Postwar Japan was severely constrained in terms of space, resources, time, cost, and their perceived low quality by the West. At Toyota, for example, there was a concern with quality and inventory levels and the costs and space consumption associated with each. Emulating what U.S. companies were doing was essentially not doable and unaffordable. As the story has it, Ohno visited an American supermarket and realized his vision of pull production. This became codified as an essential element of what was to become known as the Toyota Production System (TPS). Much of the TPS is Taiichi Ohno's evolution of basic industrial and systems engineering improvements aimed at the unique inventory, quality, space, and natural resource limitations in postwar Japan. Development and implementation of the TPS was a lot of work—relentless, never-ending work—work that turned out to go unnoticed by the Western world until it revolutionized global manufacturing by 1980. Several others, such as Masaaki Imai, father of Kaizen, also became internationally renowned for the continuous improvement work at Toyota and many other Japanese companies. The single most important factor was their deployment of improvement in a perfect cultural environment characterized by honor, nationalism, teamwork and true empowerment, a relentless commitment to quality and perfection, prevention and improvement driven, quality at the source, shame for failure, extreme discipline, concentration on process and root causes, meticulous attention to details, and long-term focus, to name a few traits. Toyota and many other Eastern corporations mastered continuous improvement under the radar screen for years. The combination of the industrial and systems engineering tools and their national culture was a match made in heaven. During this same time, some U.S. companies with an appreciation for industrial and systems engineering were also involved in many of the improvement efforts, like pull production and two-bin systems, work cell design, plant layout, preventive maintenance, and continuous flow, that supposedly originated in Japan. However, the efforts in what was primarily "command-and-control" and "good soldiering" cultures back then were not as continuous and certainly not as impressive as the results of their Eastern counterparts.

When Toyota, Honda, Canon, Sony, and many others began dominating U.S. industries in the 1980s, America received its first wake-up call of continuous improvement. American executives, and educators began visiting these Japanese organizations and brought back what they thought that they observed. These visitors did not appreciate the human and cultural elements of their observations and instead repackaged and imported a discrete series of new and improved industrial and systems engineering techniques followed by their own vocabulary of acronyms and books on the topics. The long and the short of all this is that continuous improvement was exported from the United States to the East, where it was really deployed with a best-in-class style, and then the United States imported continuous improvement back to America. The chronic problem with continuous improvement in the Western world is a different culture and a different way of thinking. In the East, their leadership styles and culture turned out to be a perfect match for continuous improvement. In the West, many leadership choices, behaviors, and actions favor instant gratification and run counter to continuous and sustainable improvement. Much of this is driven by traditional cost accounting metrics and Wall Street expectations.

Thirty years ago, America became painfully aware of the importance of quality improvement, and executives were scratching their heads as they watched the 1980 NBC documentary, *If Japan Can, Why Can't We?* This was a mammoth wake-up call for business improvement. We watched their industry success at reducing setups, defects, cycle times, costs, and inventories based on improvement techniques introduced by Taylor, Gilbreth, Ford, Shewhart, and Deming in the early 1900s. Suddenly, there was a high degree of interest in improvement, but in retrospect a poor track record of implementing and sustaining continuous improvement. A vivid memory from this time was executives making comments similar to, *"If you think things are bad now, wait until the great Shenzhou (China —Land of the Divine) awakens."* Their predictions were right on the mark! Back then, Deming talked about constancy of purpose; unfortunately, we still have not found it yet with business improvement. The average executive lasts about 2 years in his or her position. The average birth-death cycle of various continuous improvement programs has been even less time in most organizations (although Lean Six Sigma has stuck for a longer period of time than its predecessor efforts). Many of today's executives may have been through a partial or exhaustive paintball of bandwagon improvement initiatives (Figure 1.1) in their careers.

Within each of these improvement initiatives is their own vocabulary of acronyms, buzzwords, tools, and methodologies that has confused the business improvement playing field even more. Further, the experts promoted their own wares while discrediting the offerings of other competitors. They attempted to convince management with bogus advice, such as Lean is better than Six Sigma, Kaizen is quicker and simpler than Six Sigma, or the right sequence to implement improvement tools is 5S followed by Gemba walks, value stream maps, and muda analysis. Several vendors have popped up over time, offering their "canned"

FIGURE 1.1 The paintball of continuous improvement. (© Copyright 2011 by The Center for Excellence in Operations, Inc. [CEO].)

proprietary software applications, templates, and reports as an optional means to improvement. Continuous improvement has resembled an executive game of grabbing at straws and searching for the magic bullet. This spectrum of bizz-buzz combined with how leadership has deployed these initiatives has left many employees totally confused and turned off by the thought of another improvement program. For decades, organizations have been grasping at and bouncing between the improvement tools by themselves and missing the mark of how to deploy strategic improvement successfully. Unfortunately, the banners and slogans were, and continue to be, a short-term replacement for the tough work of implementing, benefiting from, and continuing onward with business improvement. I walked into a new client a few years ago, and one employee commented to me, "I know why you are here—because Mr. X [the chief executive officer] has read another book!" In another organization, an executive actually made the comment: "We need Lean Six Sigma because we finished our continuous improvement programs years ago." Regardless of the *ribbon du jour* of improvement programs, continuous improvement is more leadership and common sense than rocket science and tools.

In retrospect, organizations have been on a random walk down continuous improvement street during the past few decades. Continuous improvement has been a concept that every executive in every organization definitely embraces in concept but not as a critical and sustainable element of business strategy in daily practice. There is a disturbing and well-documented birth-death cycle that exists with continuous improvement initiatives: When things are good, improvement is the first casualty because it is perceived to be no longer necessary. When things are bad, improvement is the first casualty because people do not have the time and resources to improve and do their regular firefighting jobs. Between these two extremes, improvement has been supported by temporary and wavering commitments, token agreements, follow-the-leader fad programs, massive training, and more going through the motions of improvement. Over time, executives and their organizations ride through many of these cycles, creating the *separation disorder of improvement* culture: People view improvement as "in addition to" rather than "an expected part of" their daily work.

Another historical fact about improvement is its continuous repackaging and remarketing under a different banner as if the concept never existed before. Organizations are sold down the road with another box of improvement with a different ribbon wrapped around it and new promises, but the contents of the box remain basically the same. As mentioned, much of what exists (and has always existed) in the boxes of improvement are the basic disciplines and solid fundamentals of industrial and systems engineering—exported to the Far East, implemented with great success, and imported back to America. Most gurus packaged improvement as the latest single-point tools, acronyms, and buzzwords, with no overarching and sustaining constancy of purpose. Dozens of books have been published on individual improvement tools with Japanese names. Organizations have introduced improvement programs like a pinball game in which everyone eventually forgets which balls gained or lost points. There has been an enormous focus on the tools (the means) and not enough focus on the leadership, systems thinking, infrastructure, and cultural elements of continuous improvement—the critical success factors that create sustainability and keep the "continuous" in continuous improvement. Executives have continually underestimated and oversimplified what it really takes to plan, organize, deploy, execute, and sustain a successful continuous improvement initiative.

Let us continue our walk through continuous improvement history to the present experiences with Lean Six Sigma. The impulsive leadership actions to the recent meltdown are but another example of a natural response to disaster, leaving executives and organizations running with the best of intentions but vulnerable to many bad choices. One of the most disturbing leadership choices through the recent economic crisis has been the across-the-board freezes on improvement when organizations need it the most. Through the meltdown and slow recovery, this expediency of impulsive leadership has trumped the propriety of logical improvement thinking, often creating a dazzling display of illusive short-term success. When people perceive improvement as a low priority, they tend to go into firefighting mode and lose sight of the most obvious fundamental: The only way to get better is to improve current conditions. Improvement is the process of getting from point A (current state) to point B (the improved state) through "structured principles and deliberate actions" that enhance stakeholder value, perfection, and excellence. Instead, many executives and their organizations are stuck in this mode of *hyperinsanity:* doing more of the same things with greater velocity and emotions and expecting to achieve different results. Like it or not, executives choose to replace the "structured principles and deliberate actions" discussed with "whack-a-mole actions," hoping to achieve faster results. In many organizations, the continued reactionary management practices are becoming the new cultural norm that we refer to as *acceleration entrapment*: Organizations are so overloaded with multitasking immediate crisis after crisis that their people become ineffective at everything. Some justify their actions by blaming the fierce global economy. Other leaders revert to their great manager practices of stirring up the organizational pot and create the appearance of making things happen. However, the true root cause at play here is lack of constancy of purpose, which is driving culture backward, reducing employee commitment and trust, and placing these organizations farther behind in this new economy. In many organizations, these uncompromising leadership behaviors have created more waste and hidden costs and increased the need, magnitude, and urgency of strategic improvement. Today, for example, over 80% of Lean Six Sigma and other formal improvement initiatives are derailed and off point. Once again, executives are contributing to the *laws of unintended consequences* about improvement by their actions by repeating the same familiar birth-death cycle of continuous improvement programs since the 1980s. Organizations may have run out of steam with Lean Six Sigma but cannot afford to back-burner improvement. History shows us that the only continuous activity is the introduction of new buzzword branding for continuous improvement. This is the last thing that organizations need.

To ensure that the jargon of improvement is not complicated even further, this is a good time to provide more definition to terms that appear to be used interchangeably throughout the book. *Strategic improvement* is a large-scale improvement initiative that attempts to transform organizations to superior "breakthrough" levels of performance. Strategic improvement is a continuous process of improvement at a higher level. An example might be to reduce time to market for new products or length of stay in hospitals by 75%. *Continuous improvement* is an ongoing effort to improve products, processes, and services. Continuous improvement encompasses many activities under the umbrella of strategic improvement that tend to be more rapid and incremental by nature. In our examples, continuous improvement might involve dozens of concurrent improvement efforts to achieve these strategic objectives. *Business process improvement* is a form of continuous improvement that refers to the application of improvement to key transactional business processes to improve speed, quality, cost, or service-level delivery. *Sustainable improvement* is the combination of strategic, business process, and continuous improvement, executed to produce nonstop benefits over time without any disruptions in progress. Some may argue that sustainable is not good enough. Note that in our definition sustainable is not level; it refers to a sustainable *process* that is capable of continually increasing the rate of improvement. *Lean Six Sigma* is the most current and most popular set of methodologies and tools to enable strategic, continuous, and sustainable improvement. Lean Six Sigma is one of many means that organizations can deploy to achieve significant benefits. Strategic improvement, continuous improvement, business process improvement, sustainable improvement, and Lean Six Sigma are the means, not the ends. As you have just learned, improvement has been repackaged and coined by a variety of other buzzword terms since the 1980s. Regardless of the adjective or latest label, the art and science of improvement are powerful enablers that transform organizations to new, higher levels of strategic and operating success. It is the continuous that keeps this success sustainable.

MY EARLY LESSONS IN CONTINUOUS IMPROVEMENT

As I thought about writing this book, I reflected back to many childhood lessons that in retrospect are a collection of those unintentional subliminal stimuli that have profoundly influenced my professional career of continuous improvement. I grew up in a household with very strict and disciplined parents. My dad served in the Army infantry frontlines of the World War II European theater, and my mom was an expert at home and family management. Their backgrounds shaped the basic laws of our household: listen, do what is right, always tell the truth, and respect others around you. Like many parents in this era, their view of the world was in terms of binary choices such as black or white, right or wrong, win or lose, and good or bad. You make good choices, and good things happen; you make bad choices, and there are consequences. For as long as I can remember, as a child I was encouraged to pick up my room, put my toys away, hang up my clothes, shower daily, help with assigned chores, behave myself in church, and always listen to and respect elders. When we were asked to do something, there was a high expectation that it would be done right the first time. We learned quickly that the consequence was to do things over until it was right—no excuses, no delays, and no compromises. There was no tolerance for waste, inefficiency, and *winging it* in our house. Thanks to my parents, I learned at a very early age about teaming, a place for everything and everything in its place, doing the right things right the first time, and rewards and consequences.

My dad worked as an Underwriters Laboratories (UL) inspector and provided the familiar "UL Approved" services to nearly a hundred different manufacturers in Connecticut. At the early age of 11 or 12, I would occasionally accompany my dad to work in the summer if he was visiting a company where I was interested in how they made their products. When the manufacturer's product failed UL testing, it required a period of improvement and verification before additional testing was performed and the UL stamp of approval was placed on the product. Back then, my dad would try to explain his slide rule and manually prepared Shewhart charts, but it was way over my head. Even then, I remember my dad dealing with bootleg UL stickers, or stickers placed on noncertified product by the manufacturer so it could ship and make the numbers. My grandfather was a quality manager in one of the companies my dad visited to provide UL services. He also spent time showing me all of the measurement instruments in the quality lab and taught me how to read a micrometer, a dial gauge, and calipers. At a young age, I was exposed to the manufacturing processes of a variety of products, from electrical lighting to industrial furnaces to stereo components and fire-retardant paint. This was my version of the popular TV programs *How It's Made* and *Ultimate Factories*. I guess I have this Lean Six Sigma and continuous improvement stuff in my DNA. What I never realized at the time is that these experiences were laying the first stones in my foundation of root cause problem solving and continuous improvement.

GRANDPA HARRINGTON'S FARM

Back in my early teen years, I was too young to get a job but old enough to want a little spending money. I decided to seek work with a few of the local farmers in northeastern Connecticut. I would bounce around on demand, riding my bicycle from one farm to the other and working as a farmhand. One day I might be helping with cutting fields and baling hay. The next day, I might be picking up "drops" in the apple orchard so the cows would not eat the apples, become intoxicated, and then ruin their milk. Sometimes, it was picking vegetables or sweet corn for the farm stand. Or, I might be shoveling cow "flops" and washing down the floors in the barn, helping out with milking activities, washing down vessels and milking equipment, or herding cows in and out from the pastures. Occasionally, it was nonfarming duties like cutting lawns, trimming shrubs and trees, or cutting and burning brush. I could not understand why anyone would want to be a farmer because the work was very hard and never ending. All of these local farmers had a common work ethic: hard and long workdays, no shortcuts, do things right the first time, and work to a rigid schedule, keeping all equipment ready to go, and never putting anything off or letting things back up or go undone. They were experts at 5S and many other Lean concepts.

My first impressionable experience with continuous improvement occurred one summer at age 14. My favorite employer was an elderly third-generation farmer in northeastern Connecticut whose nickname was Grandpa Harrington to his little team of young workers. He always dressed in bib blue jean overalls, wore a straw hat, and always seemed to have his unique grin and huge twinkle in his blue eyes. Grandpa was a local celebrity who attracted many people to visit and engage in small talk. He had a colorful personality and could match wits with the best, always ending on a friendly note. I gravitated toward this farm because of Grandpa's personality and the opportunity to earn the most spending money. Grandpa took me under his wing and began teaching me about different types of work, probably because I was an attentive listener to his wisdom—and willing to work every day, all day. You get the idea. The farmer's nickname was "Grampa," and soon mine was "Tiny." Grandpa was one of those rare individuals you meet in life whose character literally overflowed with honesty, integrity, commitment, generosity, spirituality, and high morals. He was an incredible mentor—a master at management by walking around, mentoring and asking the right questions, and always being there to help us out of tough situations. Looking back, we all listened and looked up to him as if he was our real grandfather. I remember how he would throw in a few extra apples or not even charge people who might be temporarily down and out on their luck. One day while working at the farm stand on a slow day, I began asking a lot of questions about how he ran the farm. I was impressed with how he moved me and others all over the place and always got everything done for the day. I was intrigued even at age 14 how he could keep himself and the rest of us so organized. I enjoyed the farm stand assignment: helping customers select and bag produce and the one-on-one time listening to Grandpa's wisdom. It is one of those childhood memories I vividly remember and cherish like it happened last month. Grandpa had a full index finger and partial fingers on both hands, a casualty of a farming accident 50 years earlier. When I did not listen or did something incorrectly, he would "noogie" me with that open index finger to get my attention. He would also recognize extra effort and throw in an extra few dollars for the day. Work was never done; there was always a list of things that he prioritized in his head and assigned to his workers. Grandpa constantly stressed the importance of working together, always helping each other out, and letting him know about problems. During our conversation, he mentioned that he could make more money this month if he did not have to pay me for feeding the cows or picking up the fallen apples, but it would mess up his milking operation. He mentioned that he could cut out the expenses for planting corn and other vegetable seeds, spreading fertilizer, or harvesting hay. That would save a lot of material, labor, and equipment wear and tear, but his cows would starve and he would have nothing to sell in the stand next year. He could save money by not cleaning the barn, but his fields would not have fertilizer and his cows would get sick. He could choose not to repair the tractors and other heavy equipment and not plow and plant the fields—that would save a lot of money this month, but it would put him out of business. He walked over by the produce racks and began weeding out a few apples and peaches. Then he waved that single index finger at me and said:

> Tiny you never sell the customer anything but the best fresh fruits and vegetables—one bad apple or wormy ear of corn and they won't be back. Never screw the customer. Be polite, help them find the best apples or tomatoes in the racks, throw in an extra apple or peach. Check the fruit and vegetable displays. And if you don't do it right I'll give you a poke and make you do it over.

He constantly stressed with everyone the importance of making sure that whatever needed to be done got done right away and at the right time so you always know where you stood.

> Review what needs to be done every day, and then make sure all of tomorrow's work gets done and done right. Keep the routine going: no shortcuts, no stalling, no excuses, and no surprises. If you allow things to pile up, it costs a lot more because you will not have time to catch up. Then you find shortcuts and make more problems for me.

I remember those sit-downs in the farm stand, talking while biting into a juicy Macintosh apple, like they were last week. Another day, he continued with his advice:

> Never hide a problem, tell me about it because I'll find out anyway. If we don't know we have problems, we can't fix them. Always remember, Tiny ... nothing is ever right unless it is done right. If I allow people to do a half-assed job on one single thing, they will do a half-assed job on everything.

That was his philosophy to me and his entire teen farmhand team about how to run the farm. Back then, I was too naïve to appreciate his seeds of improvement and leadership wisdom. It took years to realize that Grandpa was trying to accomplish much more than getting his farmwork done through our efforts. I never realized that these fond memories and experiences would teach me about the most critical success factors of continuous improvement and describe to a T exactly what organizations are doing wrong today. Organizations worry so much about the cost of seeds, which represents the freezes on improvement, technology, and critical infrastructure needs for the future. The drop apples and sour milk represent the trade-off of short-term thinking and instant gratification results. Postponing repairs represents cutbacks in financial and human capital. Not cleaning the barn represents the toleration of waste and the proliferation of many more new problems. Not plowing and seeding the fields represents short-sightedness, lack of doing what is right regardless of the consequences, and poor talent development. There was a solid vision and balance of short term and long term, and this month's bank statement did not clutter Grandpa's thinking and leadership. He knew how to make the annual farm cycle in the black. Grandpa was teaching me about fixing chronic problems instead of containment and buying time. Finally, 95% of his activity was focused on keeping things right rather than reacting to things that go wrong. Unfortunately in this new economy, these ratios are reversed for most organizations. Most executives are spending most of their efforts on buying time than on fixing chronic problems with their organizations. Containment and buying time were not even considered on Grandpa Harrington's farm, and they certainly are not winning strategies in today's global economy. I did not realize it at the time, but Grandpa gave me the earliest and most impressionable lessons on continuous improvement that still subliminally influence how I lead and motivate others today.

OFF TO THE UNIVERSITY

Another major influence with continuous improvement occurred during my college years. Dad and Mom did not attend college, so it was a given that I was going to become the first college graduate in the family. Against the advice of all high school guidance counselors, I pursued an engineering degree because at the time the demand and starting salaries for engineers were incredible (for that time period). Although I was told by many that I would never make it, I decided to go for it anyway. Like many students, I arrived without the faintest idea about selecting a major.

While completing my undergraduate engineering courses in the core curriculum, I became very interested in industrial and systems engineering and pointed the remainder of my degree requirements in that direction. I did not want to be the guy sitting in a cubicle designing a pump, a new cake mix, or a circuit board. It sounded much more exciting to be the integrator who pulls it all together into a system of people, products, processes, equipment, materials, energy, information technology, work environment, and the like. At the time, I wanted to be the utopian guy who makes the world better by engineering growth, productivity, cost reduction, efficiency, quality, safety, financial security, and best working conditions into organizations.

I was blessed to have industrial and systems engineering professors—every one of them—who not only taught the content of their courses but also were very passionate about their expertise and previous industry experiences. They arranged for several plant visits, guest speakers, and assistance on special projects from industry. I remember how much I wanted to grow up and be one of these people, a plant manager or vice president of manufacturing. Much of the classroom and laboratory activity allowed me to internalize the processes of improvement, experience the sense of making things better, and replace the intimidation with the fun and positive experience of change. The curriculum was packed with classroom exercises and case studies, all creating a very compelling conclusion that one should never fear improvement and change. The notion of improvement and change was a straightforward process with the right methodologies and tools. One small detail was omitted that could not be packed into a course: the human drama and resistance to change.

My university experiences provided technical knowledge and created the passion, urgency, desire, and confidence to push the envelope of improvement and change. These experiences also created the compelling belief that improvement is always possible and achievable because it is a never-ending journey, not a definable destination. The limit of improvement is the self-imposed limit that people and organizations choose to place on themselves. There was a perfect blend of academia and real world that paved the way for my lifelong journey of continuous improvement. My journey has evolved into an entire career in the continuous improvement business. This journey has clearly demonstrated repeatedly that the best things in business and in life come about by challenging comfort zones, embracing change, and proactively getting better by improving current situations: now.

BENNY, THE SHOP STEWARD

I started my industrial and systems engineering career as a time study and methods analyst in one of the world's leading brass manufacturers. At the time, the job offer was for big bucks: $10,800 with a 6-month review. It was one of those old-line, 100-year-old nuts-and-bolts industries in the Naugatuck Valley area of Connecticut where Grandpa, Dad, his sons, relatives, and in-laws all worked. Academia could never prepare me for what I was about to experience during those first few years of employment. Here I was at age 22, the time study kid flouting long hair, bell bottoms, western-style blazers, and platform shoes in a conservative theory X culture (e.g., brush cut, white shirt, black tie, dark polyester suits). I had a second job in the evenings playing drums in a few popular regional bands and making more money at it than my day job. Reality smacked me right in the face as I was counseled by the general manager on my first days about appearance and dress code. I remember vividly the advice of a general manager at my first job, "If you want a successful career, do whatever GE and IBM are doing, including how they dress for work." I began thinking what a big career mistake I made by becoming an industrial engineer (IE).

I worked with a department of nondegreed, up-from-the-ranks IEs who would say, "Forget everything you learned in college, kid; you're in the real world now. None of that theory matters." The IEs would sit in the office and conduct surface-level reviews of low-performing operations and then tighten up the standards using old studies and based on their own perceived best methods. Operator involvement was not even a remote thought; the department mindset was that the operators were stupid and dishonest. Then, they would head out to the plant with their axe-man and head-chopper attitudes to implement the new standards. Before too long, everyone would get upset and go through the grievance procedures. It was a silly game of liar's poker, even to a 22-year-old.

The plant was full of intimidating, cigar-chomping union guys who resented the IE department and would tap their machines with a wrench to give everyone a heads-up that the time study guys were walking through. In my first days, one hourly guy told me a story about a time study engineer's bones found in the pickling tanks 20 years earlier. Then, he encouraged me to find another job before they found my bones in there.

A lot of these guys could not speak English, but they knew all of the time standards and corresponding premium rates. They spoke fluent English if they were cheated out of a nickel on their incentive earnings. My coworkers loved to confront and tease these guys and remind them of their superior salaried status. But, being inexperienced and intimidated, I chose a different approach.

I remember listening carefully to the operators on the floor and treating some of them to coffee, asking their opinions and getting them involved in my projects, treating them with dignity and respect, allowing them to help me implement improvements and modify the incentive system fairly so they could make a few extra bucks for good performance.

One of my first assignments was with "Benny," a second-generation employee and shop steward (Benny's son also worked there). I was warned that if I made Benny angry, he would punch first and talk later. Benny was a monster of a guy, about 6 feet 5 inches, who wore construction coveralls and had fingers like Italian sausages. Benny was a bull worker, and he knew how to work hard and smart. He was a real gentleman until something set him off—then he was like a freight train off the tracks. I heard the old stories about his infamous fistfights in the parking lot and company gin mill around the corner and decided quickly that I never wanted to see that side of him.

Benny and I got off to a good start. We collaborated on how to improve his operation, and being green, I listened a lot and gained Benny's trust. The next day, he said with a grin, "Hey kid, let me show you something. But then I'll do whatever you want me to. You're the time study guy." Benny showed me how to adjust his machine and boost output by 20%, and he showed me how to adjust the incentive system fairly, honestly, and equitably. Benny knew more about his job than anyone else in the company. When I naïvely asked him why he was not running his operation this way, he said, "The other time study men don't even talk to us when they come down here. They told us we had to do it this way. They're giving us incentive pay to do things wrong, and they will write us up if they catch us doing anything different. Pretty dumb place, uh?" Benny was testing me. We made *his* changes, everybody won, and Benny became a good friend and shop floor ally. The IEs upstairs were a bit intimidated by an inexperienced kid coming up with all of these new improvements. I always confided in Benny and tapped his advice on other assignments. Benny spread the word about my approach to other stewards. Various employees began requesting my help with improvement, and they made sure that management heard the positive compliments about my performance.

Back then, I could not spell empowerment, but I was practicing it. The operators would tip me off and show me how to make improvements, and I would adjust the incentive schedule so they were not penalized for doing things right. The more they helped me out, the more things improved. I remember their comments, like, "You stick with us kid … we know what we're doing, and we'll be happy to help you out." I learned quickly that the operators were the most knowledgeable about their jobs, not the supervisors, managers, and other IEs who never listened because they were too busy sitting in the office and chasing imaginary standards—traditional cost accounting metrics such as pounds produced, yields, plant efficiency, absorption, and equipment utilization. Management played the familiar games of overproduction, working overtime on product that was not needed, or holding the books open an extra shift to improve (manipulate) these metrics. I often huddled around machines with operators to identify and solve problems. They joked around with me about getting a haircut, and I would call them "Benny and the Jets" after the famous Elton John song (many employees were N.Y. Jets and Joe Namath fans). A few of them would show up at one of my evening gigs to hear the band. I was successful at winning over many hourly workers by making their jobs a lot safer, easier, and capable of letting them earn higher compensation. These workers would either shrug their shoulders and play dumb or avoid talking to my IE peers and other management people.

Even though shipping performance, profitability, and employee relationships were clearly improving, plant management began accusing me of getting too friendly with the union workers instead of playing the traditional hard-ass time study role. Naïvely, I developed my ally status with the workers smack in the middle of the "us-versus-them" culture and did not pay much attention to the occasional humiliation and bogus advice by management and peers. I stayed the course of doing what is right, regardless of the consequences.

Not surprisingly, I moved on to another company after a few years. But, I still reflect on those wonderful hourly union people and the valuable lessons they taught me about the gray "human engineering" areas in my oversimplified, black-and-white world of improvement. First, the methodologies and tools of improvement by themselves are no match for dysfunctional leadership and the entrenched cultural values and practices. Second, you can be very successful in business and in life by proactively and constantly practicing the core virtues and values of honesty, vision, integrity, candor, courage, dignity, respect, commitment, credibility, passion, empathy, listening, and talent expansion of, with, and through others.

The vast majority of people are not bad by nature; it is their choices and decisions that create a perception of their badness. Many of these choices are driven by the wrong short-term metrics. The only way to turn this situation around is through the active and visible practice of the core virtues and values mentioned. I am blessed by my exposure to these valuable life lessons in my early twenties and how it has positively influenced my career and my own personal life.

THE LATEST WAVE OF IMPROVEMENT

Back in 1999, my company, The Center for Excellence in Operations, Inc. (CEO) was approaching its tenth anniversary as a firm specializing in strategic and operations improvement. We watched the "new" Six Sigma craze unfold and recognized that it included many methodologies and tools routinely used in our client operations improvement engagements. Suddenly we were being excluded from potential engagements because we were missing our rite of passage: a "Black Belt." Based on the early experiences of GE, Honeywell, ABB, and other highly publicized successes, executives became very insistent about people having belts as a prerequisite for improvement. Coincidently, we were working on a large Lean implementation with a division of a Fortune 500 organization that made Six Sigma a corporate mandate. We worked out an arrangement to attend the training and become certified in return for a free project with a $250K savings. After the six month process, I attended the graduation ceremony for the latest group of certified Black Belts. This ceremony was held in New York City on a Saturday evening, and I returned to work on Monday fielding questions about our Six Sigma practice like a true expert, and able to handle the tough questions like "Do you have a belt?"

Let me be totally candid about my experience by starting with the certification process itself. My first exposure to Six Sigma was in the mid-1980s through Motorola and a consortium of other companies, one of which was my employer at the time. I was participating with the consortium on developing an industry accepted statistical problem solving course for the high tech industry. The technology at the time was scientific calculators, an Apple Lisa, or Lotus 123. For me personally, certification was another one of many of my "you know you don't know it all when" life experiences and I enjoyed the process immensely. Being blessed by one of the first Motorola founding Six Sigma fathers as my instructor probably had a lot to do with my positive experience. I learned about Minitab and realized that this technology simplified statistical engineering and root cause analysis in the same way that Microsoft Office has enabled widespread graphic communication by the masses via PowerPoint presentations. As for the belt itself, certification is a respectable achievement but it is just the very beginning of improvement expertise. It is analogous to getting a driver's license; it is a step in the right direction but there is so much more to creating the long term, world class NASCAR racing team.

Let's now talk about the broader profound experience of certification. There is a larger lesson in the data-driven, fact-based methodology of Lean Six Sigma: People become vulnerable by their own intuition, opinions, and perceptions because "they don't know what they don't know." The more experience, knowledge, and confidence people accumulate, the more they tend to rely on their quick *"already know the answer"* instincts. Too many executives and managers in all industries are making bad decisions based solely upon their own personal experiences and intuitions. Some act as the consummate decision makers and tend to run over anyone that disagrees with their position. Intuition in the absence of facts also drives others in the organization to make incorrect decisions, take the wrong actions, and achieve poor results. The structured discipline of Lean Six Sigma (DMAIC) is all about great leadership through true problem definition, metrics for baseline performance, improvement goals, root cause problem solving, empowerment and engagement, project management, execution and sustainability of improvements, and accountability for results. Lean Six Sigma literally strips a process butt-naked and exposes the deeper hidden causals of poor performance. Lean Six Sigma teaches one that when the onion of a complex process is peeled back, what was originally thought to be the problem is not the problem at all. The real problem is something else, typically a root cause that has never been discussed previously.

By the way, this discussion applies to me as well . . . the seasoned expert on improvement. Sure, I am well versed on the various methodologies and tools of improvement. After working with over 300 clients on thousands of improvement projects over nearly four decades, I also don't know what I don't know. But I have learned through these experiences how to listen, create continuity of purpose, mentor organizations, ask the right questions, adapt improvement to unique situations, resolve barriers, develop talent, engage and empower people where they work, and achieve breakthrough results. My clients have taught me well that the largest improvement opportunities are the ones that we do not know about yet. Continuous learning outside of the comfort zone and in the wilderness of your intuition is what really develops one into a respected expert and enlightened leader. The other important take-away in all of this is that without data, you are just another person with an opinion – plain and simple. Executives must understand that because of their level and status, their opinions and intuition can become perceived facts to everyone else in the organization. When executives and managers refuse to acknowledge that they don't know what they don't know, they cannot lead their organizations to take the right actions and achieve the right desirable results. Enough incorrect intuition always defeats well intentioned organizations.

IMPROVEMENT EXCELLENCE™: THE NEW MODEL OF IMPROVEMENT

The silver lining to the recovery is that there are more global opportunities for improvement, growth, profitability, and global competitive success than any other time in history. The next generation of improvement is *Improvement Excellence*™: a legitimate core competency that enables organizations to *improve how they improve.* Improvement Excellence™ is part *back to basics* and part *innovative adaptation* to new global improvement needs. To accomplish this successfully, organizations need a more nimble and targeted, rapid deployment and rapid results model of improvement. In short, this requires a new *process* of improvement and a shift in focus to technology and the emerging global network of transactional processes. Improvement Excellence™ recognizes the need to stop the parade of buzzword improvement programs and implement continuous improvement for real, using the basic methodologies and tools that have existed for decades. This requires an unwavering focus on the leadership, infrastructure, and cultural elements of continuous improvement. These are the proven success factors that enable organizations to affix and retain the word *continuous* in continuous improvement. The old continuous improvement model of top-down, executive-mandated, train-the-masses, knock-off fad programs and metaphoric shotgun improvement is obsolete in this new economy.

REINVENTING DEMING'S FOURTEEN POINTS

In the famous book, *Out of the Crisis*, Dr. Deming revealed his famous fourteen points for transforming businesses. That was back in the 1980s, his book receives credit as the major impetus of the total quality management (TQM) movement in America. Many of Deming's points remain valid today, especially constancy of purpose. In the context of continuous improvement, the purpose is to improve continuously, which has not happened in most organizations. However, the urgent need to improve in the new economy makes the 1980s vintage improvement approaches look like a cakewalk. Back then, continuous improvement was centered largely around domestic manufacturing and assembly. Today, it must be adapted in every industry sector (e.g., interconnected global supply chains, hospitals, financial services, governments, etc.). Furthermore, improvement must be spread across the extended enterprise, focus on more interdependent transactional and knowledge processes, address many more complexities, and be executable at warp speed. No one is exempt from improvement.

The purpose of this book is to help all organizations and their people reinvent continuous improvement in our ailing and dawdling economy. When one thinks about process improvement as a "process," our process has not changed in decades. Consequently, many organizations are stuck in this "square-peg-and-round-hole" puzzle of improvement.

A good place to start is by updating Deming's fourteen points to reflect the requirements of our new economy. Figure 1.2 displays the original and revised fourteen points. Throughout this book, the reader will learn that success in the new economy requires the right mix of simple back to basics, reengineering some of the basics, and creativity and innovation in adapting improvement to these new requirements. Continuous improvement has not been very continuous in the past, and it is important to design the future around root causes of past failures. Organizations that reinvent continuous improvement by following the prescribed

New (N) or Basics (B)

Deming's Original 14 Points		Deming's 14 Points Revised		
1.	Create constancy of purpose.	1.	Create constancy of purpose with a living sustaining infrastructure and a disciplined, evidence-based approach to strategic improvement.	*B*
2.	Adapt the new TQM philosophy.	2.	Develop continuous improvement as the enterprise-wide cultural standard of excellence, and build expectations into the performance and reward system.	*B*
3.	Cease dependence on inspection.	3.	Rediscover a new, rapid deployment and rapid results process of improvement for the new economy.	*N*
4.	Move towards a single supplier for any one item.	4.	Adopt DMAIC as the structured, universal standard and common language of improvement.	*N*
5.	Improve constantly and forever.	5.	Recognize that strategic improvement is a continuous journey, not a destination.	*B*
6.	Institute training on the job.	6.	Embrace a customized, rapid deployment approach to education and talent development.	*N*
7.	Institute leadership.	7.	Exercise and recognize leadership best practices behaviors.	*N*
8.	Drive out fear.	8.	Develop dynamic and technology-enabled communication and change management best practices, using different media approaches for different audiences.	*N*
9.	Break down barriers between departments.	9.	Finally empower and engage people to improve where they live every day.	*B*
10.	Eliminate slogans.	10.	Develop the core competency of Improvement Excellence™ or "improving how you improve."	*N*
11.	Eliminate management by objectives.	11.	Implement the right performance measures that drive the right behaviors and achieve the right results.	*B*
12.	Remove barriers to pride of workmanship.	12.	Put the CEO, the Executive Core Team, Champions, Executive Sponsors, Process Owners, and other essentials of sustaining infrastructure to work on improvement every day.	*N*
13.	Institute education and self-improvement.	13.	Continuous improvement education and talent development is also continuous.	*B*
14.	The transformation is everyone's job.	14.	In the new world of interdependent transactional and knowledge processes, no one is exempt from improvement.	*N*

FIGURE 1.2   Deming's original and revised 14 points.

best practices of this book will discover more opportunities for improvement *now* and in the future than they might have missed in the past.

INFRASTRUCTURE: THE FOUNDATION OF CONTINUOUS IMPROVEMENT

Success or failure with any strategic improvement initiative lies within a well-designed and well-orchestrated implementation infrastructure. The importance of this critical foundation has been underestimated, oversimplified, or skipped altogether in the interest of expeditious activity. Infrastructure is the bricks and mortar of planning, organizing, and setting up continuous improvement for success and sustainability. Because it requires time, resources, and prior implementation knowledge and experiences up front, infrastructure has been the weakest link in continuous improvement for decades. It remains the weakest link in continuous improvement today. If organizations are serious about keeping the continuous in continuous improvement, they must go back and build the formal implementation infrastructure. This includes three major components:

1. *Strategic Leadership and Vision:* These align the strategic plan, the operating plan, and the improvement plan through a process called policy deployment.
2. *Deployment Planning:* This ensures the objective targeting of the highest-impact improvement opportunities, the most effective and efficient

use of talent and other limited resources, and the formal prioritization of improvement activity consistent with achieving the strategic plan.

3. *Execution:* This is the efficient completion of improvement projects and the transition of continuous and sustainable improvement to process owners and stakeholders.

I discuss these in greater detail throughout the book. Formal infrastructure provides the necessary day-by-day checks that guide planning, deployment, execution, and sustainability of continuous improvement. A well-crafted infrastructure ensures that the accumulated knowledge of organizations is engaged on the right things in the right place at the right time and in the right way. The point here is that without leadership and improvement infrastructure best practices, there is no hope for continuous and sustainable improvement. The absence of these two best practice factors sets organizations up for an improvement journey characterized by symbolic storyboards, beautification exercises, dress-up improvements, poor results, and a negative effect on culture.

BEHAVIORAL ALIGNMENT: THE BEDROCK BENEATH THE FOUNDATION

There were underlying reasons for sharing my early experiences with improvement and the childhood lessons learned. Strategic improvement initiatives are usually structured to appear logical and straightforward, but they are definitely not easy to implement and sustain successfully. Sustainability requires leadership and improvement infrastructure best practices. Some of the fundamental leadership best practices have been introduced in this chapter through my early personal experiences with continuous improvement. Leadership begins with character. These are the core virtues and values of honesty, vision, integrity, candor, courage, teamwork and empowerment, dignity, respect, commitment, passion, discipline, empathy, listening, and talent expansion of, with, and through others. Many of these core virtues are part of Toyota's culture and Eastern culture in general. Grandpa Harrington was showing me the Toyota Way over 40 years ago. Grandpa Harrington has long since passed away, but it is not surprising that his farm is one of the few working farms remaining in the area.

There is no doubt that short-term performance and reward pressures can temporarily take executives off the bead of these core virtues and values. However, executives must step up and proactively practice these core virtues and values if they hope to create a living and sustainable improvement culture in their organizations. These core virtues and values are not in conflict with success; they are the very essence of success. Every executive in every organization has the capacity to learn, personally master, and develop widespread practice of these core virtues and values. However, it requires constant awareness and self-discipline, cognitive practice by actions, and the strong conviction and charisma to influence the same behaviors in others. I discuss best practices leadership behaviors in greater detail in Chapter 3.

SUMMARY POINTS

Chapter 1 has introduced you to the underlying detractors of continuous improvement: the character and fundamental virtues and values of leadership. Enlightened leadership creates the cultural center of gravity for formal improvement. Success is also dependent on the ability of leadership to remain committed and focused on improvement as a basic strategic need and a sustainable infrastructure. These are the 80% factors of improvement that lead to growth, competitiveness, talent development, and superior operating and financial performance. These are also the most difficult leadership challenges, especially over the longer term. Organizations have focused on the easier, lower-impact factors, such as mass education of tools and methodologies, followed by executive mandates for their use. History has also taught everyone that the Western short-term "Ramen noodles" approaches to improvement do not work. This is not intended to be a leadership criticism but merely a statement of the ugly facts. Continuous improvement is unequivocally a culture created and sustained by leadership—not the latest improvement *du jour* program with its own rebranded methodologies and tools. History clearly demonstrates that continuous improvement has been implemented more like the latter.

Improvement is an investment with a positive return on investment (ROI). Improvement is not intended to be an incremental cost or another chunk of overhead. The problem with many strategic improvement initiatives is that they are not structured, planned, executed, and managed as an investment. Accordingly, the interest, commitment, effort, and results all dwindle. In the latest 80% failure rate of Lean Six Sigma deployments, it is not the fault of Lean Six Sigma. Leadership sets the course for success or failure by its actions. Leadership is ultimately responsible and accountable for making the right choices about how to implement continuous and sustainable improvement successfully. There is nothing new here—Deming talked about the same thing 30 years ago in his famous book, *Out of the Crisis*. The reality is that crisis situations are inevitable; however, the basics remain the same:

- How do organizations respond to and manage their way out of the crisis so that their time, risk, financial jeopardy, and cultural impact are minimized? The only way to get better is through authentic improvement of current conditions. Organizations must do a better job of learning from the past to accelerate their future success with crisis situations.
- How do organizations weave strategic and sustainable improvement into their culture? When improvement is truly continuous, it occurs before, during, and after crisis situations. Well-engrained improvement buffers organizations from many of the potential negative impacts of crisis situ-

ations. For these organizations, the journey through crisis is faster and more predictable, and they rise out of crisis as much stronger and superior competitors.

The bottom line is that executives and organizations must and can change their approach and *process* of improvement to avoid "the same with a different name" track record of intermittent, ineffective, and fading improvement. The next generation "process" of improvement is a simplified, laser targeted, rapid deployment, and rapid results model that, at the same time, mitigates the risks of improvement by the proactive search and elimination of root causes of risks before, during, and after improvement.

Continuous improvement is like a huge gorilla in the room, and many executives have not chosen how to deal with it effectively time and again. The problem with the improvement gorilla is that it becomes very condescending when organizations fail to pay attention to it. To complicate matters further, the new economy has rewritten the rules for success, creating the need to reengineer the process of improvement in organizations. There is absolutely no doubt that the most successful road out of the recent economic meltdown and slow recovery is a deliberate cycle of rapid improvement followed by rapid and sustainable results. The new game is one of who is implementing and sustaining improvement and transforming culture at a faster rate than that of the competition. Strategic improvement is not an option in the new economy. The new global opportunities for improvement in every organization are enormous and so are the consequences of doing nothing. Executives who are sitting on their hands and on their cash and not investing in the future will lose—plain and simple. The recent meltdown combined with everyone's claim to have some continuous improvement initiative (e.g., Kaizen, Lean, Six Sigma, enabling technology and cloud computing, etc.) under way has leveled the improvement playing field. Yesterday's successes and awards matter a lot less than the rate and magnitude of improvement needed now and in the future. Nevertheless, improvement is still the fast lane to recovery and future global success. In today's economy, organizations are either aggressively improving their businesses or are falling behind at an increasingly rapid rate.

BIBLIOGRAPHY

Deming, W. Edwards. 1982. *Out of the Crisis*. MIT Center for Advanced Engineering Study, Cambridge, MA.

Ford, H. and Bodek, N. (Foreward). 2002. *Today and Tomorrow, Commemorative Edition of Ford's 1926 Classic*. Taylor & Francis, Boca Raton.

Liker, J. 2004. *The Toyota Way*. McGraw-Hill, New York.

Taylor, F. W. 1911. *The Principles of Scientific Management by Frederick Winslow Taylor*. A monograph. Harper & Brothers, New York.

Zandin, K., and Maynard, H. 2001. *Maynard's Industrial Engineering Handbook*. 5th edition. McGraw-Hill, New York.

2 Infrastructure Overview: Accelerating Continuous Improvement

INTRODUCTION

In the new economy, organizations must not only get continuous improvement right, but also must accelerate their rate of continuous and sustainable improvement. The need for improvement is rapidly becoming greater than the capability and capacity to improve of most organizations. This chapter provides an overview of the most critical leadership, strategy, and sustaining infrastructure elements of successful continuous improvement initiatives. Over many years and consulting engagements, we have developed proven accelerators of continuous improvement that are embedded in this sustainable implementation infrastructure: Strategic Leadership and Vision, Deployment Planning, and Execution.

In our complex, technology-driven global economy, there are many unmastered lessons from the history of continuous improvement. So much of business improvement has focused on the tools, training, and acronyms themselves. The real what-really-matters factors have been downplayed in most textbooks and education and historically by many who claim to be the experts of Lean Six Sigma and other previous continuous improvement initiatives. In all fairness, many of these self-proclaimed experts were great educators and entertainers but poor implementers and even poorer executive mentors and organizational change agents.

A QUICK LESSON ON THE BASIC ESSENTIALS

What do we mean by the basic essentials of leadership, strategy, and sustaining infrastructure? These are the most critical success factors that place and keep the word *continuous* in continuous improvement and transform culture. Leadership, strategy, and sustaining infrastructure require commitment, time, and resources up front, but the payoffs are enormous on true continuous improvement and cultural transformation. The problem with these basic essentials has been threefold:

1. Convincing leadership about the significant importance of these elements as the foundation of success, especially when they have learned just enough about continuous improvement initiatives to be dangerous and are anxious to improve now. Continuous improvement is not as easy as it looks, and it has been viewed more as an acquired skill through massive training and osmosis rather than a core competency that organizations must learn to develop over time.
2. Committing to the small amount of planning time and resources to select and define mission-critical projects, create the sustaining infrastructure, develop talent correctly, and set strategic initiatives on the right course out of the gate. In the interest of making quick improvements, the basic elements of success are the first casualty. Eventually, the entire improvement initiative joins in and becomes a casualty.
3. Following a deliberate process of continuous improvement through the multitude of activities of the formal sustaining infrastructure. Lack of understanding or underestimating the importance of these basic essentials combined with the anxiety of instant gratification often results in executives claiming that their organization does not need to go through all of this. Satisfaction (or dissatisfaction) with a certain level of improvement causes executives to wander from this formal and sustaining infrastructure. This is nothing more than Planning 101, in which a few days up front will circumvent weeks or months of waste and lost opportunities down the road.

Organizations never seem to have the time to do the right things right the first time, but they always seem to find the time to do the same wrong things repeatedly. History demonstrates that these basic elements are the lost essentials of continuous improvement. For decades, organizations have had the best of intentions when implementing various improvement initiatives, but their actions have turned out to define the laws of unintended consequences with improvement. Furthermore, close enough is no longer good enough because the acceptable losses from waste and inefficiencies are no longer tolerated in this economy. Improvement has evolved to a commodity level at which organizations either improve or become victims of improvement by their competitors.

Successful strategic improvement initiatives incorporate the basic essentials of continuous improvement (Figure 2.1). These basic elements include leadership, vision, strategy, structure, processes, talent, technology, and metrics. The illustration describes the "main effect" consequences of missing these basic essentials as if they are mutually exclusive. Recognize that in reality, there are significant interaction effects of one or more deficiencies in the model on other essential elements. The degree of success or failure in one element of the model influences the success or failure in other elements.

While the basic essentials are depicted as a linear, two-dimensional framework, they are a dynamic network of concurrent activities that drive, restrain, or produce no effect on improvement. At any given moment, they can also rise

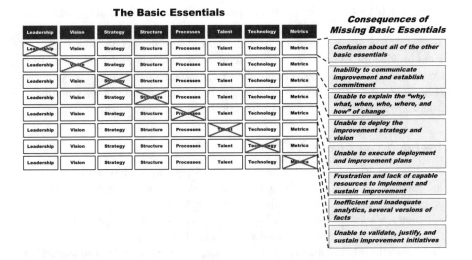

FIGURE 2.1 The basic essentials of continuous improvement. (© Copyright 2011 by The Center for Excellence in Operations, Inc. [CEO].)

to the foreground, fade into the background, or temporarily disappear off the screen. Get the picture? Leading continuous improvement is like juggling balls that others are moving around on you (or randomly throwing at you). These essentials never remain in a steady state because they are most influenced by leadership and human behaviors. Each of these essentials is like a block on a finely lubricated incline, moving uphill with the right positive forces and sliding downhill with negative forces or the absence of positive forces. In statistical terms, the essentials are closely correlated and produce both main effects and interaction effects on each other. Every process, including the process of improvement, includes variation, which creates shifts in performance. "Shift happens": Changes in priorities, a major customer or supplier problem, people entering and leaving the organization, complacency, new leadership, human frailties that require reinforcement, perceptions, economic news, politics, and thousands of other reasons temporarily take improvement initiatives off point. Effective leadership of the basic essentials pulls improvement back on the right course, albeit a slightly different course. Lack of the basic essentials creates what we refer to as a separation disorder of improvement: Improvement is viewed *in addition to* rather than *part of* daily work. In practice, this model is a living network that requires constant balance, checking and validation, readjustment, and constant course corrections. Otherwise, the improvement initiative begins to unravel itself and eventually fade away.

This is the very essence of the basic essentials of leadership, strategy, and sustaining infrastructure. Continuous improvement is not an exact science; there are many unknowns and even more surprises. Unfortunately, organizations have treated improvement more as an exact science by their excessive focus on the improvement tools themselves. To add more challenge, the world of opportunities changes at warp speed, so success is also directly proportional to the capability and velocity of improvement. In short, the basic essentials of continuous improvement provide the living framework to identify and quickly execute on emerging improvement opportunities. The basic essentials are the superglue that holds strategic improvement initiatives together and transforms the notion of continuous improvement into the cultural standards of thinking and working.

THE IMPROVEMENT BATHTUB CURVE

After years of involvement with Lean Six Sigma and many other strategic improvement initiatives, nothing in organizations changes much until people embrace and are ready and willing to change. Change usually occurs by two extremes: pain and pleasure. Pain is usually associated with change from negative forces, while pleasure is associated with change from positive forces. One is not easier than the other is, and the results from improvement come back to leadership behaviors, decisions, and actions. Years ago, we described this with our familiar *improvement bathtub curve* (Figure 2.2) and how organizations postponed serious improvement until they entered one of the two extremes. Organizations in either the pain or the pleasure zones are committed to improvement and achieve the most success with improvement. Between pain and pleasure is the "empty tub," which represents organizations that are comfortable with their current situations. These are the most difficult organizations to change because they have strong convictions that everything is fine and they have things under control. A closer look at this segment exposes weak spots in leadership and culture: lack of vision or recognition of the need to improve, a casual go at improvement programs

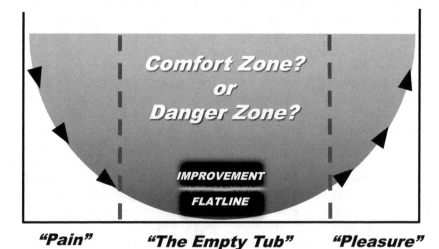

"Pain"   "The Empty Tub"   "Pleasure"

FIGURE 2.2   The improvement bathtub curve. (© Copyright 2011 by The Center for Excellence in Operations, Inc. [CEO].)

with few expectations, postponement of improvement, lack of critical competencies to improve, favoring quicker ad hoc management approaches, reactionary changes, or waiting and hoping that potential threats change direction and go away. Their improvement initiatives do not exist or are flatlined. These are cultures of unknowing and unintentional complacency, and their comfort zones can turn quickly into danger zones. These cultures typically take action when crisis smacks them in the cheek.

There is a dynamic to the improvement bathtub curve. Everyone wishes to be in the pleasure zone. For the organizations that keep continuous in continuous improvement, they expand and remain in the pleasure zone. Their choice is a deliberate and unrelenting one. As soon as they lose momentum, they slide back into the empty tub zone. Similarly, organizations in the empty tub zone can shift to the pleasure zone through the deliberate disciplines of continuous improvement. They can also be pushed into the pain zone by a do-nothing response to negative forces, which creates a crisis to change. Regardless of how they arrived there, organizations in the pain zone must use deliberate improvement (temporary or continuous) to shift to the other zones. Again, the zone they shift to is dependent on the strength of continuous in continuous improvement.

Many of the more recent, well-publicized Lean Six Sigma deployments were motivated by mutual pleasure. The economy was in good shape, and organizations took advantage of great opportunities and potential to improve. It was the all-around right thing to do. Individuals were provided with a great professional development opportunity to attend workshops in a popular destination spot, or become certified as a Black Belt, a distinctive and valued career achievement. Another common motivator of pleasurable improvement is when revenue growth and demands exceed the ability to service customers, which is a good problem. Toyota is in this segment because it has experienced the pain after World War II and the pleasure during the past six decades of never looking back and becoming the world's largest and most successful auto manufacturer.

As we look around at the postmeltdown economy, improvement is motivated more by the consequences of remaining the same, whether it is pain or pleasure. Where there is pleasure improvement, there is great, enlightened leadership. Most of what we see is pain without the appropriate leadership responses. Many organizations are actually experiencing lots of pain but remain sitting idle in the empty tub. Or, they begin by taking all the wrong, short-term swings at improvement. Keep in mind that pleasure can also go away or turn to pain quickly in the new economy. The forces of change may be unpredictable and based on chance. The location of an organization on the improvement bathtub curve is not chance; it is a leadership choice. Once the right choices are made, the rest of the improvement journey falls into place. The purpose through this book is to raise consciousness about the power of reinventing strategic improvement and convince the reader that risk of doing nothing is much higher than the risk of improvement.

THE RELATIONSHIP BETWEEN DIMINISHING VALUE AND WASTE

Another challenge for all organizations is this concept of diminishing value. The relative value-added content of work is always declining from the customer's perspective. Therefore, value has a direct relationship with waste. The term *value added* has been defined as anything the customer is willing to pay for, but that is changing in the new economy. There is a value war of sorts going on; customers and suppliers want to avoid as much of the cost as possible, even though value exists. Much of this is due to the declining perception of value and the need to reduce costs. For example, if an organization implements Lean Six Sigma and achieves benchmark quality and delivery capabilities, the value is high to the marketplace. In 6 months, customers grow accustomed to these service levels and expect this level of performance 100% of the time. The initial value is now diminished. When every competitor implements Lean Six Sigma and develops the same capabilities, the value is no longer a differentiator. We live in a world where the life cycles of value are much shorter than in the past. Globally, everyone is trying to leapfrog the competition, which continues to drive down value and costs. The bar of expected operating capabilities is rising faster than organizations can improve and keep up with it.

Current performance has an associated level of value. *Delight performance* is the result of maximizing the total customer experience with a higher associated level of value. The gap between current performance and delight performance is waste. The word *waste* has negative connotations, but no one has done anything wrong. Waste is dynamic and results from a changing world with rising expectations. The only thing wrong with waste is allowing it to grow while choosing to do nothing about it. The risks of doing nothing are much higher than taking action, and doing nothing has far-reaching consequences on others in the organization. The challenge with waste is that it is often hidden or unknown until it is too late to avoid a problem. Closing these gaps represents the largest improvement opportunities for organizations. The improvement strategy should include a serious rethinking of how the organization can improve its value proposition at multiple levels of product or service delivery. Lean Six Sigma and other improvement initiatives must be focused to mine and eliminate the wastes proactively. The future is all about maximizing the total customer or patient experience, through all of the touch points. For an individual organization, the future is about who can *improve how they improve* faster than the competition. This theme rings clearly throughout the book.

PAYOFFS THROUGH LAYOFFS ARE NOT IMPROVEMENT

Some of the most common leadership actions in times of crisis are the across-the-board layoffs and spending freezes. Asking individual divisions and functions in the organization to ante up 10% of their people or budget is not improvement; in fact, this is also not leadership. Sometimes, this approach is fine to shake up organizations that are literally plagued with visible inefficiency and waste. Another logical reason might be the decision to close a facility and move manufacturing and related support functions to China (although the decision process itself may be in question). However, for fairly efficient organizations that have been through several of these cycles, their organizational fat is now down to the meat and bones. It does not require much creativity and innovation to order across-the-board spending freezes or to walk out 500 terminated employees on a Friday afternoon. This trend is occurring increasingly in hospitals under severe changes in reimbursement and rising double-digit costs. When this happens, morale suffers a big hit because the organization perceives the decision as heartless and always results in walking the wrong 500 people out. If organizations choose arbitrary layoffs and spending freezes as a short-term measure, they need to communicate frequently with the organization to manage people quickly through this anguish stage and restore productivity and morale.

The major point here is that arbitrary layoffs and across-the-board spending freezes are not improvement because these actions usually do not improve anything but imaginary financial numbers. Layoffs and freezes only buy executives more time and make situations worse—for themselves and everyone else. These decisions also take the wind out of the sails of strategic improvement for sure. There are serious flaws in these decisions that every executive knows but chooses to ignore them under much larger pressures of improving the short-term numbers. Employees in organizations that have been through a few of these cycles also understand these flaws. Improvement (e.g., a solid root cause analysis) on the topic of spending freezes would reveal that some functions should cut their budgets by much more than 10%, while others like new product development should increase their budgets; the net goal may end up exceeding 10% through science, not hip shooting.

In the case of arbitrary downsizing, these decisions are the exact opposite of business process improvement. Everyone forgets that these people who are let go served a purpose in the organization's key business and service delivery processes and took vital knowledge and skills with them. When they disappear, the remaining employees (who are already overloaded) are asked to pick up the slack. The result is the addition of more hidden inefficiencies and waste as people search for work-arounds to keep their heads above water. Recently, a manager commented to me: "We are all so overloaded that it's a joke. … My job has turned into coming to work every day and doing whatever people ask me to do to keep myself from getting in the least amount of trouble." Success in this organization has become minimizing failure by obedience. Business process improvement is a much better approach to downsizing because process improvements may eliminate the need for people and at the same time improve efficiencies and eliminate waste. If organizations embraced *continuous* improvement all along, downsizing could occur continuously (instead of in batches driven by crisis) and naturally through attrition or other means that would be better understood by employees. Some employees might enter a reserve pool; they are retrained and redeployed in the organization. Strategic and sustainable improvement is a much better way to achieve these results and is much less disruptive than across-the-board downsizing and spending freezes.

The Next Generation of Improvement

The purpose of this book is not to recommend another enchanting improvement mantra or some magic improvement dust under a new banner. The basic methodologies and tools of improvement have served organizations well for the past 75 years; another new buzzword program is not the answer. As we have mentioned several times, the issue at hand is that the "process" of improvement has served its useful life. Think about it. How many processes in your organization have remained virtually the same since the 1980s? All processes require improvement and tweaking as the dynamics of business change over time.

Years of involvement in successful improvement initiatives enables one to learn invaluable lessons and experiences from the associated human drama and cultural side of continuous improvement. These lessons in executive leadership and human engineering are often difficult to envision, predict, explain, replicate, standardize - and even more difficult to package into an illusively perceived recipe like the stand-alone improvement tools. The real challenge in the new economy is *improving how we improve* – To learn how to implement continuous improvement correctly with all the necessary leadership, strategy, and sustaining infrastructure elements . . . within the real constraints of executives and their organizations, while adapting improvement to the complex requirements of the new economy.

The next generation of improvement is not another buzzword program at all. The next generation of improvement is a challenge of how to design and implement continuous and sustainable improvement successfully in the new economy with the right approach, velocity, focus, and ease – while eliminating or working within the dynamic operating models, realistic constraints, and absorption bandwidths of organizations. What this means is the combined strategy of Deming back-to-basics, innovation, enabling technology, and adaptive improvement. The future of improvement is a nimble, systematic execution of this combined strategy that creates the continuous cultural standard of excellence. This is a well integrated *system* of improvement similar to the Toyota Production System (TPS) but a more dynamic system that leverages technology and harvests the larger enterprise and extended enterprise opportunities.

THE PHILOSOPHY OF IMPROVEMENT EXCELLENCE™

Improvement Excellence™ is the mastery of developing and implementing successful strategic and continuous business improvement initiatives, transforming culture, and enabling organizations to *improve how they improve*. It is a continuous journey of striving for excellence through a flawless presence of the Strategic Leadership and Vision, Deployment Planning, and Execution infrastructure and a broader, more creative, and innovative application of improvement methodologies and tools. Improvement Excellence™ integrates all improvement methodologies into a uniform and laser-targeted powerhouse initiative and a broad scope that encompasses the end-to-end "idea to pleasurable customer experience" cycle. There is no such thing as a standalone Kaizen, Lean, Six Sigma,

> *"Improvement Excellence^{TM} is the mastery of developing and implementing successful strategic and continuous business improvement initiatives, transforming culture, and enabling organizations to improve how they improve."*

information technology (IT), or other single-point improvement initiative. It discourages the age-old obsession with specific improvement tools by themselves. Rather, Improvement Excellence™ integrates these methodologies and tools into a master improvement tool box of sorts because no single-point improvement effort is all encompassing or all inclusive. Global enterprises, healthcare organizations, financial institutions, and government agencies all have a full spectrum of improvement opportunities that require the right approaches to achieve the right results. The goal is to identify and successfully deploy the right combination of improvement methodologies to the highest-impact opportunities. Improvement Excellence™ builds capability and competency for this new transcendent state of continuous improvement.

For most Western Hemisphere organizations, the greatest missing link is that continuous improvement is first and foremost a cultural standard of excellence that is created and sustained by leadership. This is accomplished through the right improvement vision and strategy, best practices leadership behaviors, and a rock-solid sustaining infrastructure. When organizations fail at making continuous improvement a cultural standard, the word *continuous* always drops out, and they backslide to less-effective and less-efficient practices. Like it or not, this is the story of (dis)continuous improvement over this time frame. Now, let us think about Toyota, which, despite its recent brake system problems (which were resolved quickly), has been winning at the global game of continuous improvement for nearly 70 years. The largest single reason is culture, not a continuous parade of buzzwords and improvement tools.

Successful change is never easy, and it often requires patience, commitment, and devotion levels far beyond initial expectations. Organizations have a tremendous opportunity to turn things around in the future by focusing on the core competency of Improvement Excellence™ or improving how they improve. The best practices leadership behaviors, strategy, and sustaining infrastructure that serve as the underpinnings of Improvement Excellence™ are introduced in this chapter and discussed in greater detail throughout the book. The specific elements of Strategic Leadership and Vision, Deployment Planning, and Execution begin this destination of continuous and sustainable improvement success by driving a huge wedge into the norms of organizations and creating the proven path toward Improvement Excellence™.

THE IMPROVEMENT EXCELLENCE™ FRAMEWORK

Figure 2.3 provides an overview of Improvement Excellence™ as an integrated framework. This framework includes three distinct and important components:

1. The *Formal Sustaining Infrastructure* of Strategic Leadership and Vision, Deployment Planning, and Execution. Embedded in each of these infrastructure elements is what we refer to as the proven "accelerators" of strategic improvement. The Ten Accelerators are covered in more detail in this chapter.
2. The *Integration of Improvement Methodologies,* which ensures that the right improvement methodologies and tools are applied to the highest-impact opportunities correctly, creating breakthroughs in systematic performance followed by continuous improvement best practices. This is covered in more detail in Chapter 6.
3. Our *Rapid Deployment and Rapid Results Improvement Model* is called Scalable Lean Six Sigma™. The model is based on the simple Pareto principle: Target the largest opportunities and focus limited resources on these opportunities with the necessary limited set of improvement methodologies. The idea is to focus on the right big things that keep everyone awake every night. Scalability in the model is achieved mathematically: 80% of the improvements are represented by 20% of the possible opportunities, and 80% of improvements require 20% of the methodologies and tools. This is also covered in more detail later in this chapter.

Note the center section of the diagram. Enlightened Leadership is the engine of Improvement Excellence™. The detailed process of enlightened leadership and the components and accelerators of Improvement Excellence™ are covered extensively in Chapters 4 through 6. The remainder of this chapter provides an overview of the model.

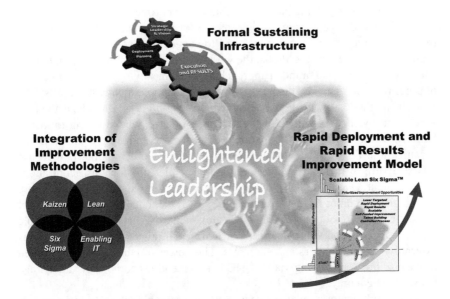

FIGURE 2.3 The Improvement Excellence™ framework. (© Copyright 2011 by The Center for Excellence in Operations, Inc. [CEO].)

DMAIC THE COMMON LANGUAGE OF IMPROVEMENT

Many organizations still use Deming's PDCA (Plan-Do-Check-Act) cycle in their continuous improvement activities. The benefit of PDCA is that it provides a structured methodology and common thought process about improvement. In practice, PDCA is usually used in a teaming environment where much of the results tend to be *compensating improvements* based on brainstorming around group experiences and perceptions. This is fine for the more obvious "low-hanging-fruit" opportunities. DMAIC (Define-Measure-Analyze-Improve-Control) is the structured methodology followed in the evolution of Six Sigma deployments and is very much an integral part of success with improvement. DMAIC is a more robust version of Deming's PDCA cycle, Eight Disciplines (8D), and other company-specific step-by-step programs because it demands more data-driven and fact-based analysis. DMAIC is an effective gate-keeping process in the pursuit of *perfection-driven improvement* through more evidence-based root cause analysis and sustainability of improvements.

Successful continuous improvement initiatives require a common structured approach and more permanent universal language of improvement. A common language and structure like DMAIC provides the detailed GPS for the *process* of improvement. On a broader scale, DMAIC provides this effective roadmap for all continuous improvement initiatives. DMAIC has a strong analogy to a roadmap or atlas because in practice it becomes evident that the true benefit of DMAIC comes from the universal ability of people to follow a repeatable, proven approach to solving business problems. Over time, DMAIC becomes the successful standard communication protocol for improvement. On the surface, this seems quite logical, yet this is one of the major reasons for recent Lean Six Sigma successes. Since the 1980s, the world of improvement has chosen to take a more exploratory and branded approach to problem solving, resulting in cycles of programs, confusion by the buzzwords, and disappointment with results. The DMAIC methodology is not just a problem-solving process. DMAIC is the universal improvement language of the seasoned mentor, who is trying to install DMAIC as the common cultural standard and protocol for improvement in the organization. Following this structure, and coaching others about how to use this structure to their advantage, is a major enabler of successful continuous improvement. Over time, DMAIC grows into something much larger and more powerful: It becomes the new way that people think, act, and work—and expect the same behaviors in others. DMAIC fundamentally changes the way people think, work, communicate, and interact with each other internally, as well as externally with customers and suppliers. The power of fact-based, data-driven root cause problem solving via DMAIC is a tremendous competitive advantage in the new economy.

Successful mentoring is dependent on closely following the DMAIC methodology. This is a conceptual problem-solving and project management structure that must be flexibly adapted to a wide array of problem-solving situations. The DMAIC methodology provides an effective structure and gate-keeping process of improvement with formal and deliberate checkpoints. The specific elements of each phase are not all used all of the time, but exist for practical application when their use is warranted. In the case of an atlas, not every page of the atlas is used for every trip. The pages used depend on the destination in mind. Likewise in DMAIC, the specific steps and tools applied depend on the specifics of the particular problem. In addition, similar to taking a trip, the secret to completing the journey successfully is first to understand where it is you want to go (*define*). Once the starting point is established, it becomes critical to characterize the problem and the process (*measure*). At this point, improvement teams define potential root cause diagrams, value stream mapping, and other analysis that quantifies the current process and its associated baseline performance.

Moving further into the DMAIC process, teams perform root cause analysis and other analytics to diagnose and analyze the current process (*analyze*). At this point, the problem is more defined and understood than ever before. The onion has been peeled back, and the true root causes are known and calibrated. Next is the point at which improvement alternatives and options are evaluated (*improve*), and the best improvement course of action is decided on by the team. Finally is the implementation of recommendations (*control*) and the handoff to process owners. Some have argued that Control should have been called Continue. First, using a rock-climbing analogy, the tricams and other protective devices must be set before the climb continues. This is Control, so the climber does not fall or the improvement progress does not backslide. Also, there is very visible evidence and well-defined corrective actions to keep progress moving upward. Continue is a given in continuous improvement. As defined, DMAIC never claimed that improvement concluded with C, although it did end there for those purely interested in getting their Black Belt. Continuous improvement is exactly what it says: One begins the process all over again on the same or different improvement initiative.

The DMAIC process is so logical, and it is the lifeline of strategic improvement. Unfortunately, DMAIC and structured root cause problem solving are the first casualty in times of crisis. It takes strong, unwavering, and seasoned leadership to take DMAIC from a novel concept for a few teams to an accepted standard of behavior and logical thinking in organizations.

Some criticize DMAIC for its linear, waterfall approach to problem solving. This is not a problem of DMAIC; it is a problem of an inexperienced improvement practitioner trying to fit every problem into the standard recipe. DMAIC is not a simple recipe, and it should not be followed blindly for every improvement opportunity. The experienced practitioner recognizes and adapts many implementation factors outside the standard DMAIC process. DMAIC does not need to follow a true linear process. Often, individuals find themselves looping back to a previous phase to clarify forward direction or to conduct an additional analysis based on new information.

Many of the more high-complexity/high-impact improvement opportunities in organizations, particularly the technology-related projects, are about dealing with what is referred to as *wicked problems*. These challenges are typically characterized by significant ambiguity and uncertainty, no single correct and fixed definition of the problem, multiple views about the problem with conflicting solutions, lack of information, different participants with different motivations, and multiple connections to other problems. Some examples of these complex improvement opportunities include research and development (R&D), technology development, concept engineering of new products, software development, advertising and promotional effectiveness, and global product development and commercialization. Indeed, it is this *social complexity* of these problems, not their technical complexity, that overwhelms most current problem-solving and project management approaches. DMAIC can also be applied to these totally nonlinear creative and innovative process improvements. The fundamental link in these situations is fact-based, data-driven root cause analysis (without locking creativity and innovation in a box), which actually enables more effective levels of creativity and innovation.

IMPLEMENTATION INFRASTRUCTURE

Figure 2.4 provides an overview of the critical infrastructure elements of a successful continuous improvement initiative. Success or failure lies within a well-designed and well-orchestrated implementation infrastructure: the Strategic Leadership and Vision, Deployment Planning, and Execution success factors.

Within each of these elements are proven accelerators of continuous and sustainable improvement. As mentioned previously, these are the most critical

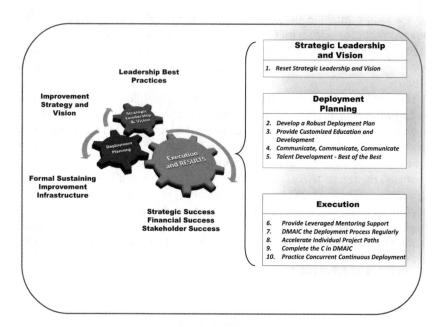

FIGURE 2.4   Critical sustaining improvement infrastructure. (© Copyright 2011 by The Center for Excellence in Operations, Inc. [CEO].)

success factors, but they are also the most overlooked, underestimated, and difficult make-you-or-break-you factors. Keeping infrastructure productive requires time and resources, but not nearly as much as doing the wrong things or doing things over. Based on our experiences, the benefits of success are millions of times higher than the costs of failure. Everyone knows this intellectually, yet formal improvement is always the first casualty of crisis and *immediate reason*: the act of attempting to correct a situation at hand with unreasonable actions based on opinions, perceptions, or direct orders from others who are missing the facts. Logic and root cause thinking are replaced by reactive improvement and firefighting, and the "continuous" falls out of the equation again. The root causes of recent failures of Lean Six Sigma and every other continuous improvement initiative are traceable to lack of, or poor performance in, implementation infrastructure. These factors are much tougher to get right and sustain (and a lot less fun than training in some exotic location), and it requires a long-term level of attention, commitment, resources, time, and effort from the chief executive officer and his/ her executive team.

BUILDING THE SUSTAINING IMPROVEMENT INFRASTRUCTURE

Continuous improvement initiatives have evolved to their own turning point. Looking backward, the traditional top-down, executive-mandated, train-the-masses implementation approaches are no longer valid. These approaches are too costly, too slow, and too bureaucratic. The same thinking that got us here will not get us where we need to go. The fine art of *hyperinsanity*—doing more of the same things with greater speed, effort, and emotions and expecting different results—is also out. Looking forward, technology is placing our ability more in real time to improve by a process we refer to as Sense-Interpret-Decide-Act-Monitor (SIDAM). In the past, everyone talked about going to the Gemba (the workplace), but today the Gemba is coming to our fingertips. There is absolutely no doubt that organizations must continue to improve to remain competitive. This all adds up to the urgent need to change the *process* of continuous improvement, to adapt improvement to the new economy in a more targeted, rapid deployment and rapid improvement model, finally to achieve continuous and sustainable improvement, and to secure our global competitive and financial success.

As I say repeatedly, setting up a strategic improvement initiative like Lean Six Sigma looks logical, but it is not easy. Laying the groundwork for a successful and sustainable improvement initiative that becomes interwoven into the daily cultural fabric requires the right long-term commitment, expertise, and effort up front. This groundwork is like any planning exercise: Every minute up front will save days or weeks down the road. Success is also dependent on the nurturing and reinforcement aspects of the sustaining infrastructure throughout the continuous journey of improvement. A solid sustaining improvement infrastructure makes the difference between harvesting "the money" versus harvesting "the empty motions."

The remainder of this section provides an overview of the formal implementation infrastructure and their respective accelerators of continuous improvement:

INFRASTRUCTURE ELEMENT: STRATEGIC LEADERSHIP AND VISION

1. **Reset Deployment Leadership, Strategy, and Vision.** This accelerator helps executives rationalize business strategy, understand gaps between current and desired performance, and align Lean/Six Sigma improvement activities with business strategy. Right up front, executives must prevent Lean Six Sigma and other strategic initiatives from becoming another fad, improvement-for-improvement's-sake program with illusionary results. Interest and enthusiasm alone without substance allow these initiatives to roll out of the gate on a wrong course. This accelerator includes the following objectives:

   - Develop the improvement strategy and vision
   - Build a leadership deployment infrastructure
   - Assign a formal executive leadership team and a balanced deployment core team
   - Identify executive sponsors
   - Create a shared sense of executive knowledge via Champion-level Lean/Six Sigma education and executive coaching and mentoring
   - Establish high-level strategic improvement needs

- Begin to build stakeholder commitment and engagement

All of these topics are covered in greater detail in the next chapter on leadership, strategy, and vision.

INFRASTRUCTURE ELEMENT: DEPLOYMENT PLANNING

2. **Develop a Robust Deployment Plan.** This accelerator identifies the major themes of improvement required to meet or exceed the business plan. It also involves a formal process for stepping down the major improvement themes into specific project opportunities. In our strategic improvement initiatives such as Lean Six Sigma, we have developed several templates to guide our clients through this process:

   - Macro Charter: A template used to collect and identify potential project information such as problem, probable root causes, cost of quality/waste, proposed project name, objectives, improvement goals, benefits, and deliverables.
   - Project Selection: This template allows executives to evaluate projects against each other relative to business plan contribution. Projects are scored and ranked against attributes such as cost reduction, growth, level of resources, time, availability of data, capital investment, and others. The object is to remove subjectivity or executive preference and focus on the organization's most high-impact/lower-effort and -resources projects.
   - Project/Resource Alignment: This simple template evaluates potential participant resources against a variety of required skill sets and direct experiences, facilitates the identification and selection of team leaders and team participants, and helps to align people to projects with a level of objectivity.
   - Team Assignment: Another objective within deployment planning is to spread and develop critical mass as much as possible. In our deployments, we exercise the one resource-one team rule, which forces a deeper development of bench strength. When everything needs the involvement of a handful of people in the organization, something is definitely wrong.
   - Project Charters: These are the team's reference documents for the specific project. Project Charters define a specific team leader and team, executive sponsor, and the project title. Project Charters also include a crisp problem statement, probable root causes (Clue data), project objectives, scope, boundaries, performance metrics, current baseline performance and Cost of Poor Quality (COPQ) data, improvement goals, quantified benefits, expected deliverables, and a rough timetable for the project.

These and many other details of Deployment Planning are also covered in greater detail in subsequent chapters.

3. **Provide Customized Education and Development.** The objective of this accelerator is to shy away from the traditional boilerplate education structure and develop the custom-tailored curriculum and module content that delivers the specific skill set needs of a particular client with a specific set of challenges and projects. Successful continuous improvement initiatives do not provide mass education on rarely used topics and theory and instead focus on a more targeted approach with the practical and most widely used improvement tools. In addition, this customized education should include skill set development on the soft side of improvement, such as project management, performance measurement design, teaming and team dynamics, change management, and other improvement leadership topics.

4. **Communicate, Communicate, Communicate.** There is no such thing as too much communication as long as the message is consistent and value adding. The most important part of communication is to establish the recognition of the need to change and why the organization must embrace change. The why of change is often inadequately explained or explained with emotional reasons. Well-executed and frequent communication builds commitment and trust, reduces confusion, sets expectations, builds continuity and interest, removes fears of change, provides a medium for publicizing success and recognizing people, and builds momentum for larger successes.

5. **Talent Development—Best of the Best.** This accelerator means simply putting the best of everything into the deployment: best projects; best leadership; best team leader; best team members; best innovative approach; best implementation plans; best use of limited resources, time, and capacity; best implementation path; and best results. The underpinning of this accelerator is proactive talent development because organizations cannot put up their best without having their best on the bench ready to go. Although some organizations have attempted it, improvement is not something to be assigned to less-desirable people with time on their hands. We want to pull these people in and develop their expertise at some point, but not at the front end of the deployment. Sports teams do not go at it with their third string—they go with their best players. The same holds true with Lean/Six Sigma and improvement in general.

INFRASTRUCTURE ELEMENT: EXECUTION

6. **Provide Strong Leveraged Mentoring Support.** These activities are the most important in a Lean Six Sigma deployment or any other strategic improvement initiative. There is a significant opportunity to

reduce project completion cycle times and results while still developing people in the improvement methodologies and tools. This requires project leadership and mentoring by very experienced professionals with proven executive mentoring and development expertise, a thorough understanding of key business processes, deep knowledge in leading and implementing large-scale improvement initiatives, and several previous experiences with the same or similar projects in a wide variety of environments.

7. **DMAIC the Deployment Process Regularly.** Variation exists in all processes, including the DMAIC process. There is no magic mantra for success: The series of events that happen during a deployment are unpredictable and therefore subject to course corrections. Things such as delays in projects, a team pulled and assigned to an important customer issue, the departure of an executive or team member from the organization, misunderstandings in project objectives, shifting in priorities, problems with acquiring data and information, workload conflicts, absenteeism, dysfunctional behaviors, poor team performance, a trip to a supplier, unexpected quality or engineering development problems, and thousands of other events introduce variation and disruptions to the implementation process. Successful continuous improvement initiatives require the leadership, DMAIC thinking, and know-how to recognize these detractors and take the right swift actions to reset the course.

8. **Accelerate Individual Project Paths.** This is the creative fusion of Accelerators 2 and 5. One of the largest challenges for teams is refining and targeting the true scope of their projects. Even a good job on defining and scoping out projects in Accelerator 2 results in a funneling down in direction once the onion is peeled back and data drive the team to the true, prioritized root causes. The objective here is to guide teams and projects down the 80/20 path, with 80% of the problem improved by focusing efforts on the 20% of the root causes. As mentioned in Accelerator 5, implementation know-how and experiences count a lot more than self-proclaimed know-how or elfin knowledge of individual improvement tools.

9. **Complete the C in DMAIC.** In the DMAIC cycle, C is the most important step. It turns out that C is also the weakest link in the DMAIC chain. This is the actual point of implementation and process owner handoff. There are several important activities that must take place to ensure a smooth transition from a team project to the improved process norm. Failure to address the critical elements of C is a sure bet to sliding backward to old norms—and no improvement. Keep in mind the importance of this risk in the new economy: What was once "staying the same" is the equivalent of falling behind at an increasingly rapid rate.

10. **Practice Concurrent Continuous Deployment.** The traditional rollout of a Lean Six Sigma deployment has occurred in waves, similar to groups of soldiers completing basic training and military boot camp. The term

wave refers to a sequential process for developing people and completing projects. There are defined start and end times to a wave and a deadline for certification. Waves tend to stretch out the smaller-content projects and compromise the larger-content projects in the interest of everyone marching to the same certification deadline and scheduled graduation day. Between the so-called waves, a lot of progress and momentum can be lost. In contrast, concurrent deployment is the development of people and completion of improvement projects continuously and based on current critical needs. Although a deployment may begin with teams and projects leaving the same starting gate, improvement activities do not end at the same time. Some projects end earlier or later than others do. Concurrent deployment embraces projects, priorities, and resources that are always "teed up" ready to go, opportunities are continuously targeted and prioritized based on strategic impact, individual project launches are staggered based on availability of resource availability, and improvement capacity is managed. The deployment process is deliberately scheduled to be concurrent and continuous.

Collectively, the accelerators embedded in the implementation infrastructure provide a proven architecture for a successful Lean Six Sigma deployment and lasting sustainable strategic and continuous improvement. Infrastructure is not a bureaucracy but provides just enough edifice to keep initiatives together and in the right positive direction. The accelerators provide the right level of leadership, discipline, structure, and accountability that has been missing in many Western Hemisphere improvement initiatives. These accelerators should not be limited to a Lean Six Sigma deployment: Many of the accelerator concepts are directly transportable to other strategic initiatives whether it is evaluating, purchasing, and integrating a new acquisition or facility; rationalizing global supply chains, regional sourcing, or internal logistics; implementing a new integrated enterprise architecture; planning new product and service delivery offerings; or conducting a cost-benefit and risk analysis on various government services.

SCALABLE LEAN SIX SIGMA™

Scalable Lean Six Sigma™ is the Center for Excellence in Operations' proprietary accelerated improvement model for rapid deployment and rapid results. In 2001, the company adapted the conventional Lean Six Sigma deployment model to our smaller and midsize client needs. Figure 2.5 provides a graphical view of Scalable Lean Six Sigma™.

One of the problems with the traditional big-bang, top-down, train the masses, mandated Lean Six Sigma is that it takes too long before actual improvement begins. It assumes that a belt is a prerequisite for improvement, and it has created an improvement bureaucracy of Master Black Belts, Black Belts, Green Belts, Yellow Belts, and White Belts. This approach is a major overkill for smaller and midsize organizations. Even very large corporations are groups of smaller

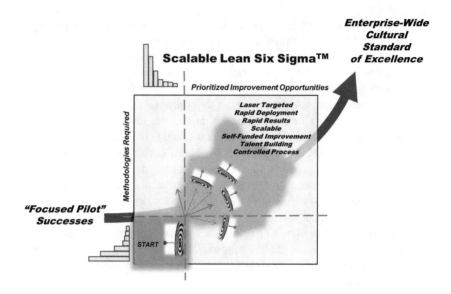

FIGURE 2.5   Scalable Lean Six Sigma™. (© Copyright 2011 by The Center for Excellence in Operations, Inc. [CEO].)

and midsize organizations. When one looks closer at this traditional process of improvement, it is not surprising that leadership has abandoned Lean Six Sigma in search of a more accelerated approach.

Another element of waste in the traditional Lean Six Sigma deployment is that belts end up applying much less of the content that was covered through the exhaustive certification process. Most improvement opportunities require what is referred to as the basic blocking and tackling tools of Lean Six Sigma (e.g., value stream mapping, check sheets, templates, basic charting and data analysis tools, 5S, fundamental Lean tools, Failure Mode and Effects Analysis (FMEA), process capability, measurement systems analysis, etc.). This is particularly true in the professional, knowledge, and transactional process space. There are definitely exceptions to the rule, but they are exceptions, not common practice. Through dozens of successful deployments, we have applied the Pareto thinking to the design of our high-performance Scalable Lean Six Sigma™ model, namely:

- 20% of the improvement opportunities yield 80% of the benefits;
- 20% of the improvement methodologies and tools are used to achieve 80% of the benefits;
- 20% of those in the organization become the outstanding champions of improvement and attempting to make this 100% is a game of diminishing returns;
- 20% of the supply base creates 80% of the sourcing and procurement issues.

Scalable Lean Six Sigma™ is a simplified and streamlined approach to the traditional Lean Six Sigma deployment model. We have applied much of the thinking embedded in Lean Six Sigma to the process of improvement, and have eliminated the non value-added improvement activity. Certification is still valued, but it is viewed as a longer term professional development activity for the real champions of improvement, rather than a prerequisite for improvement for the masses or another "check the box" for the resume.

The meltdown and slow recovery created a need for a more nimble and fast-track approach to continuous and sustainable improvement: a different approach that is more laser targeted to the highest-impact improvement opportunities, incorporates the attributes of rapid deployment and rapid results, is flexible and scalable to emerging needs, and positions organizations in a self-funding mode of improvement. As it turns out, the requirements of the new economy are very similar to smaller and mid-size organizations that Center for Excellence in Operations, Inc. has worked with since 2001 with our Scalable Lean Six Sigma™ model. They cannot fund Lean Six Sigma like GE, are very risk averse, do not have full-time resources to devote to improvement, will not wait years to achieve an ROI, need to build internal capability quickly, and demand results now. Through the years, our smaller and mid-size clients have achieved benchmark results in a much tighter deployment window (6–18 months). On a scale of magnitude, some have outperformed the deployments of larger corporations, including GE, Honeywell, and other shining stars of Lean Six Sigma. Scalable Lean Six Sigma™ fit the bill for these clients, and with a bit of tweaking, it fits the bill for an accelerated approach to Lean Six Sigma in the new economy.

Scalable Lean Six Sigma™ is the essence of rapid deployment and rapid and sustainable results. The formal sustaining infrastructure of Strategic Leadership and Vision, Deployment Planning, and Execution enables organizations to identify, prioritize, and laser target the highest-impact opportunities. This is very different from the scattered, "improvement-for-improvement's sake" approach of traditional deployments. The strategy behind Scalable Lean Six Sigma™ is to ensure that an organization's improvement initiative is an investment with a significant entitled ROI and not a sunk cost. The model is also designed to position organizations quickly in a self-funding mode with Lean Six Sigma.

CONTINUOUS IMPROVEMENT: NO LONGER A FAD OR OPTION

The philosophy of improvement, combined with the methodologies and tools used to mobilize people to a higher standard of productivity and quality of life, is one of humankind's most important social technologies. As organizations evolve globally and technologically, so do their complexities and inefficiencies. Technology is transforming business, healthcare, financial institutions, and government into interdependent and interconnected networks of transactional enterprises. Technology is also enabling organizations to do more than they might have thought was possible a decade ago. This transformation is creating the greatest opportunities for organizations to improve, leapfrog competitors, and dominate global markets in the new economy. To be successful, organizations will need to become much more committed and aggressive about continuous improvement— for the long haul. They will need to build organizations that proactively seek and act on every improvement moment.

Organizations are facing improvement challenges today that they never had to deal with before. For example, how do we improve a Web-based global product development process with people, R&D and development labs, manufacturing, and distribution scattered around the world? How do we define, develop, and deliver more prevention-based services to patients at half the cost and length of stay? How do we simplify and grow the Web-based transactions process for 80% of consumer banking activity? How do we release a new product on time and on budget, including product availability, and multilingual literature and customer service in a dozen different markets around the world? How do we improve asset utilization and patient experiences in operating and emergency rooms via increased throughput and cycle time reduction? How do we meet the bank's profitability and growth objectives in a slow recovery with new regulatory and compliance requirements? How do hospitals operate within budget with lower reimbursements, reduce costs, mitigate risks, provide surgeons with the capabilities of the latest equipment and procedures, and meet the compliance requirements of dozens of state and federal agencies trying to justify themselves? How do we remove the political and self-serving forces of government and reduce the deficit strategically, logically, and via root cause thinking? All organizations are working on challenges that they never had to deal with in the past. What is next? We have entered a future in which we will all need to solve more complex, multidimensional problems at warp speed that we do not know about yet. You can be sure that the future holds technology-enabled improvement using devices and applications yet to be developed. This evolution is already rewriting the rules of improvement rapidly, with a reversal of going to the process for improvement (going to the Gemba), to the process coming to the user's fingertips, awaiting their actions for immediate improvement (the Gemba is continuously streaming to me).

There is a simple but powerful message from this chapter. All organizations can and must improve to remain competitive and financially sound. In terms of numbers, most organizations have the opportunity, the means, and the competitive need to generate annualized "economic value added (EVA)" or economic improvements that are equivalent to 3% to 10% of revenues or more. Think about how much equivalent incremental revenues this represents to generate an additional 3% to 10% of EVA profit or budget surplus. The EVA aspect of this statement is important because once the checks are written for the required returns to shareholders and executive compensation, the improvements are translated into sunk costs. In other words, they are a "wash," albeit a necessary takeaway from the rate of improvement. Furthermore, all organizations should be using strategic improvement as a growth strategy to the tune of 10% to 20% annually.

The opportunities and urgent need for improvement in all industries and organizations are higher than ever before in the history of continuous improvement.

Manufacturing has led the charge of improvement for the past 75 years, and there is a lot to learn from these experiences. This urgent need has reached a crisis point of insurmountable proportions in industries that are less seasoned in continuous improvement, such as healthcare, transportation, financial services, education, and government for sure. Every organization is no longer exempt from improvement, including our federal, state, and local governments. In the case of our federal and state governments, they should be looking at shrinking their operations by these numbers based on current costs. The traditional "tax-and-spend" practices of government are no longer a viable strategy for success without severe consequences for generations. Parliamentary procedure or covering up bad processes with additional revenues is not the answer. Through deliberate and well-structured improvement initiatives, governments can replace the emotional "cut-and-negotiate" legal maneuvers with a logical and evidence-based process—and it is hoped offer improved service delivery with substantially reduced waste, service risk, and cost. A realistic improvement goal of many government agencies is in the neighborhood of 30% to 50% without impacting critical service delivery. These numbers represent a huge decrease in the future deficit and taxes. But rather than debating numbers, the point here is that organizations cannot be successful in the future by rationalizing away waste, trying to be all things to all people, arguing about the relevance and applicability of continuous improvement, or by pretending that bad performance is good performance.

There is an old corollary with improvement: The same people plus the same process plus the same thinking plus the same metrics equals the same results. In this economy, the same thinking that got us here will not get us to where we need to go. For those who have never been serious about improvement, it is time to stop buying time or explaining how improvement is irrelevant to the waste and inefficiencies in your unique organizations. For those of us who have been funding this waste and inefficiencies in other industries, it is time to demand rapid improvement and accountability—and stop giving more money to people who have consistently proven that they are wasteful and irresponsible. Waste and inefficiency in all forms (e.g., time, cost, quality, risk mitigation, complexity, customer service, etc.) constitute a universal dilemma in all organizations. The only difference lies in how the waste is created and eliminated around the unique operating models and constraints of various operating environments.

For executives and all other leaders, it is an opportune time to rethink their previous approaches, experiences, and *process* of continuous improvement. The concept of continuous improvement is a universal need. There is no need to wait for the next repackaged buzzword program to come along and jump on the improvement treadmill again. The methodologies of Lean Six Sigma and all other improvement initiatives of the past provide a solid means for improvement. What is now needed is an update and renewed focus on the Strategic Leadership and Vision, Deployment Planning, and Execution elements of continuous and sustainable improvement. Improvement Excellence™ and its respective elements of leadership, strategy, and sustaining infrastructure provide this updated and transcendent model of improving how we improve.

These factors are the foundation of continuous improvement: a solid foundation that yields continuous and sustainable improvement and breakthrough results.

BIBLIOGRAPHY

Burton, T. 2011. *Accelerating Lean Six Sigma Results: How to Achieve Improvement Excellence™ in the New Economy.* Ross, Ft. Lauderdale, FL.

Rother, M. 2011. *Toyota Kata: Managing People for Adaptiveness, Improvement, and Superior Results.* McGraw-Hill, New York.

3 Leadership: Building a High-Performance Culture

INTRODUCTION

This chapter begins to peel back the onion and expose the leadership-related root causes of continuous improvement failure. The purpose is not to point blame at our executive friends, discredit the thousands of people *giving it their all* with continuous improvement, or self-promote Lean Six Sigma or some new improvement program as the magic bullet of success. An important fact to keep in mind is that the recent meltdown and slow recovery, globalization, technology, and many other forces continue to present disruptions and insurmountable challenges to executives. This is not new, but when it happens, it changes the rules of perceived success with executive choices, decisions, and actions that run counterintuitive with continuous improvement. Today, the single largest executive challenge is constancy in leadership aptitude: exercising the right consistent behaviors, decisions, and actions among the many options available—on hundreds of daily tasks. It is funny how Deming said the same thing decades ago. Wavering leadership produces a serious multiplier effect because just a single executive working on a single task may impose abundant complexities, inefficiencies, or repercussions on the organization.

In spite of these growing complexities, all organizations must quickly figure out how to reverse this 30-year trend of failed improvement programs by challenging the elegant theories and approaches of strategic improvement initiatives of the past and present with the ugly facts.

LEADERSHIP TRANSFORMATION IN THE NEW ECONOMY

Leadership is often cited repeatedly relative to continuous improvement success and total business success. The recent meltdown and slow recovery have introduced a whole new breadth and scope of operating issues in all industries, rendering the traditional notions of leadership as out of touch in the new economy. For example:

- Strong industry expertise and experience are no longer enough to guarantee success. Conventional industry structures are becoming increasingly complex, with a higher content of externally distributed activities and more regulatory requirements, causing executives to rely heavier on the leadership capabilities of others.
- The sheer scope of leadership responsibilities is far greater than any other time in history. Leadership has a threefold challenge: (1) leading their organization to make their monthly and quarterly financial numbers, the short-term performance criteria that significantly influence all behaviors, decisions, and actions; (2) leading and influencing their organization down a successful and sustainable path in the future; and (3) leading and managing a large number of diverse relationships across their end-to-end supply chains and stakeholder chains.
- Traditional industry models are rapidly being replaced by the need for newer, more profitable industry models and hence new leadership models. Organizations are now facing challenges that often appear to be in the "hopeless" category. Hospitals are laying off employees and initiating legal actions against their state governments because they are seriously challenged by declining reimbursements and rising double-digit costs. Where will the money come from? State governments are also broke. Domestic manufacturing that was once housed in a single Illinois factory is now scattered across a complex supply chain network in 25 different countries; more and more people are commuting to work via a jet and a passport to resolve many new complex customer, supply chain, technology, and quality issues. Financial institutions are sitting on tons of idle cash due to strict regulatory requirements that have decreased loan activity, increased foreclosures, and are driving increases in miscellaneous fee activities to offset the interest revenue losses. To top things off, President Obama is trying to backdoor bill HR 4646, which would place a 1% tax on all bank transactions. The value creation propositions in all types of organizations are being significantly challenged, and many of their choices to address these new challenges are shortsighted, lack creativity, and are strategically incorrect.
- Federal, state, and local governments have also reached a tipping point in terms of passing rising costs and inefficiencies on to taxpayers. In this particular case, the model of government has not changed in the last 100 years. The other challenge is that leadership and improvement have totally different meanings in these organizations, primarily due to their legal and entitlement models of leadership thinking. Federal, state, and local governments are the ripest environments for continuous improvement, with aggregate benefits in the trillions of dollars.

So, how do organizations create their new mind models of leadership and improvement? For many organizations, this is going to require bold strategic, structural, and fundamental changes in their business models—a more radical reengineering approach followed by continuous and sustainable improvement. Before this can begin, the executive team needs to think about more strategic, structural, and fundamental changes as a cohesive group. Organizations like government agencies, public utilities, law firms, hospitals, financial institutions, and many other complex service industries that are in the "infancy stage" of strategic improvement will need to become more familiar with the improvement basics that have existed in manufacturing industries for the past 75 years:

- Increase awareness and acceptance of the importance of leadership, improvement strategy, implementation infrastructure, process improvement or risk mitigation, the right balanced performance metrics, accountability for results, and rewards and consequences.
- Appreciate the concept of "process." Everything in organizations takes place through processes: efficient and inefficient processes, multiple processes, nonstandardized processes, work-around processes, and lack of processes.
- Understand and retrofit the fundamentals of continuous improvement (e.g., Kaizen, Lean, Six Sigma, constraints management, etc.) and how to best adapt these improvement methodologies to their specific operating challenges and new business models.
- Recognize that Lean Six Sigma and other continuous improvement initiatives are not a business strategies but powerful enablers of business strategy when planned and executed correctly.

For more seasoned improvement organizations, an effective first step in the new economy is "talent alignment": The executive team recognizes the gaps and need for injections or recruitment of new talent and expertise from outside their industry. We have mentioned Improvement Excellence™ as a critical core competency in the new economy. The combination of globalization with the recent meltdown and slow recovery has placed organizations in a frustrating position where the new requirements greatly exceed their capabilities and competencies to deal with these challenges now. After nearly four decades in business, I am convinced that continuous improvement is a core competency and natural mindset that must be widely developed and practiced daily and rigorously deployed in a variety of situations. Organizations that make their living at strategic and continuous improvement develop this as their primary core competency. In organizations that fabricate metal, provide patient care, or manage motor vehicle registration renewals, improvement is a core competency far down the list. Their core competency is their primary core competency, providing their products and services. This is not a criticism but a fact. In my own organization, we would be clueless about how to design a circuit board or conduct surgical procedures on patients. However, when one actively practices the art and science of continuous improvement every day and in a variety of organizations while dealing with an unpredictable set of executive styles and egos, politics, and human drama situations, it becomes a core competency. The main point of advice here is to leverage success off the core competencies of external partners. The largest risk in the new economy is the risk of doing nothing. Organizations must approach strategic improvement as an investment, not a risk—with an expected return on investment (ROI) and consequences for failure. Strategic improvement is never risky with this kind of leadership behind it. Furthermore, failure is not the fault of improvement.

Finally, there is a severe need for many executive leadership teams to shift from a directing and meddling mode to a more mentoring, development, and influencing role. The current leadership behaviors are understandable, considering that we are all in the midst of the largest economic disaster since the Great Depression. The overwhelming array of challenges continues to grow for all industry segments. These times require great leadership to get through it all. Executives are not supposed to be overwhelmed, but the economic events of the past few years have created a lower hybrid form of leadership post-traumatic stress disorder (PTSD) in many organizations. Executives are stuck in so much day-to-day firefighting that they cannot return to the great leaders they once were or have the capacity to become. However, the continuation of these behaviors will accomplish nothing more than paralyze talent development and organizational bench strength, escalating the need for more directing and meddling. Executives must take a much more collaborative and cognizant view of their own leadership roles in the new economy, garnering expertise and insight from a wider range of external partners, colleagues, and associates. Organizations simply do not possess all of the internal capabilities for their new spectrum of operating challenges and new paths to success. A leadership transformation is desperately needed in many organizations—one that recognizes the complexity, magnitude, scope, and velocity of change necessary to achieve success in the new economy.

HISTORY LESSON: IS LEADERSHIP THE REAL PROBLEM?

Every time continuous improvement fades away (fails), it is easy for everyone to blame leadership and explain the failure away by moving on to other pressing issues. When strategic improvement initiatives fail, placing the blame on leadership and leaving it at that is a cop-out for failure—now and in the future. Placing the blame without understanding and correcting the underlying root causes of failure leaves organizations destined to repeat this cycle. The fact is leadership determines this degree of success by their choices and actions, which are highly influenced by understanding root causes of success or failure from previous experiences. The capability to succeed and the degree of success with continuous improvement, and everything else for that matter, are established by leadership through the strategy, structure, talent, processes, technology, and metrics they provide to their organizations. Deming said approximately the same thing 30 years ago, so therefore it is all leadership's fault. This is dead wrong. Do you think executives wander away from continuous improvement intentionally? Do you believe that leadership for continuous improvement is restricted to the executive suite? In the case of continuous improvement, no one ever stops to conduct a due diligent root cause analysis about what just happened—and how to resurrect and avoid the same mistakes in the future. An evidence-based postmortem reveals that leadership-related root causes are assignable and explainable—and therefore correctable. Whether executives admit it or not, they are motivated by instant gratification; however, a successful continuous improvement initiative takes more commitment, time, resources, and patience. It also pays off thousands of times more than knee-jerk reactions and several failed fad improvement programs.

A ROOT CAUSE ANALYSIS ON LEADERSHIP

Everyone is intellectually committed at some level to continuous improvement. The problem arises when it is time to put the rubber on the road and keep it there. This is a great opportunity to conduct a simple "Five Whys analysis" on this topic.

1. *Why do continuous improvement initiatives fail?* Executives do not view failing at improvement as failure; they believe that they are always in improvement mode and fail to recognize it as a true discipline and core competency. "They don't know what they don't know" about strategic and sustainable improvement.

2. *Why?* Improvement is not viewed as a rigorous, never-ending formal core competency that is practiced daily and enables strategic success. In many cases, improvement is viewed as a temporary action for an emerging set of problems or the vogue thing to do. Executive commitment and interest level always drift away to more shorter-term issues that are perceived to be more pressing, especially when they become disappointed with the delusionary results. Some improvement initiatives have produced more overhead costs than benefits.

3. *Why?* Improvement is managed as a short-term program not a cultural standard of thinking and working, a cultural standard of excellence. Therefore, improvement has been deployed incorrectly for the long term, with the absence of strategy and sustaining infrastructure. Instead, the approaches have been repetitious, top down, mandated, training of the masses, and poorly executed magic bullet improvement programs.

4. *Why?* Executives perceive improvement programs as a tactic to produce more immediate results. They look around and see what other organizations are doing and jump on the bandwagon in hopes of an instant lottery of new financial performance. Improvement is a lifelong organizational commitment to excellence that is perceived to be in conflict with quarterly performance and earnings per share (EPS).

5. *Why?* Short-term performance and reward systems often drive organizations into an operating mode of *immediate reason*—the act of attempting to correct an immediate situation with unreasonable actions based on perceptions, opinions, or direct orders in the absence of the true facts. This is certainly counterintuitive to root cause problem solving, data-driven and evidence-based decision making, and a logical process of improvement.

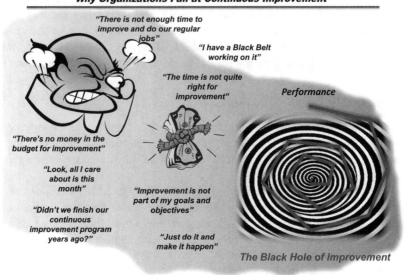

The Familiar Dilemma
Why Organizations Fail at Continuous Improvement

"There is not enough time to improve and do our regular jobs"

"I have a Black Belt working on it"

"The time is not quite right for improvement"

Performance

"There's no money in the budget for improvement"

"Look, all I care about is this month"

"Didn't we finish our continuous improvement program years ago?"

"Improvement is not part of my goals and objectives"

"Just do it and make it happen"

The Black Hole of Improvement

In a troubled economy with high unemployment and cost cutting, people in organizations tend to do as they are told because this is a less-risky choice than pushing back with the need for improvement and root cause analysis. Hence, organizations become improvement dysfunctional: Leadership for continuous improvement is paralyzed in all directions: top down, bottom up, laterally, horizontally, and middle out.

This Five Whys analysis has repeated itself in organizations for decades. The problem with continuous improvement is that it is extremely difficult (but not impossible) to resurrect initiatives and get them back on a sustainable track. Usually, it requires a change in leadership and strategy and the renewal and rebuilding of credibility through the help of a respected outside expert. When people in organizations live through a few of these birth-death improvement cycles, they become frustrated with the hyperbolic leadership behaviors, become skeptical about commitment and trust, and lose interest in participating in another improvement initiative. Executives must think, approach, and execute improvement as if they only have a single shot at getting it right. It requires a strong and cohesive leadership team that is willing to admit to past failures, even if they did not occur on their watch. At the same time, they must create a compelling vision and strategy for the future. Finally, they must regain organizational commitment by their consistent messages, behaviors, and actions. Believe it or not, leadership for continuous improvement is very real and very visible stuff. Executives are on center stage while the rest of the organization observes and interprets commitment, priorities, and other signals of wavering direction. A seasoned practitioner can walk into an organization and tell quickly how serious it is about continuous improvement, but it requires looking beyond the symbolic storyboards, beautification exercises, color-coding practices, and other window dressing evidence of continuous improvement.

There is a delicate balance here that has been out of balance for three decades. With all due respect to executives, their role is to make organizations successful within a defined time period. The related anxiety levels run counter to setting up a successful and sustaining improvement infrastructure, so it has rarely happened in the history of improvement. Many executives pride themselves on how much they know about improvement and fail to recognize it as a legitimate core competency. There is a big difference between *knowing how to* improve and implementing continuous improvement for the long haul. Why? It looks easy—just do what everyone else is doing because it must be right. They want the improvements now and choose the organic approach, but many are not willing to make the commitment and investment in expertise, time, and resources to implement improvement successfully. I have heard executives talk about "wrapping up improvement," which is definitely not a sustainable strategy. Consequently, executives fail to create and sustain the desired culture for permanent continuous improvement. For decades, executives have lined up like lemmings jumping off a cliff with the latest fad improvement programs. Executives have also been baited by many "one-size-fits-all" consulting organizations and their continuous improvement programs branded and presented with their own overhead and front-end costs (e.g., training the masses, top-down mandated approaches, unrealistic expectations, etc.). The consultants walk in with their "improvement-in-a-box" program and the "magic Kool-Aid" and say, "Let's roll." Many consultants have the intellectual (50,000-foot) grasp of improvement tools and the associated training skills, but they are missing the most important implementation core competency elements of leadership, strategy, infrastructure, execution, and sustainability. The consultants are long gone with their revenues as organizations find out about the questionable ROIs too late in the process. So, what happens? The plug is pulled because the value of continuing just is not there. The most recent fiasco is Six Sigma certification. There is no doubt that Six Sigma certification is a worthy professional development endeavor. But, why did organizations buy into the silly bureaucratic structure that promotes ratios of Master Black Belts, Black Belts, Green Belts, Yellow Belts, and so on before there was a well-defined improvement strategy? This was flash-in-the-pan improvement at its best. Did all of these people need a "belt" as a prerequisite to implementing improvements? Of course they did not, but certification in a much better economy was a nice professional development offering to gain people's commitment and involvement. Everyone wanted a belt, and in some organizations it became mandatory for promotional opportunities. Organizations got caught up in this "mad belt" disease; today, over 80% of people who went through formal Black Belt certification (at a cost of around $80,000 each) are no longer actively involved in improvement. The remaining 20% who are still actively involved in improvement use about 20% of what they learned during Black Belt training on a daily basis (e.g., the basic, simpler improvement tools). Worse yet, many are totally frustrated because they are immersed in daily crises and do not have the time and support for data-driven root cause problem solving. At present, 80% of Lean Six Sigma deployments are failures in organizations. Once again, crisis leadership has sucked the oxygen out of their improvement initiatives. Many executives and their organizations continue in their freeze-frame mode of improvement and expect success. Others are slow-walking improvement to maintain the right impression for headquarters. In some troubled industries, risk-averse executives are watching their financial crisis unfold before their very eyes, waiting for the tsunami to strike land before they decide to take action. A fact about improvement is that organizations either pay now or pay much more down the road.

Those who seem to have benefitted most from the Lean Six Sigma movement were the large training firms that acted as the certification factories and then disappeared when the tough work of implementation was most needed. Many firms did not possess the implementation core competencies, so it was highly unlikely that they could develop these core competencies within their client organizations. Many of their resources were trainers, not practitioners. A big lesson from all of this is that continuous improvement is not a simple recipe: It is a highly complex, creative, and continuous process of integrating people, processes, assets, information, capital, and other resources into a winning strategy of success and superior performance. If one looks back in history, there is a trail of failed moon shots to implement and sustain improvement with TQM (total quality management), JIT (just in time), reengineering, Enterprise Resource Planning (ERP), Lean, Six Sigma, and now Lean Six Sigma. Like the past continuous improvement experiences, executives again shrug their shoulders and fall prey to plausible deniability with that decades-old excuse: "I don't know what happened—we did everything just like GE, Honeywell, John Deere, and everyone else … and we used the same prominent consulting firm. We did all the right things and never could have predicted that this would happen." This all-too-familiar rationalization is not the fault of Lean Six Sigma or the label

of the specific improvement initiative; the root causes are directly related to leadership, strategy, and sustaining infrastructure. History demonstrates that it takes a lot more than the Wizard of Oz behind the curtain to keep the *continuous* in continuous improvement.

BREAKING OUT OF THE LEADERSHIP QUAGMIRE

Like it or not, executives must and will continue to be accountable to their corporate headquarters and ultimately Wall Street. It is a basic requirement for keeping their seat in the organization. There have been only a few executives in my lifetime who could fend off Wall Street with their infamous genius, such as Dr. Edwin Land during the high times at Polaroid (when analysts at one stockholders' meeting asked about profits, he answered, "The bottom line is in Heaven," and "Marketing is what you do when your product is no good"). Hospitals, financial institutions, and federal, state, and local governments will continue to be challenged with reducing spending and services while keeping everyone happy. The bottom line of this paragraph is that all of the challenges related to successful continuous improvement initiatives are clearly dependent on leadership, strategy, and a solid sustaining infrastructure. The Five Whys provide an explanation of the self-repeating vicious cycles that undermine continuous improvement. Nevertheless, leadership is ultimately responsible for turning this 30-year trend around—period, end of story. This turnaround must begin in the executive suite with the right choices, behaviors, and actions surrounding continuous improvement. A failed improvement initiative is like a tired old race horse. Sometimes it is possible to nurse the horse back to a healthy champion for a few races, but most of the time the horse is "dead money" (e.g., hopeless, no chance of ever winning). Leadership is responsible for not only the turnaround but also *how* the turnaround must take place based on the circumstances. Failed improvement initiatives are extremely difficult to turn around. Most of the time, the best approach is a fresh start and a clean slate.

It is no secret that most executives (and everyone else) are already in overload mode these days. This is a fact, not a leadership excuse. The point here is that executives need and welcome help in improving the organization's performance and well-being. The rest of the organization must also step up and take on the risks of doing the right things right the first time. Hopelessness is a self-inflicted emotion, and buying time and keeping a low profile are not viable improvement strategies. So, to everyone in every organization I say, "Step up." Executives never shoot people with great ideas and a common purpose. Executives are also very intelligent people who are willing to listen to a logical presentation of fact-based ideas and benefits. The real power of continuous improvement occurs when solid opportunities for improvement are identified autonomously by everyone in the organization.

I have mentioned previously that through the meltdown and slow recovery, organizations have placed a freeze on improvement when they needed it the most. However, there is a silver lining in this cloud. For many organizations, this has turned into an opportunity to purge their non-value-producing improvement infrastructure and rethink their future improvement strategy with a better and more relevant model. There is a simple lesson in this paragraph: If you are leading or involved in an improvement initiative that is not working, it is time to make the right choice. Executives can either step up, change the process of improvement, and make it successful or keep the freeze on improvement and remain in organizational churn-and-burn mode. It all comes down to a simple binary choice: performance or excuses for nonperformance. Success with improvement is an executive choice based on behaviors, decisions, and actions.

THE MOST IMPORTANT CHOICE: BEHAVIORAL ALIGNMENT

No executive is (expected to be) perfect at everything 100% of the time because mayhem, chaos, uncertainty, and ambiguity are givens in our economy. This chapter and this book are not intended to beat up on the majority of executives who are giving their 150% to achieve success. But, these behaviors are very real and set the pace for the organization. With all of the crazy demands placed on organizations these days, executives can easily forget just how powerful their behaviors can be at accomplishing great things with and through others. The purpose of behavioral alignment is to boost executive awareness of their center-stage role and their underemployed powers. Executive behaviors are so powerful because people are observing these behaviors closely and acting accordingly.

BEHAVIORAL ALIGNMENT BEGINS IN THE EXECUTIVE SUITE

Leadership of continuous improvement and everything else for that matter is not within a title or position in the organization. Leadership is also a continuous process of behaviors, decisions, and actions—of executives and potentially everyone in the organization regardless of title, status, or position. Behavioral alignment begins with the chief executive officer (CEO) and the CEO's executive team. The most important choice executives must make in reversing this 30-year trend of failed improvement is to view their behaviors and leadership styles from an "outside-in" perspective. The intent of this outside-in view is to step out of the routine and consider the following:

- **Take a fresh objective look at the organization.** The same people plus same thinking plus same processes plus same information equals the same results. This is defined as *insanity*: doing more of the same things and expecting different results. Since the meltdown, many organizations have graduated to *hyperinsanity*, which is doing more of the same things with greater urgency and speed and expecting different results. Improvement requires a continuous change in one or more of these inputs.

- **Think about the leadership behaviors of yourself and those around you.** What are the enabling and detractive behaviors of improvement and success? How do others really feel about the leadership of yourself and others? Are people sincerely committed? Would they stick around in a great economy with a wealth of employment opportunities? The old adage of "I'm not here to make friends" is obsolete thinking in our complex economy. Executives need to develop, mentor, and leverage every ounce of talent in the total value stream. Organizations need to develop the core competency of improving how they improve more than ever before.

- **Take a deeper dive into leadership behaviors on an individual basis and as an executive team.** The purpose here is to become more familiar with behaviors that are detrimental to improvement and best practice leadership behaviors that excite, motivate, and develop talent in organizations. The past has provided organizations with a variety of stand-alone leadership assessment tools, such as Myers-Briggs, 360 assessments, situational leadership indicators, management effectiveness profiles, and dozens of other instruments. We also provided our best practices leadership behaviors model at the end of this chapter. It is not easy to accept that the problem with sustaining improvement may be in the mirror, but discussions and exercises around executive behaviors are beneficial at creating a cohesive, improvement-ready executive team.

- **Accept that rapid and continuous improvement is a basic requirement for business success.** It can no longer be perceived as a program off to the side or something "in addition to" the organization's normal business activities. Executives and their organizations fail to recognize the most obvious fundamental: The only way to get better is to improve the current state. The shortfall is that executives are extremely challenged about how to fit improvement into the daily cultural fabric of how people think and work without jeopardizing the other thousand things that need to get done. Nevertheless, the answers to this question are also a basic requirement for business success.

This is a difficult process that is best accomplished via individual and executive team mentoring by an objective professional outside the organization. Like everything else, many leadership assessment exercises of the past are becoming a bit dated in our present economy. All of these instruments are informative awareness exercises, but they tend to be static in terms of implementation and daily practice. The best practices leadership behaviors model is a more practical guide of proven behaviors that drive strategic and sustainable improvement and breakthrough results. All of these instruments are only as good as leadership's awareness and choices to practice and encourage these improvement-enabling behaviors. Regardless of the instrument, executives must put their behaviors in check and think about how these behaviors are either promoters or inhibitors of success. It is nothing personal—these are unintentional, good faith behaviors in the strife for leading the organization down a successful path. Leadership is more about step-ping up to the challenges that others perceive as risks, learning from successes and failures, and mentoring others continuously through the same process.

So, where are organizations relative to where they need to go? Since the 2008 meltdown, many executives have their organizations ping-ponging around with short attention spans and total confusion about what they should do next. In a challenging economy, the behaviors of many executives suppress creativity and innovation and resurrect old habits of mind. Behaviors such as across-the-board spending moratoriums and belt tightening; wavering or sending mixed signals on direction and commitments; openly expressing despair, uncertainty, and panic; imposing conflicting rules, directives, and edicts; and "going back to the well" are behaviors that create huge barriers to business improvement and drive culture backward. Their effects transmit themselves swiftly and bamboozle the entire organization. Everyone knows that this is not intentional, but organizations act exactly and directly proportionally to the perceived directions of their leaders and executives. Behavioral alignment is the initial process of transcending this organizational chaos and turbulence to a higher level of order and laminar flow.

So, How Do We Align Organizational Behaviors?

The process of behavioral alignment is not difficult once the executive team makes the commitment to have a fresh look at its leadership practices. Aligning organizational behaviors is an extension of this process with significant input and mentoring of everyone in the organization. Keep in mind that this is not a one-shot activity but a process of defining and maintaining alignment. Executives and managers can achieve significant ongoing benefits beyond continuous improve-ment if they practice the following simple routine:

1. *Stop, Look, Listen, and Reflect.* Today is a good time for executives, organizations, and their people to look back at all that they have accom-plished through the meltdown. These accomplishments may have come at the expense of negative effects on culture. Now it is time to set some new priorities for the new challenges ahead—new challenges that require new thinking, new talent and skills, and new actions for success. The continuous piling on of new assignments and requirements is not the way out of survival and on to success. There are activities in the pile that are no longer essential or no longer relevant.
2. *Reset and Realign Priorities.* This requires a quick sanity check on the business strategy and performance to date. This step involves recruiting help by listening to the voice of the organization. One effective approach is to ask key people throughout the organization to make a list with three columns: (1) Which activities are essential and mission critical (value adding) to customer requirements and meeting business objectives? (2) Which activities are clearly disruptive and not value adding to both

of these needs? and (3) Which activities need to be either canceled or postponed due to a reset of priorities or lack of realistic bandwidth?

3. *Take Out the Trash.* Many organizations are not good at this step. It is time to move aside the emotions and deal with the true value-adding facts. This is what we refer to as tall-pole leadership, borrowed from the analogy of a Pareto chart. The CEO and the executive team should be able to translate the organization's inputs into precise and prioritized actions ("the vital few") that visually demonstrate a resetting of the course. The other aspect of this step is to recognize that human capacity to do things well is not an unlimited resource, just as a piece of equipment running beyond its intended use will break. Over time, people have been given so many directives ("the trivial many") that keep getting added to their roles that they cannot be effective at anything. The pile of directives becomes larger, and nothing is taken off people's plates. Instead, it is managed by superficial statements like "it has to be done" or "make it happen." In fact, there is a lot of trash on people's plates—non-value-adding duties that are not needed for broader organizational success. This step should reduce total workloads so that people can do a better job on the remaining priorities or new initiatives, such as Lean Six Sigma.

4. *Acknowledge and Communicate.* Many organizations are loaded with employees who come to work every day with their eyes glazed over from change. They do not understand the "whys" of all of the changes around them. Much of this change has been necessary, but it has not been communicated well. People have been through so much change in the past few years that many have thrown up their hands in frustration. This is the worst environment for improvement because people wait to be told what to do next, and (in their minds) they do not have time to improve and perform their regular duties. Organizations need to hear, understand, see, and believe in the resetting of priorities from reactionary survival to success mode. This must be visible both in executive behaviors and in how their work environment is improving every day.

5. *Stay Out of the Traps.* This is simply creating a living routine practice of keeping the most important organizational activities in the forefront and aligned to customer and business success. This also includes a regulated and disciplined process for prioritizing and adding new requirements into the organization. There are always exceptions, like a major customer or quality problem, and the right first step is quick containment. But, do not stop there. When executives choose to deal with these exceptions in the realm of structured and disciplined improvement, it takes a lot less time, resources, and costs than dealing with the same issues repeatedly. Why? Because the root causes are embedded in process, some weakness in process. The other part of this routine

practice is continuously managing and weeding out the nonessential, nonrelevant activities that seem to find their way into all organizations, intentionally or not.

BEST PRACTICE LEADERSHIP BEHAVIORS

The recent meltdown and slow recovery have also resulted in unintended consequences on leadership behaviors. Today, many well-intended executives find themselves spending too much time and focus on day-to-day meddling and not enough focus on the more important strategic issues of their organizations. Not to be critical, but executives find themselves in this situation because of their own choices, behaviors, and actions. It is these same choices, behaviors, and actions that shift executives toward building a high-performance culture.

There is nothing new about leadership behaviors that enable the long-term success of Lean Six Sigma and continuous improvement in general. The purpose of this section is to remind versus teach these behaviors to the reader and to increase awareness about executive behaviors and how they influence a strategic improvement initiative such as Lean Six Sigma. The following discussion does not follow any particular leadership model. This model reflects proven enabling executive behaviors of CEOs, executive deployment champions, executive sponsors, and other members of the executive team. This may not be an all-inclusive list; however, it represents the leadership behaviors we have observed and experienced in Lean Six Sigma benchmark deployments.

Best practice leadership behaviors can be grouped into five major categories:

1. Vision
2. Knowledge
3. Passion
4. Discipline
5. Conscience

Figure 3.1 provides an overview of these best practice leadership behaviors. Within each of these categories is a set of behavioral power triggers that contribute positively to Lean Six Sigma success and, in fact, personal leadership success. The remaining discussion provides additional details about these best practice behaviors as they relate to a successful Lean Six Sigma deployment. Keep in mind that these behaviors are transportable to any strategic leadership challenge.

VISION

Vision is the ability to see beyond current challenges and define a new direction for improvement. Vision is only attainable for individuals willing to pick their heads out of the reeds, take a time-out, stop the *insanity*, and dream a bit about how the business can and will improve. Vision is a reverse process beginning

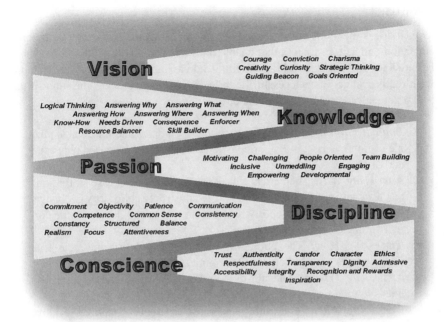

FIGURE 3.1 Best practice leadership behaviors.

at a more fuzzy utopian state of improvement (e.g., zero inventory) and working backward to a more realistic state (e.g., reduce supply chain inventory by 20%)—one that is a believable but doable step function improvement over current conditions and one that requires the collaboration and cooperation of many improvement activities to eliminate dependencies. The supporting best practice leadership abilities include acting as or with

- *Courage:* The ability to confront fear, pain points, risk/danger, uncertainty, or internal and external intimidation.
- *Conviction:* The art of convincing oneself and others about reality, risks, and the consequences of not improving.
- *Charisma:* The magnetism, communications skills, and personal being to persuade and convince others about improvement.
- *Creativity:* The ability to imagineer, think beyond the box, and think and act divergently.
- *Curiosity:* The desire and inquisitive interest to learn from others.
- *Strategic Thinking:* Thinking beyond next quarter and thinking big.
- *Guiding Beacon:* Behaviors followed by actions that attract others.
- *Goals Oriented:* Setting the bar of expectations high but achievable; also raising the bar of expectations above current performance to encourage continuous improvement.

KNOWLEDGE

Knowledge is the ability to act based on true facts and data. Knowledge is self-education and self-awareness that enable one to understand how the vision may be possible. This includes taking the time and having the patience to understand what really matters in a successful Lean Six Sigma deployment. The supporting best practice leadership abilities include

- *Logical Thinking:* The ability to reduce a complex and unsolvable puzzle of improvement into a rational and orderly set of proposed plans and activities.
- *Answering Why:* The patience to develop the business case so that one can lead with facts and truth and data to construct a solid story of change.
- *Answering What:* The ability to synthesize facts and decide on the correct strategic corrective actions.
- *Answering How:* The ability to understand and prioritize the true requirements of a challenge and recognize internal shortfalls.
- *Answering Where:* The ability to prioritize where the organization needs to focus improvement efforts.
- *Answering When:* The timing and sense of urgency required to move the business forward.
- *Know-How:* Taking the time to build intelligence combined with objectivity so that one avoids reactionary problem solving, underestimating efforts, or hip-shooting leadership.
- *Needs Driven:* The ability to understand implementation requirements and admit to barriers to success and gaps in internal expertise.
- *Consequence Enforcer:* The ability to take a tough stand on fact-based controversy or confrontation or noncompliance to improvement goals and objectives.
- *Resource Balancer:* The ability to help the organization balance priorities versus the perceived piling of additional assignments on current workloads.
- *Skill Builder:* The ability to recognize skill and experience gaps and inject these competencies into the organization.

PASSION

Passion is the compelling emotion that drives leaders to success. Passion is the "fire in the belly" that gets leaders and organizations through any and all obstacles to success. In all of our client Lean Six Sigma benchmark deployments, these engagements were started with significant leadership mentoring until the momentum of "failure is not an option" was established. These were not flowery words: Executives and the organization deployed Lean Six Sigma in a manner in which there were no individual failures, no leadership failures, and hence success. Deployments were truly team based; everyone helped each other through individual projects and other deployment issues. It is always amazing to watch particular individuals who some may have written off rise to the occasion and accomplish what others in the organization thought was nearly impossible. When leaders possess and transfer passion to the rest of the organization, it is powerful stuff. Organizations with the fire in the belly are more successful than organizations that throw around the cliché "I already know how to" because there is always an immense force to figure the unknowns out. One of my previous books referred to these experiences as Eureka moments or personal discovery moments. When organizations and individuals experience these victories, it builds commitment, confidence, and an even larger fire in the belly. After decades of business experience, an individual with deep passion will always outperform the passive individual with knowledge. A person with passion will learn, apply this education, and gain knowledge—and continue to repeat this cycle. Many people with enough knowledge to be dangerous are the "I already know how to" people who typically sit idle and tell others how much they know. We have a nickname for this: "vaporbility." It is similar to vaporware in software, the features and functionality that everyone is out there selling, but it has not been developed yet.

Under the category of passion, the supporting best practice leadership abilities include those that are

- *Motivating:* The ability to activate and energize goal-oriented behaviors in the organization.
- *Challenging:* The ability to positively call out individuals to explain, justify, or rationalize plans and activities.
- *People Oriented:* The ability to encourage employees to use all of their talents and skills and to be productive in an organization where learning is a priority.
- *Team Building:* The ability to mentor people to work in cohesive, cross-functional teams, regardless of their home organization.
- *Inclusive:* The ability to recognize and tap people's experiences and expertise from a variety of backgrounds.
- *Unmeddling:* Recognizing that leadership is not meddling in or second-guessing others' roles and responsibilities. Leadership is developing others to conduct themselves with excellence in their roles and responsibilities so that meddling is not required.
- *Engaging:* Developing positive, enthusiastic, and effective connection with people regarding their work in a way that motivates an employee to invest in getting the job done, not just "well" but "with excellence" because the work content energizes the individual.
- *Empowering:* The ability to give away power and authority to the organization because the organization has developed the sense of responsibility to accept power and authority and act in a correct manner.
- *Developmental:* The ability to encourage and mentor systematic growth in individual job content skills, broader business skills, communication skills, interpersonal skills, or supervisory/leadership skills.

DISCIPLINE

Discipline is the ability to adhere to rules of conduct and expectations for the organization in a manner that establishes logical business conduct and order. The other side of discipline is "walking the talk." Discipline lays down the moral compass and serves to guide organizational behaviors to pursue the right decisions and achieve the right results. Discipline that encourages root cause problem solving develops abilities in individuals to make choices that will help grow the business over the long term, rather than to take advantage of the short term. Discipline forces people to follow a proven path and not jeopardize the future for some short-term, knee-jerk actions. The new economy has introduced competitive forces that are reducing the ability of organizations to maintain discipline. In a world of now, any color, any volume, any size and shape, and changes in demand for any of these is irrelevant, discipline is being replaced with chaos. Leaders must realize that chaos is not necessarily bad because there is ultimately order in chaos. Chaos is just the hypersonic ride to the next level of order and the next level of discipline. Chaos brings out the best in people because they do not have time to think, pontificate, or think of reasons for not changing. Chaos is also an enlightening organizational state because it exposes individuals' true capacity and capability for change.

The supporting best practice leadership abilities of discipline include the following characteristics:

- *Commitment:* The ability to make a personal pledge or emotional contract to a particular course of action without being disrupted by other arising issues.
- *Objectivity:* The ability to express or deal with facts or conditions as perceived or measured without any bias and distortion by personal feelings, prejudices, interpretations, political implications, or personal implications.
- *Patience:* The ability to endure and stay focused in the most difficult situations.
- *Communication:* The ability to foster interchange of the right thoughts and actions by translating information into understandable messages.
- *Competence:* The ability to engage and complete various actions, to demonstrate true commitment, and that one is not asking the organization to do something that they will not do themselves.
- *Common Sense:* The ability to exhibit sound, logical, and practical judgment.
- *Consistency:* The ability to display cohesive, non-contradictory behaviors.
- *Constancy:* A behavior that relates to the quality of unwavering direction and steadiness or faithfulness in action, affections, and purpose.

- *Structure:* The ability to create, follow, and reinforce accepted standards of conduct such as DMAIC (Define-Measure-Analyze-Improve-Control) and root cause problem solving.
- *Balance:* The ability to strive for a fact-based state of equilibrium or parity characterized by understanding and stabilizing the organization's driving and restraining forces.
- *Realism:* The ability to deal with people, objects, actions, or business conditions sensibly and levelheadedly as they reveal themselves in actuality.
- *Focus:* The ability to concentrate on a particular challenge, combined to create clarity that allows others also to concentrate on a particular challenge.
- *Attentiveness:* The ability to listen to all sides of an issue with objectivity and without interrupting and providing an answer. Another aspect is the ability to mentor and ask the right questions and develop subordinate decision making.

CONSCIENCE

Conscience is the leadership ability to distinguish whether the organization's actions, or individual actions, are right or wrong. Some refer to this as the inner voice of the subconscious mind. The subconscious mind is always acting as a secondary reflector of leadership thoughts and ideas in the body. This inner voice is shaped by values or emotional rules established in one's personal, social, cultural, educational, and business life. Conscience is the inner voice that justifies and rationalizes what is right and what is wrong. When leaders go against what the inner voice is saying, the result is a guilty conscience, emotional anxiety, and a disengaged organization. The inner voice is always right most of the time because it knows us better than others and probably even ourselves. Conscience is the daredevil child of the intuitions held since childhood. Intuitions about conscience are correct most of the time because they are the response of synchronism between our mental and physical being. Stated simply, most leaders know the difference between right and wrong, and there are many cloudy spaces in between. Intuition supplemented by data and facts reduces the risks of right or wrong. Eventually, the inner voice, our best listener, picks us up and alerts us to learn from our experiences, get on with business, and leave the past behind.

The supporting best practice leadership abilities of conscience include the following characteristics:

- *Trust:* The reliance on another individual's integrity, abilities, commitment, enabling behaviors, performance, and mutual surety. Trust is the nucleus of leadership.
- *Authenticity:* The truthfulness of origins, attributions, commitments, sincerity, devotion, and intentions.

- *Candor:* The quality of being frank, open, and sincere in speech or expression.
- *Character:* The moral and ethical traits and qualities of a leader as observed by the organization.
- *Ethics:* A leader's observed moral principles and values.
- *Respectfulness:* The ability to exhibit positive esteem and in turn receive the respect of others.
- *Transparency:* The ability to act in a "what you see is what you get" manner and work *with* the organization.
- *Dignity:* The ability to grant the right of respect and ethical treatment to others.
- *Admissive:* The voluntary admission of truth, even if it is a mistake; also the acceptance of other's mistakes and the mentoring of corrective actions as part of the normal learning and development cycle.
- *Accessibility:* The ability to be reachable and in the presence of the organization; also the ability of others to work with leaders without fear.
- *Integrity:* The honesty and consistency of actions, values, methods, measures, principles, expectations, and outcomes as demonstrated by both communications and actions.
- *Recognition and Rewards:* The ability to celebrate and recognize organizational successes and reward high-performing individuals and teams, but follow the "Great Job" comments with "How good do you think we can get? What are the team's next actions?"
- *Inspiration*: A divine influence, action, or power of leaders to motivate intellect or emotions or to influence great behaviors followed by great actions and great satisfactions.

The collective works of the great Mark Twain teach us many profound lessons about humanity, morality, and courage. One of my personal favorites is *The Damn Human Race*: a collection of essays and topical writings, mainly and most eloquently concerned with the themes of American civilization and social justice. In his wisdom, Twain talks about the behaviors of dogs, cats, birds, and many other animals and then draws comparisons to human beings. He also draws the distinction in morals between these animals and humans in his witty, humorous style. Mark Twain's underlying message is that from birth, animals all understand and assume their natural role in life. Humans on the other hand, possess intellectual capacity at birth but are totally unaware of their natural role in life. Humans spend their entire lifetime searching for who they are, who they want to become, and how to evolve this potential into a higher role in life. Mark Twain's wisdom is timeless; therefore it provides one of many elements to the different kinds of leadership needed today and into the future. First of all, the massive training programs of improvement programs since the 1980s need to go away. One trains animals because that is what works for animals. One must continuously educate, mentor, and develop the talent, the intellectual capacity, and full potential of people. Second, all executives and managers have the moral responsibility to proactively practice the virtues and best practice leadership behaviors, and reach for new levels of leadership achievement. The basic virtues of success, an adjustment of the moral compass, and the best practice leadership behaviors are not options, they are "must dos" in the new economy. Executives and managers also have the moral responsibility to fully develop the intellectual capacity and talent in their organizations so that collective entity achieves new levels of achievement and superior performance over and over again. No excuses! Enlightened leadership is about making money and developing management and their organization's full potential. Both are a requirement for success in the new economy

EXCELLENCE IS A JOURNEY

The ultimate purpose of behavioral alignment is to create the trickle-down effect of others in the organization. We have discussed best practice leadership behaviors, but we have not discussed that these behaviors are the sole responsibility of executives. Granted, it must begin with the executive team and be consistent in terms of decisions and actions. In successful Lean Six Sigma deployments, leadership evolves from the top down, bottom up, and middle out. Leadership is not limited to the executive suite. Success requires that everyone play a leadership role and practice the best practice leadership behaviors. The most successful and innovative Lean Six Sigma deployments were implemented by creative and enlightened leadership with committed organizations and talented people. (The term *enlightened leadership* is not used here in a humiliating way; it is a new and distinctive leadership state of rediscovery introduced in the next chapter.) The executives in these organizations are bright people who can grasp concepts and understand quickly what needs to be done. In addition, they have developed a culture that has graduated from fad, magic bullet programs to faster-than-a-speeding-bullet improvements.

BEGIN THE JOURNEY RIGHT

Creating a high-performance culture is a journey, not a destination. However, a word of caution is in order. This journey should never be packaged as slow, casual effort that the organization will implement over the next 3–5 years. The most important part of the journey is the initial departure and planned route. Organizations that enter into their improvement initiatives with a mindset of "let's pick a few random areas, train a few people, get our feet wet, and not be too worried about any initial results" are doomed to failure. When executives allow expectations to be set too low, improvement becomes another fad program with no results. These executives are typically the most worried about risk, but they add artificial risks to their deployment by their own unknowing choices. History bears this fact out, over and over. Think about this logical improvement dynamic: When the actual magnitude and timing of results are low, executives lead themselves down a path on which they need to focus on other things because improvement is not working well enough. The all-too-familiar cycle is usually the slow abandonment of improvement for more important issues, firefighting, and backsliding to business as usual until crisis levels rise to fuel the need for another improvement program.

The best way to implement Lean Six Sigma and other strategic improvement is through a bold commitment and the right full-bore approach to success. Relatively few organizations can accomplish this on their own; the best-performing Lean Six Sigma organizations reached out to external expertise to help organize and structure their journeys. Strategic improvement is not a part-time or casual activity, and the organic approach to implementation is like learning how to play golf like Phil Mickelson on your own. Those who are experts at improvement live, breath, and implement improvement in a variety of environments and under a variety of conditions every day. This is the rationale for strategic improvement being a core competency. Many organizations waste valuable time with the perceived simplicity of improvement and the complexities of planning, deploying, executing, and sustaining improvement correctly.

Strategic improvement must be approached as an investment with an expected positive ROI, not a risk. The departure must begin with a "redline" level of urgency, commitment, and expectations—and produce quick tangible results in a few high-impact areas. This sets the attention, motivation, and momentum of the organization on the right course because it becomes difficult to say something will not work when people stare in awe at the initial successes. The journey must be structured to be aggressive-exponential, not passive-linear. Successful improvement is a series of stacked "S-curves" because any long-term initiative approaches maturity and reinforcement periods. Sustaining infrastructure provides these gates, checkpoints, and course corrections. It should take no longer than 12–18 months to negotiate the first S-curve, where the organization reaches millions of dollars in annual documented benefits. For the remaining S-curves, these periods are where the improving-how-we-improve mastery gets organizations to that next-higher level of improvement and sustainable results. In summary, when an organization commits to the improvement journey, it should travel with greatness in terms that achieve velocity and magnitude of results. Like everything else in life, a trivial, lightweight approach to improvement will yield mediocre to no results. Any strategic initiative that takes a long time without any visible progress also results in a loss of interest and failure.

The role of leadership is to provide the vision and ecosystem for this relentless, never-ending journey. This journey is more about attitude and persistence than skill; the limits of success are determined by the self-imposed limit of leadership behaviors, decisions, and actions to achieve success. With improvement, your limit is your limit. Since the 1980s, this journey with continuous improvement has resembled many shorter trips wandering around for the destination. It is time to change this model through the right leadership and behavioral alignment. Whether you are a global Fortune 1,000 corporation, small private manufacturer, financial institution, hospital, or government agency, the sense of urgency to improve is evident and so are the risks and consequences of doing nothing. On the flip side, the benefits of successful and sustaining improvement are larger than any other time in history.

IT IS TIME TO GO DOWNTOWN

This chapter has provided a compelling prescription for executives to begin advancing their mind models around improvement and behavioral alignment. Again, the purpose was not criticism, but it was hoped to encourage executives to step back and reflect on their organization's leadership practices and how they are working. At the same time, we want to be very candid. If this economy has not forced a radical positive change in leadership thinking and actions regarding improvement, it's time to check the pulse of yourself and others. You may be leading your organization down a terminal course. If you and other executives and senior managers are driving your organization crazy with your postmeltdown leadership styles, it is time to put the keys down and rethink the destination—but quickly. Organizations cannot afford to stall getting on the right course of action. It is time to go downtown, rediscover improvement in the new economy, and accelerate our way out of the present crisis. Strategic and sustainable improvement is the fast lane in the slow recovery. So, what is everyone waiting for? Leadership will continue to be the real barrier to success if executives and their organizations do not get out there and move their improvement planes to a higher altitude.

BIBLIOGRAPHY

Blanchard, K., and Miller, M. 2009. *The Secret: What Great Leaders Know and Do.* Berrett-Koehler, San Francisco.

Burton, T. T., and Moran, J. T. 1995. *The Future Focused Organization.* Prentice Hall, Upper Saddle River, NJ.

Burton, T. T., and Boeder, S. M. 2003. *The Lean Extended Enterprise: Moving Beyond the Four Walls to Value Stream Excellence.* J. Ross Publishing, Ft. Lauderdale, FL.

Collins, J. 2001. *Good to Great: Why Some Companies Make the Leap ... and Others Don't.* Harper-Collins, New York.

Collins, J. 2011. *Great by Choice.* Harper-Collins, New York.

Iacocca, L. 2008. *Where Have All the Leaders Gone.* Scribner, a Division of Simon and Schuster, New York.

Roberto, M. A., and Levesque, L. C. 2005, Winter. *The Art of Making Change Stick.* MIT Sloan Management Review, Cambridge, MA.

Mark Twain, 1962, *The Damn Human Race*, Hill & Wang Publishing, New York, NY.

4 Setting a Renewed Course of Improvement

INTRODUCTION

The objective of this chapter is to provide a formal guide for developing the Improvement Strategy and Vision, crafting communication protocols that build and reinforce stakeholder engagement. Most organizations have not begun their Lean Six Sigma and prior continuous improvement journeys with this formal process. In the interest of expediency, they have opted for a more train-the-masses, shotgun approach to improvement. While this may not seem like such a big deal, a formal Improvement Strategy and Vision makes the difference between motion versus progress, activity versus results, and intermittent or failed versus sustainable continuous improvement. Why? The Improvement Strategy and Vision provides the fact-based alignment and prioritization mechanism between business strategy and strategic improvement. Too many organizations have approached their continuous improvement initiatives like a blind wine tasting with inexperienced critics. Blind tastings do in fact serve as rites of passage in the exams for both the master of wine and the master sommelier degrees. For everyone else, blind tastings are nothing more than a fun form of ritual hazing. The results have little to do with the quality of the wine and weigh more on the perceptions of the questions being asked. In terms of continuous improvement, lack of a formal Improvement Strategy and Vision creates a similar ritual hazing by which organizations interpret the improvement strategy based on leadership signals and perceptions or individual perceptions. The Improvement Strategy and Vision is a living objective process; it should be reviewed periodically to keep the organization focused on improving the highest-impact opportunities. The remainder of this chapter provides guidance about how to reset the course of improvement in this unpredictable economy.

THE PHILOSOPHY OF IMPROVEMENT

The first challenge of most organizations in this ailing economy is to rediscover their mojo of improvement. Some executives view their unpredictable and chaotic leadership behaviors as improvement, but that is not the case at all. Discovering the mojo does not mean searching for and jumping on the next bandwagon improvement program. Executives and their organizations need to step back, cut through the clutter of current activities, and begin to reset improvement as both the enabler of strategic success and the expected cultural standard. Leaders with the best track record of strategic improvement make an evangelical or spiritual commitment to the philosophy of improvement.

Figure 4.1 provides our conceptual model for viewing the philosophy of improvement. The following is an explanation of the four tiers of the model:

What are we trying to accomplish? At the base of the pyramid are the basic objectives of what organizations are trying to accomplish through improvement. Some organizations spend most of their time spinning their wheels in this level, using improvement on and off as a temporary fix.

How do we achieve success? At the second tier is the available best practices approaches to achieve the desired objectives with improvement. The philosophy must be driven by a *continuous* improvement process that identifies and overcomes the detractors of improvement through the right continuous strategies and tactics, which drive the right behaviors, decisions, and actions. Many organizations are able to get some of the pieces going in this level, and the degree of success is usually tied to the heroic efforts of one or several individuals. When they back off their efforts, organizations slide back into the first level.

What is the value proposition? The third tier provides the benefits when organizations achieve the basic objectives of improvement. Again, the degree of success or backsliding is tied to the efforts of a few heroic individuals. At this point, the value proposition must be enlarged to longer-term sustainable best-in-class performance across all measures of value. The higher one travels up the pyramid, the more difficult it becomes to

FIGURE 4.1   The Philosophy of Improvement.

remain in this state continuously. Leadership and sustaining infrastructure prevent the loss of progress and enable the ascent.

What is the larger moral purpose? At the peak of the pyramid is the pursuit of a larger, ultimate state of consciousness. This is the moral compass view of continuous improvement and the greater philosophical reasoning for *improving how we improve.* This larger purpose goes way beyond financial success and way beyond the self in the bold pursuit of workplace security and longevity, best places to work, community relationships, or regaining "made in U.S.A." global competitiveness.

INNOVATION REQUIRES ENLIGHTENED LEADERSHIP

Leadership is usually focused on getting the best results with the existing business model and related activities and resources. When things are going well, there is no need to change; much of the leadership content is pure daily management. When things are not going so well, executives tend to *go back to the well* of what has worked for them in the past. Sometimes this turns things around, at least temporarily. When things are still not going well, leadership often spends too much time on the same course in hopes of turning the situation around. They do not understand the fundamental formula of change: same people + same thinking + same process + same information = same results. Things continue to spiral downward enough to make executives accept that "*you're losing the battle—what got you here will not get you where you need to go.*" This is the singularity stage of black hole theory where the downward momentum overpowers the traditional ways of fighting oneself up and out of the black hole. The harder executives work, the deeper they slip into the black hole. Enlightenment is an emotional "big bang" in leadership thinking, where executives experience a humbling and sometimes brutal cleansing of their current assumptions, intuitions, and beliefs. The true greatness in leadership arises when organizational success depends on innovation and doing something that has not been done before. Enlightened leaders internalize this noble new end in mind with the upmost courage and confidence of their convictions, even though they may have not worked out all of the details. Yet they strive for, and lead others down a renewed path of success, while unfolding this new strategic destination—much of what appears at first to be impossible to achieve.

Let's take the philosophy down to a workable model as shown in Figure 4.2. Enlightened leadership is a formal process of continuous personal discovery in the relentless pursuit of excellence and superior business performance. The diagram illustrates that leadership cycles through stages where their organizations hit natural performance plateaus. Enlightened leaders recognize these performance plateaus immediately and either modify the current course or rediscover a totally new course through a constant cycle of *reckoning* and *renewal.* They know when to make minor adjustments and when bolder changes in direction are necessary. They make the right, tough decisions quickly.

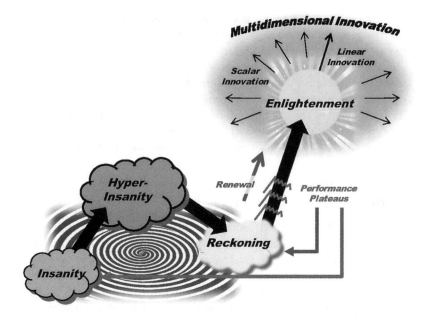

FIGURE 4.2   Enlightened Leadership Illustration showing the four stages of *Insanity*, *Hyperinsanity*, *Reckoning*, and *Enlightenment*.

When leaders fail to make the right changes at the right time, their organizations fall back to:

- *Insanity* mode – "Doing more of the same and expecting different results," which is usually followed by
- *Hyperinsanity* mode – "Doing more of the same with greater urgency and speed, and expecting different results."

Insanity and *hyperinsanity* occur when leaders choose to rabbit themselves and their organizations around from one crisis to the next. This certainly does not achieve Deming's point about continuity of purpose, and often these chest-thumping efforts achieve little to nothing and a demoralized organization. You cannot overcome challenge by doing nothing. You cannot realize new opportunities by doing nothing. *Reckoning* is virtue of enlightened leadership that creates the recognition of the need to change course. In some cases it requires proactive interventions to the current course. In other situations like our current economic predicament, it requires a bolder approach. *Renewal* is the virtue of enlightened leadership that creates a new vision, plan, and execution of change. *Renewal* is where new breakthroughs in improvement are achieved followed by new continuous improvement opportunities, all of which elevate organizations to higher levels of performance and cultural excellence. Eventually, organizations reach the next performance plateau where the need arises to repeat the positive *reckoning* and *renewal* cycle, or fall backwards into *insanity* and *hyperinsanity*. In our model, *reckoning* and *renewal* represent a continuous, relentless cycle of enlightened behaviors, decisions, and actions.

Enlightened leadership is the ability to adapt and adjust the organization's course to changing economic and business challenges. Enlightened leaders recognize the need to make these decisions immediately while time is on everyone's side. Enlightened leadership is a continuous cycle of leadership improvement. Now let's compare this to current "management by mayhem" leadership in many organizations. This is not leadership. The enduring activities of *insanity* and *hyperinsanity* are symptomatic of indecisive organizations that have lost their direction. Weak leaders procrastinate, waver, and provide conflicting direction, move quickly and accomplish little, pass off the responsibility, drive their organizations into chaos, find excuses for not making the tough decisions, and explain away bad performance. *Reckoning* and *renewal* break this vicious cycle and enable leadership to discover greater levels of self and organizational performance.

The relentless cycle of enlightened leadership leads to business model innovation through improvement. In our model, this is an advanced form of innovation that we refer to as Multidimensional Innovation. This is a new level of innovation that includes both linear and scalar innovation:

- Linear innovation is a line improvement over an existing product or process. Examples of linear innovation might include a new product feature that was once impossible, a simplified and safer surgical procedure, or significant improvements on existing processes that were previously unknown and undiscovered. We are taking the known universe of possibilities and making it better through discovery and creativity. In effect, these are line extensions of innovation.
- Scalar innovation is a brand improvement that is above and beyond existing products or processes. Examples of scalar innovation include a totally new brand of business, preventive medicine and treatment, a reinvented business model, or a totally new assembly technology. We are creating something totally new out of the unknown universe of possibilities. Scalar innovation opens up the realm of newly branded products or processes and totally different opportunities.

Enlightened leadership is the future of leadership: a process of leadership excellence that is timeless because it continuously develops leadership talent that is both current and future-focused. Enlightened leadership continuously strives to achieve a more holistic form of greatness that goes way beyond the self. Where is the enlightened leadership today? It is limited to organizations such as Apple, Amazon, Google, Fed-Ex and UPS, Research In Motion Ltd. (RIM), Southwest Airlines, Toyota, GE, BMW, 3M, and others. These organizations get it and fully understand that short-sighted, reactionary leadership is not sustainable in the new economy. Leaders that allow themselves and their organizations to twirl and toss in the modes of *insanity* and *hyperinsanity* are not innovating their business models and creating the business conditions and culture that will lead to continuous future successes. Executives and their organizations need to figure out very quickly how to spend all of their time in the Reckoning, Renewal, and Enlightenment areas of our model.

Many organizations should consider a leadership makeover because the new economy is rapidly redefining the fundamental purpose of leadership. Leaders of the present and future must first recognize the need to develop this competency within themselves because the world is moving too quickly to miss the new windows of opportunity. Executives need become swift and relentless about how they recognize and respond to new opportunities, preemptive countermeasures, or lost momentum. Constant change, increased complexity, and "improving how we improve" are givens in this new economy, and executives can no longer deal with these factors in a leadership vacuum. They must also shift from the traditional one-way management and total decision making roles to talent, growth, engagement, and empowerment—not the "lip service form of empowerment but genuine employee empowerment and accountability. Enlightened leaders must develop enlightened, connected fluid organizations that replace the random, disorganized firefighting aspects of change and adapt logically, deliberately, synchronously, and most important of all—correctly to changes in the business climate.

Maslow Upside Down

Enlightened leaders brand the emotional soul of improvement for their organizations by their courage and bold decisions, and ignore all the emotional excuses and reasons why something *can't* be done. Instead, they focus themselves and others on the positives of change and overcome the barriers with logic, facts, and communication. This is the essence of enlightened leadership. Enlightenment not only represents superiority, but it also assures the longevity, improvement, and higher standard of basic needs in Maslow's Hierarchy of Needs model for individuals, organizations, and society.

There are a few limitations to consider. Maslow's model does not consider how the economic bar rises over time and how the specific needs of different people change. The hierarchy of needs also does not recognize improvement as the basis for achieving these needs and traveling up the hierarchy.* What was once considered as a comfortable standard of living in the past is poverty today. Time, competitive pressures, and failure to change quickly enough place our hierarchy of needs in jeopardy. In the absence of Improvement Excellence™ (*improving how we improve*), an individual or an organization or a society can never sustain the

---

* The motivational models of Abraham Maslow and Frederick Taylor were at odds in terms of the specific approaches to motivation through the hierarchy of needs versus the principles of scientific management. Taylor was an early improvement pioneer, and many of his beliefs about people with natural "loafing" instincts, close supervision of elemental tasks, and punitive piece-rate incentive systems were widely adopted during the autocratic management and mass production era of the 1920s.

same standard of basic survival, security, and safety needs. It becomes increasingly difficult for employees or citizens to develop a true sense of family, friendship, loyalty, commitment, and intimacy in what people are doing when they are running around unappreciated with their hair on fire. Following the logic, it is even more difficult for organizations to provide an environment where people can experience their self-esteem needs and feel self-validated for their contributions. The difficulty increases at Maslow's self-actualization level, where people cannot continue to develop into their full capacity.

This is where the "Maslow upside down" enters. Enlightenment is this larger state of conscience that ensures the sustainability of Maslow's hierarchy of needs and a continuously improved quality of life for individuals, organizations, and society. The Plan-Do-Check-Act cycle in Figure 4.1 signifies this dynamic of enlightenment leadership. Enlightenment requires renewal. Enlightenment can never be realized in an individual, an organization, or society in general unless improvement is internalized as a universal philosophy, and the core competency of continuously improving how we improve is developed as the underpinning of this philosophy. This in turn requires enlightened leadership. The new economy demands bold enlightened leadership with the enlightened element turned on 100% of the time. This is the future of leadership: talented executives who use complexity and challenging situations to their advantage and recognize the need to improve much earlier in the game.

BUSINESS DIAGNOSTIC: THE FACT-BASED FOUNDATION

One of the most valuable efforts an organization can invest in is an objective business diagnostic. An experienced business improvement professional knows how to test an organization's processes against industry best practices and knows where to look for strategic improvement opportunities. There is often reluctance to implement this activity for several reasons:

- Many organizations have strong feelings about doing this on their own, and having an outsider conduct this activity is unnecessary and costly. The mindset is that if an outside consultant is necessary, then those in leadership are not doing their job. The problem with this thinking is two-fold: First, an objective business diagnostic is not usually objective when conducted by insiders; second, the effort produces quicker and better direction when conducted by an external improvement professional with extensive experience, competencies, and knowledge of best practices and other implementation factors.
- The organization perceives a business diagnostic as a waste of time because it believes that *they already know* most of their strengths, weaknesses, and improvement opportunities. Having an outsider reveal a different story or new root cause data might be perceived to be either embarrassing or revealing poor performance. Sometimes, the organization *knows how to* implement the necessary improvements—it is just a

matter of working it into the priorities, where improvement is usually the first casualty. These organizations either have difficulty ever leaving the starting gate or run off in the wrong direction.

- The term *business diagnostic* is usually interpreted as a lengthy analysis-paralysis study in which no one has time to participate in the process. Our version of a business diagnostic is a few days to a few weeks. The purpose is to target the right strategic improvement opportunities and identify how best to proceed within the context of a particular organization's operating challenges and environment. In effect, it is the adaptive process that leads to a tailored deployment and implementation plan. Have a look at every organization's current situation: It has more complex challenges, more uncertainty about what and how to change, and lacks resources to implement improvements and manage daily routines. These major changes have also changed how best to organize, plan, and execute rapid and sustainable improvement initiatives. Failure to recognize and build the uniqueness, complexities, and perceived barriers into the implementation process results adds significant risk to improvement. *Improving how we improve* is a core competency.

An objective business diagnostic is the foundation of a successful Lean Six Sigma deployment or any other strategic improvement initiative. The diagnostic provides the working roadmap for the deployment because it provides the upfront, deep-core drilling to the organization's key strategic, business, and operations issues. At a high level, the business diagnostic includes

- Reviewing the business strategy and operating plan
  - What are the organization's goals and expectations?
  - What are the strategies for capturing and growing market share?
  - What are the plans for new products and services?
  - How does the current portfolio of activities align to the business plan?
  - How is the organization performing against the plan?
  - Where are the voids and risks of lower performance?

- Conducting a structured business assessment to understand current performance
  - How are the current processes and practices working?
  - What key processes are working well, are working okay, and are severely "broken"?
  - What is the current performance in all areas of the business?
  - Is current performance characterized with data and facts?
  - What are the key sales and marketing issues?
  - What are the key operations issues?
  - What are the key supply chain issues
  - What are the key engineering/facilities issues?
  - What are the new product/service development issues?

- What are the key service delivery issues?
- What are the key financial issues?
- What are the key customer service issues?
- What are the current legal or regulatory issues?
- What improvements have been made?
- What have been the experiences of prior improvement initiatives?
- Where are the significant "pain points" or detractors to success?
- How are leaders and managers performing to expectations?
- Who are the organization's champions of the future?

- Benchmarking best-in-class performance
  - What are the dynamics of the cost structure and major cost drivers?
  - Is the organization aware of industry benchmarks and competitor performance in key strategic areas?
  - How do the organization's performance and key business processes stand up to industry best practices? What are these specific gaps and strategic improvement opportunities?
  - What are the accepted industry practices, and how could the organization differentiate industry performance from that of competitors? (Benchmarking is a single data point and is sometimes either outdated or irrelevant to the mission.)

- Defining gaps between current and desired performance
  - How is the organization performing vis-à-vis the strongest industry competitors in the areas of product and services availability, profitability, cost, delivery, flexibility, responsiveness, innovation, new products, financial ratios, inventory performance, quality and reliability, productivity, customer intimacy, leadership, stakeholder development, or other key performance areas?

- Developing the environment-specific Lean Six Sigma strategy and implementation approach
  - What are the specific components in the Lean Six Sigma improvement strategy?
  - What are the focal points, priorities, and plans for improvement?
  - What deployment scope and magnitude are best for the organization?
  - What level of deployment will achieve results and rates of improvement compatible with the business plan?
  - What is the right implementation infrastructure for success?
  - What is the top-level plan for moving forward with the deployment?
  - How will the organization align the customer to improvement activities?

- Defining improvement goals, benefits, and consequences of failure (failure is not an option)

- What are the strategic opportunities by key process area?
- What are the reasonable but stretch performance objectives?
- What can the organization expect to achieve and by when?

- Surfacing leadership, political, cultural, administrative, or other barriers to success
  - What needs to happen around the executive conference table to set the deployment on a successful course?
  - How do we engage the other powerful people in the organization who are not part of the executive team?
  - Who are the organization's champions, spectators, resistors, and showstoppers to improvement?
  - What is the plan for dealing with resistance to change?
  - How will the organization improve and take care of day-to-day activities?
  - Does the organization have all the right skill sets internally?

- Establishing the clear need for improvement
  - How will the organization provide a shared vision of change?
  - How will the organization communicate and reinforce the need to improve?
  - What communication media are best for various organizational segments?

These points are an abbreviated list of a true business diagnostic. The answers to these questions are constructed from discussions with a broad base of groups of people throughout the organization. These people live with their processes every day and are much closer to the root causes buried deep in the onion. As one can conclude from the questions, the business diagnostic provides valuable input to the Strategic Leadership and Vision, Deployment Planning, and Execution success factors. The business diagnostic is the working roadmap that provides specific direction for successful improvement initiatives.

The business diagnostic does not answer all the questions, but it sets organizations on the right deployment course. The pinpointing process engages people who do the work right up front: their issues, their ideas, their data-driven inputs. The business diagnostic also replaces the generic, plain vanilla approach to improvement with a highly adaptive, embraceable, and "real" approach to improvement. Many of the diagnostic participants become improvement team participants, so it accelerates the buy-in process. More details are developed in the Deployment Planning and Execution phases, which are discussed in subsequent chapters.

EXECUTIVE EDUCATION AND DEVELOPMENT

The executive education and development effort is extremely important in every organization and in particular the organizations just beginning their journey with improvement. The fundamental premise here is explained by a variation of Lord Kelvin's statement, "You don't know what you don't know. If you don't know what you don't know, you can't lead what you don't know. If you can't lead what you don't know and rely on others to lead what they also don't know, you can't execute the right actions. If you can't execute the right actions, you can't improve performance." Thanks to our new economy and technology, this premise is widening for all of us. Executive education and development are usually conducted in parallel with the business diagnostic. The objective of this effort is to build awareness and knowledge about Lean Six Sigma and the broader success factors of strategic improvement in general. This is best accomplished through the following means:

- **Educational Working Sessions (8–16 hours total):** This allows executives to become familiarized with Lean Six Sigma and continuous improvement fundamentals, the DMAIC (Define-Measure-Analyze-Improve-Control) methodology, leadership and change management best practices, and several *real* case study examples. Education is tailored to their specific environment, and their operating issues are also woven into participative discussions and exercises.
- **External Peer Visits and Communication:** It is often useful to introduce the executive team to another organization that is successfully implementing strategic improvement initiatives. Listening to another organization's why, what, where, how, and when questions is much more informative than how a specific improvement tool works. It provides executives with the opportunity to understand that there are more similarities than differences between organizations when it comes to leading strategic improvement.
- **Direct Involvement in the Business Diagnostic and Policy Deployment:** During these activities, there is a wealth of information sharing and discussions about what, why, where, how, and when of various improvement opportunities. These discussions are at a high level at this point. More specific details and priorities and improvement project details are filled in via policy deployment and other deployment methodologies. The point here is that direct executive involvement in these activities expands the shared commitment and knowledge of improvement requirements in the organization.

One of the largest mistakes that executives make is the public commitment of Lean Six Sigma without knowledge of the details and then delegating the ownership to a lower, powerless individual or group in the organization. This is guaranteed failure. Remember, the success or failure of any strategic improvement initiative is directly proportional to the executive team's behaviors, choices, and actions.

IMPROVEMENT STRATEGY AND VISION

The Improvement Strategy and Vision is the first accelerator in the critical sustaining improvement infrastructure in Chapter 2. The primary purpose of the Improvement Strategy and Vision is to communicate the compelling need to change and the consequences of doing nothing. It is developed (and updated) from the results of the most current business diagnostic. The Improvement Strategy and Vision communicates a logical and fact-based strategy of improvement at a high level, outlines the next steps and expectations, and commits to communicate more details as they are developed.

The objective of the Improvement Strategy and Vision is to

1. **Establish an unquestionable recognition of the need to improve.** This is accomplished by describing the current status of the organization, sharing customer and competitor information, and pointing out the gaps between current and desired performance. This objective includes the packaging and communication of critical business challenges (sometimes referred to as "burning platforms") and consequences of not moving forward with the changes.

2. **Create a bold and compelling image of the future.** The Improvement Strategy and Vision activates the organization's conscience and creates a renewed sense of purpose, direction, urgency, and reason. Reason is accomplished by being prepared to respond to the organization's questions and concerns with real data and facts from the business diagnostic. A fact-based image of where the organization needs to be to remain competitive appeals to people's emotions positively and builds cohesion, trust, and critical mass.

3. **Build executive cohesion and commitment.** The Improvement Strategy and Vision builds a shared sense of direction, priorities, and specific details about the why, what, where, how, and when questions. Answering these questions results in the superglue of holding the executive team together in unity of purpose and with a consistent message of improvement. Although it is often underestimated, there is so much power to improve when executives can agree on and communicate a universal story of improvement to their organizations.

4. **Build stakeholder engagement and commitment.** A fact-based and data-driven vision is effective in setting uniform direction, expectations, and "performance contracts" with executives and managers about Lean Six Sigma or any other strategic initiative. At this stage of the game, no organization or expert has all the answers to a successful deployment. Success requires a strong sense of executive and stakeholder engagement and commitment. The best way to encourage executive and stakeholder engagement is to integrate achievement into individual performance criteria.

5. **Act as the strategic reference point.** The Improvement Strategy and Vision should be constantly communicated to and referenced by the organization. This reference point serves to reinforce the message about improvement and how strategic improvement is the enabler to a successful business strategy. The Improvement Strategy and Vision is also used as a benchmark point to measure constancy of purpose against constancy of progress. However, the Improvement Strategy and Vision is just that: a strategy and a vision. The details of how the Improvement Strategy and Vision is executed and achieved must remain creative and flexible in this new economy.

The business diagnostic activities drive the chief executive officer (CEO) and the executive team to do their homework about strategic improvement. During this process, there are several excellent discussions about issues, priorities, and barriers—all of which build shared learning and commitment among executives and their organizations.

The Improvement Strategy and Vision includes the following elements:

- A recognition of the need for change (why)
- A believable but aggressive image of change (what and how)
- Bold and broad improvement goals (where and when)
- Narrower objectives (what and how—more detail)
- Specific improvement actions (what and how—even more detail)
- Accountability (who)
- Deployment timeline and expectations (what, when, where)
- The deployment monitoring system (deployment progress)
- Measurement and feedback (business improvement progress)

The Improvement Strategy and Vision becomes very powerful and compelling when, and only when, executives can communicate these questions to their organizations with a uniform story based on knowledge and facts. When the Improvement Strategy and Vision is presented to the organization with information about all of the elements outlined, it begins to create urgency, understanding, knowledge, and commitment to Lean Six Sigma.

Since the Improvement Strategy and Vision is an evolving process, I personally prefer a two-staged approach. Stage 1 is the higher-level version that is communicated to the organization early on to reduce the chatter and rumor mills and to promise more details. People by their nature will think negatively about something they know of but do not know about. What is the first thing people think about these days when a group of consultants are working in the building? Stage 2 is the more detailed version in which people learn that executive leadership has listened to their inputs and has created a strategy and vision based on their valued inputs. Establishing early buy-in and shared commitment is critical in a more rapid deployment and rapid results approach to improvement.

A common mistake that executives make is telling the organization where it needs to go but does not do justice to the why, what, how, and when of the Vision. *Why* is the most important question: If people do not understand why there is a need to change, the vision will not accomplish the momentum of drawing the organization together around a common theme. The same holds true for the what, how, and when questions. When executives gloss over these activities, the result is the same "lipstick on a pig" analogy: You can dress up a fad improvement program, you can put lipstick and cologne on a fad improvement program, but in the end it is still a fad improvement program.

THE FORMAL LEADERSHIP IMPLEMENTATION INFRASTRUCTURE

Another key element of the improvement and vision is to put the formal leadership infrastructure in place. This involves defining the organization and reporting structure, feedback and review processes, corrective action processes, and critical metrics for Lean Six Sigma or other strategic improvement initiatives. This also includes the clarification of roles and responsibilities of the CEO and executive team, the executive deployment champion, the executive sponsors, leadership champions, process owners, team leaders, team participants, and on-demand project resources.

Formal leadership implementation infrastructures share many common elements. The specific participants may change depending on availability and balance with other mission critical activities. However, the function and purpose are permanent. A good leadership implementation infrastructure manages strategic improvement initiatives through all of the typical barriers of success.

At a minimum, strategic and sustainable improvement initiatives require the following infrastructure requirements:

- Direct involvement and engagement of the CEO and executive team through frequent reviews of progress, issues, and corrective action plans. The CEO and executive team are also encouraged to participate directly in improvement activities or be present during major milestone reviews.
- A day-to-day implementation team led by a designated executive deployment champion. This is called an executive core team or steering team. Sometimes, it may be called something more generic such as the business improvement core team or business excellence steering team. The executive deployment champion is a highly regarded leader by the organization just as it says: a *champion*. The executive core team includes a cross section of competent and capable executives who can lead the overall effort and support specific improvement needs and projects. The executive core team is responsible for identifying, prioritizing, scoping, assigning, and managing improvement project activities. Finally, the executive core team is responsible for regulating and manag-

ing resources and organizational bandwidth/capacity so that the right targeted opportunities are achieved successfully and efficiently.

- Cross leadership and mentoring through executive sponsors and process owners who are usually assigned to specific improvement projects. The executive sponsor and process owner provide the overall process knowledge and ask the right objective questions but avoid steering a team to their desired conclusion. Improvement teams, executive sponsors, and process owners are all accountable for performance and positive results.

- Improvement teams are empowered to deploy the right improvement methodologies to an assigned improvement opportunity. A team leader serves as the project leader and mentor to the participants of the team. This is Teaming 101, which has been around since the 1980s, but most organizations have failed to master the approach. The executive core team manages project priorities, resourcing, and the birth-death process of teams.

- Mentors serve as deployment experts for leadership, the overall deployment process, key business process knowledge, expertise on successfully deploying the right improvement methodologies and tools, and deep experience on achieving the desired results. The best and most expedient way to develop this capability is through the use of outside consulting professionals with a demonstrated track record of success—and most important, who know how to replace themselves by developing and transferring the core competency of Improvement Excellence™ internally.

- Measurement and feedback practices that allow executives and the executive core team to monitor the progress of specific improvement actions and focus limited resources on the highest-impact opportunities. The combined rates and magnitude of improvement (validated by the finance organization for each improvement project/activity) are good metrics to track for the overall deployment. Over time, these metrics provide useful input about which areas of the organization are achieving the most and least improvement or how improvement initiatives are tracking against realization of the business plan and customer/market needs.

Leadership implementation infrastructure is clearly defined in the front end of any successful strategic improvement initiative. The chartering roles and responsibilities of each component are clearly defined and agreed on. The remaining elements of implementation infrastructure provide the visibility, controls, and metrics for keeping improvement in a continuous and sustainable state. Leadership infrastructure provides the framework for a very formal and well-defined management system for the successful strategic improvement and eliminates any confusion about executive roles and expectations.

POLICY DEPLOYMENT: PRIORITIZING AND CASCADING TARGET OPPORTUNITIES

One methodology that has gained popularity is called policy deployment. This is also called Hoshin planning or Hoshin Kanri. Policy deployment is used in strategic planning and in managing complex projects or initiatives with many components, each of which require alignment, execution, measurement, and feedback for the plan. Hoshin Kanri emerged in the World War II postwar era in Japan under the teachings of Peter Drucker. This methodology was adopted by companies such as Toyota, Komatsu, and Bridgestone Tire as a way to quality, cost, delivery, and inventory. To close the gap between strategy and execution, companies need to build strategic alignment across all levels of the business. This is the heart of policy deployment.

Policy deployment is a cascading *step-down* planning and execution process that helps in developing and organizing the strategic plan, midpoint plans, and the annual operating plan. Policy deployment is a useful methodology to translate findings from the business diagnostic into a simplified level-by-level view of the Lean Six Sigma deployment strategy. Policy deployment also links improvement initiatives and all other business activities to the top-level plans, and it incorporates features that provide early warnings about the status and alignment of specific projects and actions. Communication and status of all activities up and down the policy deployment process are achieved via documents called A3s. The name stands for the format (A3 size paper, 420 × 297mm sheets) that was originally used by Toyota and other Japanese organizations. The components of policy deployment force everyone involved in the planning process or specific projects to think crisply. A3s turn out to be 16.5″ × 11.7″ which when folded in half, is user-friendly and easily carried around for discussions by team members. The intent of the A3s is to present a crisp status of improvement by limiting the document structure and content. A3 is the metric equivalent of U.S. 11″ × 17″ which also works well. This A3 format promotes highly visual and portable planning and promotes management by walking around. Policy deployment also provides visibility to performance, which is designed to drive the right behaviors and achieve the right results.

The bottom line is that policy deployment enables laser-targeted task and resource alignment vertically, horizontally, and laterally throughout the organization's improvement initiatives. Most organizations deploying Lean Six Sigma are missing this succinct and robust planning and deployment process wrapped around their efforts. This is one element of formal infrastructure that keeps improvement initiatives on point. The intuitive leadership approach is analogous to inspection in which the odds of catching a defect are between 60% and 85% depending on the inspection criteria. Stated differently, those 15% to 40% improvement misses add up to millions of dollars in lost opportunities, momentum, and justification to continue improvement initiatives.

CONTINUOUS IMPROVEMENT
REDISCOVERED AND UNDER WAY

The failures of continuous improvement are not new. Organizations that begin their journey in the absence of a clear and concise Improvement Strategy and Vision are a leading root cause of failure. However, strategic improvement has become a no-option challenge for every executive and organization on top of all the other pressures of our disturbing economy. Regardless of the label, the art and science of improvement is the fast lane out of this slow economic recovery. The economic collapse of 2008 and our current economic situation have increased the urgency of why organizations must improve and at the same time have forever altered the process of what and how organizations must improve. This is what Improvement Excellence™ is all about: *improving how we improve.*

Today, our very sick economy has taken the shine out of Lean Six Sigma. There is no question that Lean Six Sigma is on a downslide in many organizations, when the need for improvement is higher than any other time in history. Many executives now have an "Elvis-left-the-building" attitude about Lean Six Sigma, but they must rediscover the art and science of strategic and sustainable improvement. Despite all of the publicized successes with Lean Six Sigma, most organizations are leaving annualized improvement opportunities equivalent to 3% to 20% of revenues on the table because they continue to separate continuous improvement from business strategy and culture. Boards of directors that allow their organizations to get away with not harvesting these opportunities are also asleep at the wheel.

This chapter has provided the vital guide to reset the course of improvement. A solid Improvement Strategy and Vision requires effort and know-how, but it does not need to take a long time. When attempted internally, it usually does require more time, and therefore it is either short-circuited or skipped completely in the interest of getting right into improvement activity. When there is a serious commitment to improve and internal industry expertise is combined with external improvement expertise, the result is a molecular collision of improvement success. The dynamics of this process are no secret to the best-performing organizations in terms of strategic improvement. Not to sound like a broken record, but Improvement Excellence™ *is* a legitimate core competency that many organizations are missing in the fabric of their culture.

Think about what is really going on in this chapter. The business diagnostic engages people in co-creating the early strategic improvement plans. The improvement vision is the initial instrument for creating a shared recognition of the need to improve. Executive education and development and the formal leadership infrastructure ensure that there is a consistent understanding and uniform message about improvement. Policy deployment gets the organization thinking about how to align its key business process improvement activities with broader strategic needs. Collectively, these elements begin to build stakeholder engagement despite people's discomforts and unknowns. The Improvement Strategy and Vision provides the initial beginnings of a real-time, closed-loop process of planning, deployment, execution, measurement, monitoring, and course corrections. Without these critical elements, continuous improvement is not much more than another paradox, another oxymoron.

The risks of strategic improvement are definable, predictable, measurable, manageable, and controllable. The risks of doing nothing are *not definable, not predictable, not measurable, not manageable, and not controllable.* Therefore, the risks of doing nothing are much higher than the risks of reinventing continuous improvement and getting down to business. It is not an easy road, and it may initially be a painful road for the more inefficient organizations requiring the most change. But, there is no option in our new economy.

There are four recurring comments that arise from organizations that are successful with strategic and sustainable improvement:

1. "We have achieved results way beyond our initial improvement goals and way beyond what we thought was possible."
2. "We cannot believe that we used to do things the way that we did in the past; we were too busy to recognize the obvious waste and inefficiencies in our processes."
3. "Now that we have gained more improvement experience, it's more common sense than rocket science, more basic math than integral calculus."
4. "I wonder how much better we can get."

In business and in life, there are only two outcomes: performance and excuses. The same holds true for strategic and sustainable improvement. A custodial staff, stockroom clerk, bank teller, or customer service representative has excuses because these individuals are often the victims of the processes that leadership provides for them. Their performance is only as good as the capability of the processes and cultural environment within which they work. For the CEO and executive leadership, there is no room or time for excuses. The same holds true for hospitals and in particular federal, state, and local governments. Government not only has a strange "mo' money, mo' money" perspective of improvement but also the wrong perspective of improvement and definitely the wrong priorities for improvement. Granted, the meltdown drove a gamut of survival behaviors that turned out to be grossly incorrect and counterintuitive to continuous improvement. It is time to get serious and radically change the mind models in the leaders of many organizations. There are too many people sitting in leadership chairs who should not be there. This is nothing personal—they have not discovered (or may never discover) the "right stuff" to lead their organizations down an extremely challenging road of improvement and renewed success in the new economy. In contrast, Toyota identifies over a million improvement opportunities each year, and over 90% of them are fully implemented. Toyota and a few other organizations like GE, Motorola, Honeywell, DuPont, Lockheed Martin, Raytheon, and others continue to remain the kingpins of continuous improvement. For the rest, the time to reinvent and leverage (formal, structured, logical) improvement and climb out of this slow recovery is long overdue.

BIBLIOGRAPHY

Burton, T. 2011. *Accelerating Lean Six Sigma Results: How to Achieve Improvement Excellence™ in the New Economy.* Ross, Ft. Lauderdale, FL.

Burton, T. T., and Moran, J. T. 1995. *The Future Focused Organization.* Prentice Hall, Upper Saddle River, NJ.

Jackson, T. L. 2006. *Hoshin Kanri for the Lean Enterprise.* Productivity Press, Boca Raton, FL.

Maslow, A. H. 1998. *Maslow Management.* Wiley, New York.

Strategic Frameworking. *The Brand Benefit Hierarchy.* Strategic Frameworking, Vashon, WA. http://www.strategicframeworking.com (accessed August 22, 2011).

5 Deployment Planning for Rapid and Sustainable Results

INTRODUCTION

This chapter is about putting the rubber on the road and keeping the improvement pedal to the metal for the long haul. Some organizations may have brilliant strategies, but fall down during the Deployment Planning, Execution, and Sustainability phases of continuous improvement. Deployment Planning provides the much needed answers to the why, what, where, when, and how of continuous improvement. With the sustaining infrastructure, Deployment Planning provides continuous answers and feedback about how to keep continuous improvement *continuous* and on track.

THE CONSEQUENCES OF POOR DEPLOYMENT PLANNING

One of the most frequent mistakes organizations have made with Lean Six Sigma and previous improvement initiatives is the failure to define, scope, and charter projects at a level of detail at which they are legitimately *doable* for the organization and *assignable* to an improvement team. As organizations work through their Improvement Strategy and Vision efforts, they begin to develop improvement themes of opportunities at a "boil-the-ocean" level of detail. Some examples of this might include improving the customer experience, improving global new product development, reducing length of stay or ancillary room turnaround, reducing warranty and returns, reducing the deficit, or improving quality and reliability of the global sourcing network. When organizations assign improvement projects at this level of detail, teams flounder with an assignment that is too ambitious and overly complex. Taking this a step further, teams with an ambiguous problem waste significant time because they cannot move forward, apply the right methodologies and tools, and execute their projects to a successful outcome. With enough of these fuzzy experiences that influence the team's personal performance, the organization loses its commitment. People not only internalize these bad experiences but also share them with others in the organization. In the examples, there are hundreds (or even thousands in the case of "reduce the deficit") of separate targeted improvement projects to move these performance needles in the right direction. This is related to the core competency of Improvement Excellence™: The organization is anxious to achieve improvements as soon as possible, but it fails to take the time to define, scope out, and characterize projects with data and facts. In the process, it fails to set the organization and improvement teams up for success.

Before we dive deeper into a discussion about formal Deployment Planning, let us learn from another history lesson while having a little fun about what typically has happened from previous improvement initiatives. Maybe the following outcomes have never occurred in your organization, but they are very common outcomes that stem from glossing over the Deployment Planning element of infrastructure:

- **No Traction, No Action.** Many organizations have found themselves stuck in this mode of frustration and inaction. There is a weaker recognition of the need to improve that always becomes overpowered by lack of direction and business as usual. It is a repeating cycle that begins with "we need to stop doing this," followed by attempts to improve instantaneously, a realization that it is not that easy and will require more effort, a fear of current work building up, a reassurance that things will be okay as is, and a return to business as usual. Many organizations claim to *know how to* improve, but for many reasons they fail to get off the dime. This is Planning 101, and failing to plan is planning to fail. An effective way to break this cycle is to help executive teams to quantify and recognize the costs, risks, and lost opportunities of staying the same. When this analysis is completed and validated with the chief executive officer (CEO) and executive team, it creates an effect similar to pulling the ring on a shaken can of soda pop. This always boosts the interest and urgency to change because the information is undeniable, and the profit and loss (P&L) plus hidden opportunities may range from 5% to 20% or more of an organization's gross revenues.
- **Sifting through the Snake Oil Marketing.** The recent popularity of Lean Six Sigma gained quicker and more widespread interest than any other improvement initiative since the 1980s. It was packaged and marketed with logical brilliance and the clarity of a Gemological Institute of America (GIA)-rated flawless diamond. Suddenly, the demand for people with belts for training exceeded the supply. Experience was replaced by the gating item called a belt. Some of the larger Six Sigma consulting firms were recruiting certified Black Belts (sometimes from their own clients), dressing them in a suit, and sending them out to clients with a laptop full of PowerPoint training modules to the tune of $4,000–$5,000 per day (They were actually paying these people $500–$1,000 per day). There was a significant turnover in certified Black Belts jumping ship for better opportunities. In retrospect, this mad-belt education strategy has been akin to developing a group of Michelin three-star chefs and then asking them to go out and grill a few turkey burgers. Putting the right people through a Motorola equivalent Black Belt certification is an outstanding longer-term professional development goal. However, belts were not the prerequisite for improvement that they were pumped up to

be. Furthermore, one does not need to be a master statistician to improve many of the huge commonsense opportunities in most organizations. Formal infrastructure that adapted Lean Six Sigma to an organization's specific needs would have saved organizations billions of dollars in implementation costs and given higher returns on their improvement investments. For hospitals, government, and others just beginning a formal improvement initiative, there is a great lesson to be learned from the adventures of Lean Six Sigma in private industry.

- **Mandated Improvement.** In this familiar situation, a CEO and the executive team grasp the next in-vogue improvement straw because GE, Toyota, or some other organization is on the same journey. In some organizations, a belt became a condition for advancement, which is great if the individual continues to practice and influence others on what was learned during the certification process. Sometimes, the particular improvement initiative was pushed onto an organization by a large customer as a condition of future business. From the beginning of their "me, too" efforts, the commitment is fake, and the underlying mindset is to do as much as possible with as little effort as possible. Other common characteristics of mandated improvement included decoupled leadership, overly optimistic expectations, underestimated resources and timelines, and underdelivered results. Nevertheless, executives trickled down the mandate to their organizations with a strong message that nonparticipation would negatively affect performance reviews. People began launching all kinds of improvement activities, fabricating benefits, and reporting funny money savings in fancy PowerPoint presentations to their superiors, and the news traveled up the flagpole. Many tallied up their accumulated funny money savings for their performance review discussions. They created the image that they were on board, but the entire improvement initiative was non-value-added effort. The improvement vocabulary was tossed around, but the principles are not practiced. I visited one organization a few years ago that would run around creating charts and storyboards in preparation for its customer's visit. I shook my head to think that even the customers could not see through their fabricated mirage of improvement.

- **Swallow the Whole Elephant.** Many executives enter their journey of continuous improvement with a superanxious mindset of "hurry up and improve." This is the right objective, but it is never realized continuously until Deployment Planning is in place. Instead, executives issue sweeping directives like "move everything to China in 90 days" or "fix this quality problem [which may be a design issue] by next week." On the surface, this creates the feeding frenzy look and feel of improvement, but all the shortcuts and work-arounds usually result in additional costs, quality and delivery problems, and lost customer confidence. In effect, executives are asking their employees to turn their brains off and to use brute force in the changes. Guess who ends up dealing with all of the additional problems? Organizations never have time to do the right things right the first time, but they always find the time to do things over.

- **Tool Mania.** Since improvement assignments are vague in scope, people revert to what they learned in their training. They begin acting like folks with a bag of tools looking for a problem, with a naïve application of improvement tools and magic checklists in hopes of completing their assigned projects. This usually results in a significant waste of time, resources, and direction of progress. Enough of this activity places improvement initiatives in a position of generating more cost than benefits, and the organization begins to detach itself from the effort. Improvement Excellence™ is a legitimate core competency that requires more than a few weeks of training and a belt.

- **Résumé Building.** In the recent Lean Six Sigma craze, the sole reason many individuals stepped up was to get their belts and pad their résumés. Improvement was viewed as a guaranteed promotional path instead of a philosophy and cultural standard. At the height of Lean Six Sigma's popularity, there was this leadership belief that parachuting in dozens of newly anointed Black Belts would make all of the problems disappear. In the absence of formal infrastructure, these people were either viewed as individuals speaking a different language or sucked into the daily routines of business as usual. Leadership created this motivation for people to get engaged and become a certified Black Belt because the starting salaries in other companies recruiting their own Black Belts were double or more.

- **The Magic Mantra.** Organizations have this false expectation that if their people follow the prescribed process (e.g., DMAIC [Define-Measure-Analyze-Improve-Control]), it will lead them down the yellow brick road to success. The problem with this thinking is that the process is blindly followed, resulting in many dead ends and restarts. The original objective of improvement is replaced by the bureaucratic process of improvement. Like tool mania, the efforts produce disappointing and illusionary results, and leadership commitment shifts to something else.

- **Solve World Hunger.** Failure to add detailed definition and priorities for improvement efforts creates its own inherent inefficiencies and wastes. There is another core competency missing within formal Deployment Planning infrastructure called program management: the ability to break down a broad improvement theme into manageable and prioritized *chunks* (specific projects) with their specific problem statements, objectives, improvement goal work plans, team staffing, and expected deliverables and timetable. This often leads teams down a road of solving unsolvable problems, the wrong problems, or symptoms of the real problem. Leadership has chosen to follow a blurred path of improvement with people going through the motions but nothing is changing. The difficulty and effort of improvement outweighs the benefits of improvement. Soon, it is the end of another improvement program.

- **Blind Faith.** These initiatives usually begin with training of the masses followed by a random launching of improvement projects. These organizations have chosen to skip the first two major elements of sustainability infrastructure: Improvement Strategy and Vision and Deployment Planning. Instead, their infrastructure is based on faith, hope, and wishing for change. Everyone ends up with a different interpretation of the goals and expectations of improvement. The improvement initiative unfolds to many activities everywhere—all aimed at the wrong problems and failing to deliver tangible business results. This is referred to "field-of-dreams" improvement: If enough activities are launched, the results will come. Soon, the field of dreams becomes a field of weeds.

- **Wrong Metrics, Wrong Behaviors, Wrong Results.** The improvement effort is introduced to the organization as more of a program than an expected philosophy of thinking and working. These initiatives become more of an improvement status symbol than an enabler of superior performance. Organizations measure their progress with useless metrics such as the number of people trained, the number of people and departments certified as Black Belts, the number of teams, the number of open improvement projects, or the length of time teams have been together. When organizations are not achieving true performance from improvement, they turn to metrics that show the appearance of improvement. If these are the metrics of choice, then the organization is in the improvement game for the wrong reasons. These efforts are referred to as the "T-shirt, certificate, mug, punched ticket, or banners and slogans" fad programs and are usually short lived.

Throughout the book, I reinforce the urgent need to develop the core competency of Improvement Excellence™ or *improving how we improve* in the new economy. Within the framework of Improvement Excellence™, the seasoned improvement expert quickly realizes that the major elements of sustaining infrastructure and the respective underlying accelerators are highly respected core competencies. The most challenging aspect of the accelerators is how to adapt their application to the particulars of different organizations with different cultures and business challenges. The absence of formal infrastructure has been, and will continue to be, a prescription for failure with continuous improvement.

DEVELOPING THE DEPLOYMENT PLAN

The purpose of Deployment Planning is to further define, scope, and prioritize the higher-level themes of improvement down into specific and detailed improvement activities. Deployment Planning paves the way for Execution and Sustainability

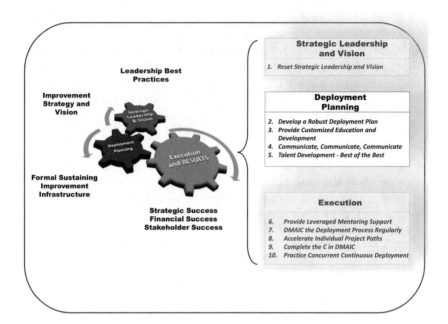

FIGURE 5.1   Deployment planning infrastructure. (© Copyright 2011 by The Center for Excellence in Operations, Inc. [CEO].)

(next chapter) and permanent cultural transformation. Figure 5.1 provides the specific accelerators of Deployment Planning.

Deployment Planning requires the fact-driven completion and updating of several activities:

- Translating strategic improvement needs into more well-defined individual improvement projects. The velocity and aggregate magnitude of improvement in the new economy is directly proportional to the level of direction and prework details provided to improvement teams. The math is simple: Rapid project completion in the same window of opportunity equals more projects with more benefits.
- Prioritization and deliberate regulation of improvement activity based on tall-pole needs. The velocity and magnitude of improvement are also proportional to how well the highest-impact opportunities are targeted and executed. The other part of this is how well these highest-impact opportunities remain in our sights—otherwise known as project and resource alignment. The historical model of *improvement everywhere* clouds the playing field and dilutes the ability to identify and follow through continuously on the greatest opportunities.
- Definition of new talent requirements and how best to develop these talents through customized education and development. This includes *what* improvement topics are most suitable to the organization's needs, *how* to

tailor education with relevant examples and exercises, and *when* to inject new skills in the most practical and useful manner and minimize disruptions to normal operations. For example, smaller bytes of education followed by direct application on an area that is a normal part of one's duties is much more effective than weeks of batch boilerplate training in large groups.

- Staffing individual improvement opportunities with the necessary cross-functional talent, leadership, knowledge, and interpersonal skills. As one of my favorite executive friends said, "You can't throw a pathetic group of people together and call them a high-performance team." First, individual teams need a well-understood definition of the improvement need and their expectations. Second, teams require this right composition of competencies. Third, teams require sponsorship through assigned executive sponsor and process owner. Fourth, teams need to be integrated into the formal infrastructure through the formal executive core team. When all of these conditions are present, the improvement goals of rapid deployment and rapid sustainable results become possible.
- Designing an effective communications and messaging strategy. Well-executed and frequent communication builds commitment and trust, reduces confusion, sets expectations, builds continuity and interest, removes fear of change, provides a medium for publicizing success and recognizing people, and builds momentum for larger successes.
- Ensuring a positive and powerful launch by putting the best of everything into the deployment: best projects, best leadership, best team leader, best team members, best innovative approach, best implementation plans, best use of limited resources, best use of time and capacity, best implementation path, and best results.

While all of this may seem to be time consuming, it really is not for seasoned improvement professionals. And, it certainly involves less time and risk than starting off on the wrong foot. The remainder of the chapter provides more detail and guidance about Deployment Planning.

HOW TO DEVELOP THE DEPLOYMENT PLAN

The business diagnostic is the main input of Deployment Planning. It usually includes a mix of attribute data (e.g., perceptions, observations, intuitive inputs from structured interviews) and variables data (e.g., standard financial reports, daily and monthly performance reports, etc.). The first step is to remove some of the fuzziness and further refine more specific opportunities. Pareto analysis is then applied to the process to segment the vital few high-impact opportunities from the trivial many lower-impact opportunities. Inherently, every organization knows it does not need to deal with every single problem to achieve large improvement hits. But, the majority of organizations do not make the effort to laser their organizations in on these larger strategic opportunities.

Deployment Planning isolates the three to five things that keep everyone awake at night.

This is not a simple and straightforward Pareto analysis, and the next steps require leadership and common sense. For example, some of the smaller issues may be big issues to premier customers, or dependencies and interaction effects may exist between the higher- and lower-priority projects. Deployment Planning requires some formal prioritization of improvement activities based on other strategic parameters. In our consulting practice, we have developed several formal "chartering" templates to guide our clients through this process. These instruments are basically an Excel spreadsheet with several tabs, where each tab represents a specific activity set of the Deployment Plan. These include the following templates: macrocharter, project selection, project/resource alignment, team assignment, project charter, and microcharters.

THE MACROCHARTER

The macrocharter is a template used to collect and identify potential project information, such as a formal and fact-based description of a problem statement, probable root causes, cost of quality (or waste) data, proposed project name, project objectives and scope, improvement goals, benefits, and deliverables.

PROJECT SELECTION

The project selection template allows executives to evaluate projects against each other relative to business plan contribution. Projects are scored and ranked against quantitative and qualitative attributes such as cost reduction, revenue growth, availability and level of resources, time, availability of data, capital investment, and so on. The object is to remove subjectivity or executive preference and instead focus the organization's limited resources on mission-critical projects that will take the least amount of effort and create the greatest impact.

PROJECT/RESOURCE ALIGNMENT

The simple project/resource alignment template evaluates potential participant resources against a variety of required skill sets and direct experiences, facilitates in the identification and selection of the best team leaders and team participants, and helps to align people with projects objectively. This template is also useful in future talent development plans.

TEAM ASSIGNMENT

The team assignment template displays a matrix of all open, completed, and planned improvement activities by individual involvement. One of the underlying objectives of Deployment Planning is to develop talent by spreading and developing critical mass across a wider base of individuals. In our deployments, we exercise the one-resource, one-team rule, which forces a deeper development of bench strength (i.e., more developed resources for future improvement efforts) and a higher degree of "improvement spillover" into daily work. This template helps leadership to expand the base of talented go-to people and to set the expectation that improvement is not limited to a team project but an expected skill set to be used in daily work.

PROJECT CHARTER

The project charter is the team's reference document for its specific project. Project charters define a specific team leader and team, executive sponsor, and the project title. Project charters also include a crisp problem statement, probable root causes (clue data), project objectives, scope, boundaries, performance metrics, current baseline performance and cost-of-poor-quality (COPQ) data, improvement goals, quantified benefits, expected deliverables, and a rough timetable for the project. Project charters are living documents that continue to evolve and target more specific opportunities as the team works its way through the DMAIC methodology.

MICROCHARTERS

Microcharters are what we refer to as "below-the-line" improvement activities. The business diagnostic process, individual improvement project activities, and daily work routines also identify several "fruit-on-the-ground" opportunities. Many of these improvement activities will not require detailed analysis or even a team. The items included in the microcharter fall into the category of Kaizen or quick-strike improvements. The microcharter avoids the slow, top-down approach to improvement by engaging people earlier in sponsored and meaningful continuous improvement. Over time, this template evolves to individual area microcharters with the capability to consolidate area activities into a summary microcharter. This microcharter is the driver of what is known in our chartering methodology to as Business Improvement System (BIS), a formal set of improvement best practices and accompanying instruments that our clients use to facilitate a uniform organizational process for identifying, assigning, completing, and summarizing the results of Kaizen or quick-strike improvements.

The Deployment Plan is the initial GPS of a strategic improvement initiative. When the infrastructure elements of Improvement Strategy and Vision and Execution are working well, the Deployment Plan becomes the living hopper for capturing, prioritizing, and queuing up improvement opportunities. Coupled with an effective communications strategy, this sends a powerful message to the organization that improvement is never ending, and proactive involvement is an expectation and condition for a rewarding career.

MORE THAN A PLAN

Since our methodology is in Excel format, there are several other residual leadership benefits, such as the ability to:

- Sort and display launched and planned projects by business unit, key process, or functional area and anticipated benefit timelines to determine how the organization's formal Lean Six Sigma initiative will contribute to the operating plan or financial plan. Organizations that are extremely committed to improvement build the planned savings into their budgets and operating plans.
- Analyze projected and cumulative rates of improvement over a specified timeline and adjust the dynamics of the improvement initiative to maintain or improve the rate of improvement. Typically, the rate of improvement becomes difficult to grow as the initial "sweet improvement fruit" is harvested during the first 2 years. Organizations maintain or increase the rate of improvement by new thinking, new innovation, extended boundaries, new people, and in general improving how they improve.
- Evaluate the relative value of launched and queued up projects by business unit, functional area, or as a baseline to measure actual project performance. It is typical for many teams actually to exceed the anticipated benefits of their projects. Some of this happens by a natural lean toward fact-based conservatism on defining projected benefits, but most of this occurs because true root cause problem solving reveals opportunities that were hidden and previously unknown to the organization.
- Ensure that continuous improvement is positioned as an organizational-wide initiative, not a manufacturing or quality initiative. No one is exempt from improvement. The Deployment Plan can quickly provide information relative to participation and results by executive, process owner, functional area, or individual.
- Plan for current and planned professional development needs, provide career exposure opportunities to individuals, develop backstop organizational skills and capabilities, or use the available information as input into recognition and rewards.
- Provide a formal knowledge repository for completed, launched, and planned improvement projects. Some of our clients have created intranet capabilities with the Deployment Plan, thus providing a searchable directory of detailed DMAIC information for each project. This capability prevents organizations from initiating efforts that might have previously been analyzed or ruled out. It also provides the ability for organizations and their divisions or business units to leverage off the knowledge of previous projects.

If an organization is really committed to continuous improvement, then it is impossible to run out of things to improve with the leadership and formal

infrastructure presented throughout this book. The "need for speed" out of Lean Six Sigma and continuous improvement is evolving rapidly, but the basic underpinnings of success will remain pretty much the same. We are entering a new era of improvement that we call *adaptive and innovative improvement*. This involves the development of an organization's capability to Sense, Interpret, Decide, Act on, and Monitor (SIDAM) improvement opportunities with technology-enabled approaches, and in near-real-time mode. These types of improvements are rapidly becoming a differentiator in this new economy.

CUSTOMIZED EDUCATION AND TALENT DEVELOPMENT

A major problem with continuous improvement has been its continued introduction through a series of single-point, disconnected, stand-alone, boilerplate approaches with their own unique buzzword vocabularies, tools, and approaches. Organizations have been continually challenged about which methodology is best for them and how to implement various methodologies in their different environments. They have also wasted time debating improvement methodologies, trying to decide which methodology was the best, which was the fastest, which fit best in their business, and what was the most popular in other organizations. This was analogous to debating which tool in a toolbox is best before one defines the repair job: Is it a screwdriver, a wrench, or a power drill? It depends, just as it depends with improvement in business. This explains the need for infrastructure. The Improvement Strategy and Vision and Deployment Plan drive how organizations implement improvement and which methodologies and tools will be most applicable to their particular improvement challenges and operating environment. Lack of infrastructure leaves people in organizations confused about continuous improvement, leaving them with no other option than to run around trying to implement tools. This has driven the historical and present fascination with the improvement tools themselves. Look at the names of seminars and workshops on continuous improvement; the majority are named and structured around tools. Some organizations begin asking questions such as, "What are we doing today? Kaizen? Lean? Six Sigma? What happened to value stream mapping, 5S, and fishbone diagrams?" The discussions about business improvement in many organizations often resemble the famous baseball comedy act of "Who's on First?" by Bud Abbot and Lou Costello.

A critical prerequisite of successful strategic improvement initiatives such as Lean Six Sigma is to understand the business improvement requirements—namely, the specific operating environment, the needs for strategic improvement, culture and other barriers to success, and how to integrate methodologies and tools into the design of the initiative. The improvement methodologies and tools are important because they represent the *means* to achieve improvement. Although the improvement tools themselves represent the minor part of success, they are collectively important, but they are not the *ends*. At the methodologies and tools level, organizations must customize their improvement initiatives around their specific requirements for improvement.

Different types of industries and organizations need a different focus, approach, and skill set for their continuous improvement journey. No doubt these factors may change or require additional skills over time. For example, if a team is improving global sales and operations planning (S&OP), that multimillion-dollar project contains dozens of Six Sigma, Lean, and Kaizen opportunities, all of which are well orchestrated and executed to create a breakthrough improvement. This occurs because there are dependencies in projects such as this one, and concurrent improvements create incredible *interaction* improvements (e.g., when an improvement in one area creates residual improvements in other areas). In the case of a typical hospital, most of the larger immediate improvement opportunities that influence length of stay, reduce ambulatory cycle time, or improve the velocity and quality of admitting are in the Kaizen, Lean, and enabling information technology (IT) arena. So, there is no need for a huge investment in Black Belts and master statisticians. However, there is a need for evidence-based improvement using the most basic analytics (e.g., Pareto analysis, cause-and-effect diagrams, value stream mapping, eight wastes worksheets, templates and checklists, etc.). Some of the Six Sigma thinking may be useful in standardizing surgical procedures and optimization around several differently weighted factors, such as risk, quality, time, and cost. The point here is focus and not delivering the entire toolkit when only 20% of it is needed. Hospitals that are considering a huge investment of time and resources to implement a big bang GE-type program are heading down the wrong road of improvement. Once again, this explains the need for infrastructure. The Improvement Strategy and Vision and Deployment Plan drive how organizations implement improvement and which methodologies and tools will be most applicable to their particular improvement challenges and operating environment.

HOW TO TAILOR EDUCATION TO BUSINESS IMPROVEMENT REQUIREMENTS

The basic premise for tailoring education and training is to accomplish the productivity and speed characteristics of improvement. In retrospect, Six Sigma and its mass development of belts has been a mixed blessing. On the one hand, it takes a tsunami to move many organizations forward with improvement. On the other hand, it has set the expectation that training the masses and creating a hierarchy of belts is the prescription for success. We cannot argue with the 20% of Six Sigma deployments that are successful and carrying on, but we can learn a good lesson from the 80% of deployments that have failed. One of the root causes is the broad, plain vanilla approach to education and talent development.

This section provides proven guidelines for customizing education and training around the basic business improvement requirements, which should be:

- *Cascading:* Education designed to deliver a uniform base of skills and knowledge to people at different levels in the organization and to deliver specific injections of skills needed for success in their specific organizational roles.
- *Integrated:* Replacing single-point tools thinking with a "toolbox and master craftsman" approach to improvement. This is the integration of Kaizen, Lean, Six Sigma, and all other methodologies and means of improvement that contribute to success. This also involves integrating other factors into continuous improvement, such as enabling IT, the human elements of change, regulatory and compliance considerations, communication, and performance and rewards.
- *Needs driven:* Curriculum design based on the organization's business improvement requirements. The goal is to provide education that goes deep into the true needs of specific organizational areas and avoids unnecessary and confusing education that is unlikely to be used in a client's operating environment.
- *Environment specific:* Infuse education with real-life pilots, examples, and data from the client's environment. The availability of real-life examples connects theory and practice and reinforces the feasibility and applicability of improvement.
- *Holistic:* Recognition that all improvement properties are not addressed by the tools alone. Education may be required on soft skills development in areas such as leadership development, teaming fundamentals,

team dynamics, change management, project management, cost/benefit analysis, implementation planning, selling, support-building skills, and performance management.

- *Participative:* Incorporates hands-on participatory exercises with relevance to real-life issues. This may include waste walks, role playing, and custom-designed simulation exercises. Participants experience how to apply the improvement tools with success and an immediate connection to their workplace.
- *Achievement based:* Education followed by successful application to a real improvement opportunity, followed by teaching and mentoring others. This was one of the best characteristics of Six Sigma because Black Belt certification required that candidates demonstrate their new knowledge and expertise through successful completion of a large and successful project.
- *Concurrent:* The best way to learn anything is in small doses, immediately applied to a real situation with specific goals and expectations. The objective of concurrent education is to tighten up the "learn-apply-improve-realize success" cycle.

The experienced practitioner understands and knows that the same improvement approaches may be applicable in concept but must be deployed with creative and innovative retrofits. Manufacturing, hospitals, financial institutions, retail, or government all have the enormous opportunity to improve. However, the leadership mind models, Improvement Strategy and Vision, Deployment Planning, and Execution elements of infrastructure are totally different. Collectively, these elements provide the capability and capacity to improve and improve how we improve. Another challenge is transactional and knowledge processes, which are technology-integrated and people-intensive processes; performance and behaviors are influenced by many factors beyond the direct process itself. In all industries, the physical content of work is being replaced by technology that is transforming the world into interdependent networks of transactional processes. Factors such as relationships, personalities, experience, maturity, political motives, egos, personal investment, security, insecurity, performance criteria, organizational balance of power, perceived priorities, and leadership expectations have significant impact on transactional processes. This is neither good nor bad—it is just a fact that influences how to improve transactional processes.

The benefits of incorporating these customization attributes into Lean Six Sigma and other strategic improvement initiatives are obvious, particularly in the performance of people after they leave the classroom. Their ability to apply, learn from the experiences, acquire new knowledge, and grow professionally is much greater than the slam-dunk, train-the-masses, get-the-belt approaches.

COMMUNICATION AND STAKEHOLDER ENGAGEMENT

Many organizations have made hasty attempts to communicate change within their organizations. Many efforts resemble nothing more than an informal "let's get everyone together and tell them what we're doing." These efforts are pursued with the best intentions but fail to address the root causes of current culture and behaviors. The purpose of communication is to create awareness, commitment, trust, inspiration, engagement, and other positive behavioral attributes of change. Communication efforts often downplay the need to understand the current drivers of people and behaviors, the potential root causes of resistance, or how people may react to the messaging. Further, the message itself has little to do with establishing the positive behavioral attributes of change. Effective communication is an open, two-way process in which people should be actively engaged and be comfortable with the process. The purpose of communication is to build the human and emotional foundation for improvement and change. There are simple rules to remember about communication:

1. The strategy that the CEO and executive team chooses to communicate the message about improvement and change (e.g., what, when, why, where, how) significantly influences the initial recognition of the need, receptivity, and acceptance on the part of the organization; and
2. The process, content, candor, method/media choices, and frequency of communication significantly influence ongoing awareness, proactive participation, reinforcement, and internalization of change. This rule determines the "continuousness" of the effort.

Why is the most important question to answer. People need to be informed of the reasons why the organization must move away from their current as-is state and of the consequences and risks of staying the same. They need to understand better the external market and competitive pressures that are driving the organization to change. They also need to understand the magnitude of these external market pressures and the sense of urgency for change. Communication is the medium that explains why the current state used to make sense, how the business environment is changing, why the organization must change to meet these new challenges, and what to expect if the organization does not change—particularly at the individual level.

DEVELOPING AN EFFECTIVE COMMUNICATIONS STRATEGY

The new economy is one in which executives must point the organizational compass in every direction except where they have been in the past. Improvement needs more creativity and innovation in the new economy. There are just too many complexities, and organizations cannot mechanize and proceduralize their improvement initiatives like the past. A more up-to-date process of improvement needs to inject new skills quickly and get people talking and working on the right opportunities. In addition, the era of talking about employee empowerment and engagement is over. In the new economy, executives need to expand and rely more on the capabilities of their organizations and truly empower people and leverage their knowledge to fashion extraordinary improvements. Another era that needs to go is the silent disengagement, "it's not my problem" element of culture. The more people become interconnected through technology, the more reason to throw this thinking to the curb. One of the largest challenges with improvement in government is that the culture is infested with this thinking. This is by no means the fault of the employees. It is leadership's fault for fostering this culture over a hundred years.

Great executives and communicators recognize how confusing the business strategy may appear to the organization, and they carefully craft their communications *before* delivering any messages. For some executives, this comes naturally; for others, it is a struggle. Communication—whether positive or negative—must be deliberately crafted, candid, and positively framed to be well received. Several preliminary questions must be considered when creating any effective communication about strategic change:

- *Who are the stakeholders?* Anyone impacted by change needs to hear the message. This includes internal and external audiences who may be directly or indirectly impacted by the change.
- *What is the communication objective?* The message of change should differ depending on whether an executive is informing, educating, persuading, seeking support, or building awareness and clarity in direction. Communication of change must be focused on the particular objective of the message.
- *What is the general attitude?* This relates to executive credibility. Like it or not, executives must think about how audiences perceive their personal credibility and trust and how to build it if it is not there. The level of hostility, ambivalence, or full support will influence how the message of change will be received by the organization.
- *How to communicate to different audiences?* The message of strategic change must be identical and consistent between organizational constituencies. However, different audience groups may need a different version of the puzzle, different levels of detail, more specifics on the impact, and information about what to expect. The overall message of change must be uniform, but the specific details are highly dependent on a particular audience's connection to the change.
- *What is the method of communication?* This relates to how the message of change will be communicated. It may include a shareholder's meeting, a quarterly review, a monthly newsletter, e-mail, webcasts, conference calls, payroll mailers, signage, and other media. The point here is that different methods of communication (media and hits) are necessary to reach and connect with different organizational constituencies.

- *What is the proper timing?* There is no right time to change except *now.* The timing of communication should be considered when delivering the message of strategic change. Generally, timing should be frequent with the goal of information sharing and stakeholder relationship building. The visible executive behaviors, decisions, and actions after the message are also important.
- *How will stakeholders participate?* Communication must become an ongoing process in which stakeholders and audiences feel free to participate and provide vital feedback about change. This builds buy-in and ownership for change. Communication of change should never be a one-way dialogue.

Any large-scale strategic improvement initiative is a process that almost every human balks at, even though the most positive career and life experiences have come about by change. Communications strategy is the enabler of managing change. When change is introduced, people internalize the perceived and often-imaginary outcomes of change. No matter how much change is planned, the response is the same. The more unknowns affiliated with change, the higher the anxiety is and the more negative perceptions there are about the change. Deep diving into people's heads usually reveals that they are not afraid of the change itself; they are afraid of the perceived loss, effort, commitment, discipline, sacrifice, the risk of failure, and disruption to their established norms. Leadership gets the organization through this very real dilemma.

GETTING OFF TO AN UNSTOPPABLE START

As mentioned, the next challenge after communication is change management. With any executive communication, there is always a mix of responses and reactions by the organization. The secret of mastering communication is not only in formal infrastructure but also in mastering change management. In a large-scale strategic improvement initiative, it is valuable to have communication and change management in the forefront constantly. There are several proven leadership approaches to provide a handhold to the organization through a major improvement initiative such as Lean Six Sigma. These approaches require patience, time, logic, and facts—and are much more difficult in practice to get right. All executives are under tremendous pressures in this economy, and the quickest leadership approach is issuing directives. Unfortunately, there are no shortcuts to reinvent organizations and transform culture.

BASIC CHANGE MANAGEMENT ESSENTIALS

As mentioned, leadership's role is to provide the positive ecosystem for success with continuous and sustainable improvement. Executives and managers will find success in deploying several familiar approaches to lead their organizations through change, namely:

- *Facilitation:* This includes open collaboration to help their people to digest and embrace the vision, mentoring people and teams to a successful conclusion on improvement initiatives, and helping people find their eureka moments with change.
- *Education:* This includes increasing awareness and knowledge about the need to change, helping people to understand the organization's burning platforms and priorities for improvement, explaining the expectations and requirements for success.
- *Engagement:* This entails getting people involved up front in the business diagnostic, creating the vision, participating in the macrocharter, and participating in other Deployment Planning activities.
- *Rewards and consequences:* Beyond talking and convincing people to get on the train and stay on the train, change and improvement must be directly tied to individual performance and rewards—the sooner the better.
- *Discussion forums:* These are smaller focus group meetings that facilitate listening and openly discussing questions and concerns, expectations, project ideas, and other potential detractors on people's minds.
- *Good teaming practices:* This includes pausing, active listening, acknowledging the other person's point of view, thinking before speaking, offering clear and consistent unwavering responses, keeping emotions out of the discussions, and continually using data and facts.
- *Cross learning:* This involves regularly scheduled peer reviews where executive sponsors and team leaders can collaborate on the progress of their improvement activities and any other dynamics of change that they are experiencing within their teams and the project.
- *Best practice leadership behaviors:* These are the vision, knowledge, passion, discipline, and conscience behaviors discussed in Chapter 3. Executives should be creating not only a vision of improvement but also a vision of the organization's desired culture and how people think and work every day.

The best that executives can do is follow these proven approaches. In some instances, there will always be the naysayers, who will not step up no matter what the organization does or accomplishes. Some of these people will resign because of the emotions of peer pressure or because they are not interested in a future that includes Lean Six Sigma, improvement, or collaborating in teams. Active talent management also sifts out the bad apples. Following these approaches and other advice in the Leadership Vision, Strategy, and Deployment Planning phases will initially win over a critical mass. These factors combined with execution will eventually engage the entire organization (with a few irrelevant exceptions) in the pursuit of Improvement Excellence™.

THE POWER OF POWER HITS

Effective change management efforts reach out and listen to the organization's questions and concerns and clarify the confusion about change. Communications strategy is the medium to accomplish this continuous process of managing change. One of the most powerful practices of executives is the continuous *power hits* to their organizations. Power hits are the quick, informal, conscious 15-second messages that demonstrate commitment, interest, and expectations. Examples of executive power hits might include

- "How's your project going? Your team's results mean a lot to the company's X." Demonstrates interest and reinforcement of importance.
- "Where are you in your project? Are you beyond D&M and into A&I yet [DMAIC status]?" Demonstrates an understanding of the improvement process and how it works and reinforces teams to follow the process.
- "Looking forward to the team's improvements." Shows interest.
- "I am both surprised and impressed. May I see your analysis?" Shows an understanding of the DMAIC data-driven process.
- "Has the team identified root causes? How do you know? What data are you looking at?" Reinforces knowledge of process and reinforces fact-based results.
- "I always suspected that the problem was Z. I'm glad you're all peeling back the onion to find out what is really going on." Admits to human frailties, reinforcement of process, reinforcement that the team will be more knowledgeable than anyone about the problem and root causes.
- "This project is extremely important. A lot of thought went into who we should put on this team." Obviously reinforcement and individual and team kudos.
- "When do you expect to identify improvements?" Communicates sense of importance and urgency.
- "Let me know whatever you need." Demonstrates commitment to the team.

One of leadership's roles in continuous improvement lies not in giving answers but in asking the right questions or making the right value-added comments. When this does not happen, people begin kibitzing about interest and commitment and whether their efforts matter. Their chatter is not always justified, but it happens. Making the effort to stop by an education session or occasional team meeting also sends a strong message of commitment, interest, and expectations. An old Chinese proverb comes to mind: "Tell me and I forget. Show me and I remember. Involve me and I understand."

Power hits are most effective when personally structured and communicated effectively, and they require a conscious effort. Also, power hits should never be limited only to teams working on improvement projects. Executives interested in building a fact-based, data-driven, root-cause-oriented culture should be consciously "power hitting" everyone on every activity in the organization. Executives should appreciate the fine leadership line between power hits and meddling or directing individuals down a personal road. Sincere power hits and the right questions really drive the desired spillover effect of continuous improvement from an individual project to the expected cultural standard of thinking and working every day.

BIBLIOGRAPHY

Burton, T. 2011. *Accelerating Lean Six Sigma Results: How to Achieve Improvement Excellence™ in the New Economy.* Ross, Ft. Lauderdale, FL.
Scoble, R., Israel, S., Barbosa, D., and Merkle, G. 2009. *The Conversational Corporation: How Social Media Is Changing the Enterprise.* Dow Jones, New York.

6 Execution and Sustainability

INTRODUCTION

Throughout the book, I raise awareness of the rapid changes in the world, which have turned the old rules of how organizations develop and improve upside down. The new economy demands different types of leaders with a broader perspective and range of qualities. For organizations to succeed, executives must better understand what key leadership behaviors and practices are paramount in driving their organization toward mass collaboration, rapid improvement, rapid results, and sustainable success. This is much more than just getting people to make the right decisions and produce the right outcomes. It is about getting people to be committed to the organization, be passionate about their work, and have a deep desire to grow personally and handle the challenges ahead. The best organizations have already figured this out and are busy executing and sustaining rapid improvement. Figure 6.1 provides an overview of the accelerators of Execution and Sustainability.

All continuous improvement initiatives are customer driven, right? During a dinner meeting with the chief executive officer (CEO) of one of our firm's clients, we discussed his perspectives about being customer driven. We talked about how everyone has always embraced the notion of listening to the voice of the customer and focusing on the customer (at least in words), until his initial experiences leading the Lean Six Sigma deployment. He mentioned, "For as long as I have been an executive, everyone has promoted the customer-driven philosophy. I believe that there's something fundamentally wrong with this thinking." He talked more and said, "I'm on a new mission, although I probably can't state it publicly without being crucified. The customer is not number one to me anymore. My people and my organization are number one. If we don't have great loyal people with talent, motivation, working together doing the right things, with shared success—we can't be successful with customers or anything else we try to do." He made a great point: The notion of customer-driven work is an empty wish unless it is backed up by the right actions.

THAWING OUT THE FREEZE

During the recent economic fiasco, discretionary spending on professional development and improvement were the first funds to be frozen. This has repeatedly been the case when organizations face negative dips in the economy. It is a familiar age-old pattern of freezes and layoffs, both of which are not improvement

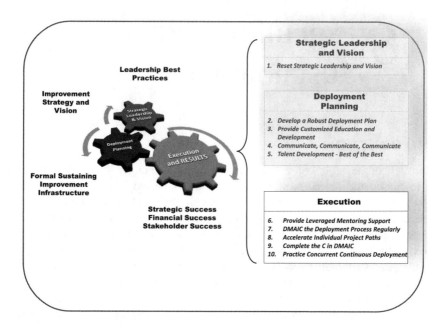

FIGURE 6.1 Execution infrastructure. (© Copyright 2011 by The Center for Excellence in Operations, Inc. [CEO].)

actions. Executives in these organizations view people not as an asset but as an expense, and they cut the expense as much as possible in a recession. Executives fail to recognize that they may have cut off their lifelines as they make hollow statements like "We'll come back to improvement later" or "We will improve organically." Leadership behaviors, decisions, and actions combined with the lack of competency, time, resources, or all of these on the part of the organization to improve send continuous improvement on another downward spiral. The leadership responses to the recent meltdown have again sent strong messages that formal improvement is no longer a priority, and the effort required to resuscitate improvement in these organizations is a significant leadership dilemma. One time-proven fact about continuous improvement initiatives is that when organizations turn down the commitment and focus, it takes only about 6–8 weeks for initiatives to disappear off the radar.

Whether an organization chose to pursue or freeze improvement aggressively during the meltdown is irrelevant in today's economy. The need for improvement is facing both types of organizations, especially those that are cautiously thawing out after the freeze. When organizations think about *best*, the first thing that they must focus on is creating a best company, best strategy, and best organization. This is a prerequisite for strategic and sustainable improvement. Simply overlaying a collection of improvement methodologies and tools (that worked well in some Fortune 1,000 corporation) on leadership and talent-deficient organizations will not cut it.

Some executives believe that the best time to change tends to be when things are slow and people have the time and opportunity to focus on development. Others believe that the best time is when times are good. Yet most executives postpone improvement until their backs are up against the wall. The problem with all of this logic is that, in the interest of the moment, improvement is always the first casualty. These organizations suffer from "can't afford to, can't afford not to" disease. Leadership gets organizations through this impasse. Great organizations recognize that they need to inject new skills into their organizations to deal more effectively with the emerging challenges of this economy, and the best time to change is always now. For these forward-thinking organizations, the underpinnings of best are organizational and talent development. They recognize organizational development as a continuous living process of developing their most valuable asset—their people. They invest in this asset because the investment earns a lot more than the cost of capital. For these organizations, this human capital philosophy does not waver in a recession, and they are now the emerging leaders of our slow recovery. Nevertheless, it is time that all organizations thaw out their freezes on improvement.

LAUNCHING WITH THE BEST IN MIND

The components of this element of sustaining infrastructure are highly correlated to talent management. When we talk about organizations putting their best foot forward with continuous improvement, there is an assumption about the existence of the best resources. Best assumes that organizations have an ongoing talent development process for developing the best and putting up the best—they go hand in hand, and it is difficult to have the latter conditions without the prior conditions. Successful and sustainable improvement involves putting the first-string players in up front and developing others to become first-string players in the future. Bill Belichick, head coach of the New England Patriots, is a coaching genius at talent management.

The Components of Talent Management

Talent management (Figure 6.2) is a process of aligning resources and skill sets to business needs. Best organizations recognize the importance of talent management in the new economy because the need for change is challenging the capabilities and capacities of many organizations to respond successfully to immense change.

The process occurs by managing six clusters of talent management:

- *Talent planning:* Defining and planning the strategy for acquiring, developing, and retaining people with the types of skills required to support future needs. Talent planning also includes the identification of internal individuals with the potential for development and growth.

FIGURE 6.2 Talent management process. (© Copyright 2011 by The Center for Excellence in Operations, Inc. [CEO].)

- *Talent acquisition:* Attracting, recruiting, and acquiring new talent. This is a well-planned, proactive activity that targets specific talent sources. A critical element of talent acquisition is to provide information beyond the current open positions, such as culture and values, professional development opportunities, flexible and work-at-home options, and career development roadmaps.
- *Talent deployment:* Verify that people's capabilities are understood and deployed to match present and evolving business requirements, and that they also meet an individual's need for orientation, assimilation, performance and expectations, motivation, recognition, and career satisfaction.
- *Talent development:* Leveraging existing talent through targeted education, professional development, and exposure to several career exposure opportunities and highly visible special assignments. Every organization should make its best effort to develop the existing talent pool because total replacement costs (visual plus hidden) fall between 30% and 80% of compensation.
- *Talent retention:* Holding on to the existing talent pool, particularly the most-valued resources and future leaders. Executive responses to the economy have tarnished loyalty and commitment, so the risk of

departure of key individuals is high. It is estimated that as many as 92% of people are seeking other employment options. This is not a big deal in a recession with high unemployment because there is no place to go. Organizations may see a mass exodus when the economy gets better.

- *Talent rationalization:* Identification of employees who clearly do not have a future with the organization due to skill sets, changes in circumstances, or performance issues; assisting these people through outplacement and transition. Although this may seem like the cruel part of talent management, this is the right decision for the organization and for the individual.

Many are predicting that the most important corporate resource over the next 20 years will be talent—smart, sophisticated businesspeople who are technologically literate, globally astute, operationally agile, and willing to grow through exposure to a variety of career assignments. In today's economy, baby boomers with significant business experience are beginning to retire at a rapid rate. This is creating a major imbalance between talent leaving and talent entering organizations. The emerging workforce is much different demographically from that of the past, and organizations are faced with enormous challenges in backfilling positions and succession planning. The success of organizations rests on the speed at which they can transform their people into intelligent, flexible, multiskilled resources.

There are many predictions out there that note as the demand for talent escalates, the supply will spiral downward, culminating in a corporate war for talent. To win the talent war, organizations will need to be skilled at hiring and promoting people and, even more important, be able to keep others from stealing their talent. For best organizations, their future is all about creating a learning organization that can withstand constant change and can truly focus on continuous improvement and continuous success—collectively for the enterprise and individually to the people who actively and openly contribute to the success.

LEVERAGED MENTORING

Organizations have been trying to get teaming and empowerment right since the 1980s. A deep dive into this situation reveals that organizations have endorsed the mechanics of teaming, but for one reason or another, they have not nurtured the human dynamics, knowledge gaps, and relational aspects of teams. They have also failed to develop deep continuous improvement competencies with their history of "on again, off again" programs. The mechanics of working in a team are simple, but emotional intelligence and the leadership, behavioral, developmental, knowledge, and interpersonal relationship factors determine team performance. Effective team mentoring expertise does not come wrapped around a Black Belt, yet organizations placed all of their faith in Lean Six Sigma and the mechanics of DMAIC (Define-Measure-Analyze-Improve-Control) to achieve success. In our new economy, the Lean and Six Sigma tools and weak team mentoring of the past are definitely insufficient for rapid deployment and rapid and sustainable results.

Mentoring is the most important factor in the execution phase of strategic and sustainable improvement, and many organizations have underestimated the importance of mentoring. The resources and time consumed for mentoring represent more than 80% of successful Lean Six Sigma deployments, in contrast to 10% or less for training. "Leveraged mentoring," shown in Figure 6.3, is a reinvention of traditional team facilitation. The idea behind leveraged mentoring is to accelerate continuous improvement through a more seasoned mentor's combined leadership and technical skills, knowledge, and experiences. The seasoned mentor is the *chief execution officer* of strategic improvement, making sure that the right things are being done in the right places and at the right times to produce breakthrough results. This is not often a comfortable role but a very necessary role for success.

There are three important attributes of leveraged mentoring. They are

- *On demand:* The seasoned mentoring professional helps to establish the right formal deployment measurement and feedback processes and understands where and what type of mentoring is necessary at all times. These professionals provide mentoring support on all issues as quickly as possible to resolve any issues, conflicts, or bottlenecks with the executive leadership team, executive sponsors, the deployment process, process owners, or teams and the particulars of their individual projects.
- *Leveraged:* This is the equivalent of using debt financing to increase shareholder value. Organizations borrow the extensive background

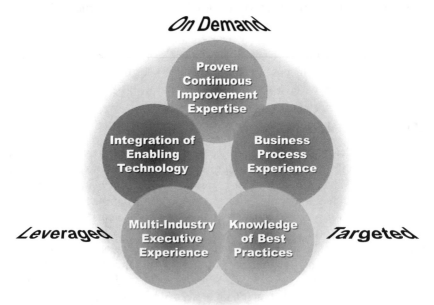

FIGURE 6.3 Leveraged mentoring.

and experiences of the seasoned mentor. The velocity and magnitude of improvement are amplified by their collective skills, knowledge, and implementation experiences of hundreds of previous initiatives and thousands of successfully completed projects.

- *Targeted:* Mentoring is proactively provided based on continuously reaching out and identifying critical leadership, deployment, or project needs.

These attributes are backed up by a strong combination of competencies that increase the quality, speed, value delivery, and development of continuous improvement teams. Leveraged mentoring develops internal talent by transforming ordinary improvement teams into proficient alpha improvement teams. The five key facets of leveraged mentoring are described next.

PROVEN CONTINUOUS IMPROVEMENT EXPERTISE

The proven continuous improvement expertise component of leveraged mentoring is straightforward. This includes mentoring on the DMAIC methodology and specific improvement tools of Lean Six Sigma. An important factor in this area is the ability to help improvement teams understand opportunities well enough to select and deploy the correct improvement tools. Too often, this process tends to be a misguided teaming effort in which improvement tools are naïvely applied in hopes of finding a solution. Improvement teams waste valuable time and resources in their inexperienced journey through DMAIC, and a trainer limited to the mechanics of Minitab or the tools themselves is not much help. Narrow experience increases the risk of *right-data, wrong-tool, wrong-answer* outcome. Knowledge and proven expertise of the methodology and tools are essential, but the more important ability is in mentoring on the deployment of the right improvement tools to the right opportunities in a project. Another critical factor here is creativity and innovation in applying the power of Lean Six Sigma to the high-impact, enterprise wide transactional processes. In retrospect, there has been too much tunnel vision mentoring by improvement facilitators focused on the tools themselves and manufacturing opportunities. Improvement needs to move way beyond shop floor activity and repeatedly demonstrating concepts to breakthrough results. The new economy is a new world, and Lean Six Sigma or improvement in general requires new thinking and new deployment best practices.

BUSINESS PROCESS EXPERIENCE

Business process experience element of mentoring is often overlooked. In many deployments, the same individuals teaching the mechanics of Minitab and the improvement tools end up mentoring improvement teams. Most of these individuals are less experienced on business process knowledge than the team they are mentoring.

Business process improvement experience includes deep expertise and knowledge of the integrated architecture of business processes and experience in analyzing and improving these complicated processes. This experience is invaluable in mentoring and managing teams to a successful conclusion while understanding the upstream, downstream, and interrelationship impacts on other parts of the organization. This part of leveraged mentoring also recognizes the integration and interaction of business processes so that improvement teams avoid suboptimized improvement—improvements in one localized area that may negatively affect the end-to-end business process. In fact, this component of leveraged mentoring increases residual improvements in other areas. Business process improvement experience is a major factor in accelerating projects and the overall deployment, especially in the transactional process world.

KNOWLEDGE OF BEST PRACTICES

Expertise in the knowledge of best practices also helps to accelerate improvement down a proven positive path. Very few organizations look externally, especially outside their industry, to learn more about best practices. Instead, they choose to go ahead inwardly with their own version of continuous improvement. The risk of this approach is akin to "the fish who does not know that he is wet." There are no other reference points beyond internal perceptions to guide the implementation. The seasoned external mentoring professionals gain the voluminous and continuously evolving skills, knowledge, and experiences through working in a variety of organizations. They are familiar with best practices and are often the "continuous improvement best practices architects" in their client organizations. Full-time improvement professionals collaborate with many other external organizations and have a more complete data set of best and emerging business improvement opportunities and practices. They also gain valuable experiences through porting and adapting of best practices across various industries and cultures. In short, they are actively engaged in improvement 100% of the time. The seasoned professional also knows how to balance best practices with innovation in improvement because best practices are sometimes a moving, declining target in our challenging economy. Simply copying best practices only makes you as good as everyone else, and by the time these are implemented, someone else has created a new level of best practices. With improvement, the *continuous* comes from thinking about and implementing new stretch possibilities. This element of leveraged mentoring helps improvement teams strive for the best, with some inclination of how to achieve best.

MULTI-INDUSTRY EXECUTIVE EXPERIENCE

The most important element of leveraged mentoring is multi-industry executive experience. The reality here is that organizations, admittedly or not, are missing the core competency of Improvement Excellence™. When an organization embarks on a major strategic improvement opportunity such as Lean Six Sigma, there is always the false sense of executive confidence in deciding how best to proceed with the deployment. Often, executives look at other organizations in their industry as a reference point.

During a large-scale strategic improvement initiative, many related organizational issues are revealed, such as executive commitment, individual performance, organizational development, or succession planning. Beyond the details and requirements of the deployment itself, executives benefit from the opportunity to discuss these issues openly and in confidence with an external and experienced sounding board or business peer. Some examples might include, but are not limited to, the following examples:

- There are lack of continuity, trust, confidence, consensus on direction, and serious personal conflicts within the executive team.
- Organizations and employees may be overconfident about *knowing how to* change but are completely unaware of what they do not know.
- Organizations have a desire to improve but are missing the leadership inertia and infrastructure to begin their improvement journey on the right course.
- Political, ownership, personality, hidden motive, and other barriers get in the way of a candid discussion about strategic issues and improvement needs.
- CEOs and executives receive value from candid discussions and objective feedback about their people, growth potential and options, organizational dynamics, or performance-related issues.

The CEO and executive staff appreciate the opportunity for an objective sounding board on these and other strategic issues that arise during a deployment, such as customer retention, organizational realignment, input on organizational changes, and fast-track career planning of superstar resources.

There is no substitute for executive leadership and implementation experience in hundreds of different organizations. These competencies enable the seasoned mentor to begin on day one leading executives, the core steering team, and individual project teams on the unpredictable journey of improvement. With the right set of conditions in place up front (e.g., leadership, improvement strategy and vision, deployment infrastructure), executives and their organizations power up the learning curve quickly.

Executives who have been through many strategic improvement initiatives in a variety of industries recognize that there are more similarities than differences—and the dissimilarities of a particular environment always have several immediate solutions when people work together. For the little brainteaser differences, the combination of internal and external experiences always wins out. The answers are usually obvious; it is the human drama and closed mindedness that make improvement the most difficult.

After nearly four decades in the improvement business, I am both amazed and still challenged about how much more there is to learn about improvement. I am also amazed at how many improvement similarities exist between industries that others within their specific industry fail to recognize, including automotive, hospitals, pharmaceuticals, government, biotechnology, aerospace, software, consumer electronics, industrial equipment, financial services, and other industries. Many of the improvement needs in these industries are similar, especially in the knowledge process space. Sure, there are definitely differences in leadership, functional organization structures, and traditional industry norms, but it all comes back to viewing improvement in terms of "process." The unique factors are also transportable and adaptable in many cases. For example, if a metal fabrication supplier needs to implement lot traceability for a customer, the pharmaceutical and aerospace and defense industries are masters at this. If a hospital is interested in improving throughput and patient flow, there are thousands of great examples of continuous flow, bottleneck management, and cycle time reduction in manufacturing industries. If anyone wants to learn about supply chain excellence, consider learning more about the banking industry.

Here is a great personal lesson. One of our clients was having trouble with excess paint sitting in inventory and then matching the original batch with orders at a later date. The client lived with this problem forever. They tried adding ingredients and dozens of other lab experiments to shift the color to no avail. An idea came to mind while enjoying a Starbucks frozen frappuccino® while waiting for my flight at an airport. I noticed that the longer the frappuccino sat, the more the original contents separated. Mixing and swirling the contents brought it back to its original state—an "Aha" moment. At the following client visit, we assembled a team and documented the various recipe ingredients, weights, and viscosities and modeled how the different SKUs (stock-keeping units) of paint would separate over time. Different colors or different products would act in different ways due to differences in pigments, storage times, and other variation factors about in the recipes. When there was an order, one person would dip into the drum without any stirring. Another would stir the drum a few times before filling the order. Another would roll a balanced barrel back and forth for a few minutes. The problem was about coming up with a standard remix time and method that would reproduce the original color of the paint. The development folks were not impressed with the team's approach and made comments like "That's not the problem; it's not that easy. It's a chemistry problem." To make a long story short, a standard method was developed (surprise: it was a larger version of a mixer/shaker used at the local paint store), and the variation in color shades was removed. Their age-old problem was gone. I was amused when the team members asked me how I knew so much about paint chemistry.

A few years ago, we spent a few days with a prospect talking to a cross section of executives and managers, kicking their tires, and looking under the rugs of their business. Then, we presented a proposal to improve their business significantly and provided options about how best to proceed. There were a few arrogant and doubtful executives in this meeting. Finally, one of them said, "Look, this all sounds great, but there is over 150 years of experience in our business sitting around this table. How can your organization possibly help us?" I thought for a moment and decided that candor was the best policy. I responded:

Please let's agree not to shoot the messenger, and what I am about to say should not be viewed as a personal shot. Our expertise is very different from your expertise ... not better—different. If the 150 years of experience was the answer, then the $25 million in savings opportunities that we all agree exists would be implemented, and we would not be sitting here for the past month talking about it. The last thing you need is someone who thinks like all of you to come in here and try to help you.

In the middle of a few rebuttals, the CEO stopped the discussion and said to his staff, "This guy has a lot of balls standing there and saying that to us, but unfortunately he's right. The largest problem in this organization is sitting around this table, and it's going to change effective today." The company contracted with us and realized $15 million in savings in the first 14 months. It happened because of the power achieved by combining committed internal and external expertise. On the very last day of our engagement, I was walking around saying my good-byes and thanks to everyone, and one of the arrogant executives at the initial proposal meeting called me into his office and asked me to close the door behind me. He was no longer arrogant; he was a brilliant executive who was humbled by our collective experiences. He grew into the evangelist and best leader of strategic improvement in the company. Over those 14 months, we became close friends, and he was promoted to senior vice president. During this meeting, he began crying and apologized to me for being so arrogant and uncooperative and how he and the entire organization were blessed by this experience. After a few minutes of deep personal talk, we shook hands and hugged. That was almost 20 years ago. He has been CEO at three different companies, and we are still great professional friends.

The lesson in this example is another shoot-the-messenger comment. When someone asks, "How much experience do you have in our industry?" the person might as well be saying, "I do not want to change." Improvement Excellence™ is a core competency, and it is not industry specific. It definitely does not exist in organizations that ask these types of questions. There are so many downright silly reasons for postponing improvement that it is like a child postponing a bath. Technology and automotive industries have traditionally been the most open to improvement, and they have led the way with continuous improvement initiatives. Industries can learn a lot about strategic improvement from the experiences of others outside their industry. Some industries, such as hospitals, financial services, and government, really need to port this expertise into their organizations from external industries if they are serious about making the necessary changes in our new economy.

INTEGRATION OF ENABLING TECHNOLOGY

Two trends are radically changing the face of improvement: the rapid emergence of enabling technology and a higher value-added content in transactional processes. With physical processes, one can observe a machine, talk to the operator, count and categorize scrap, listen for tool vibration, or feel a leaky air hose— so the problems are very visible. As the shift in improvement occurs from the manufacturing floor to the transactional process areas, our ability to use our natural senses to solve problems diminishes greatly. The level of reporting and metrics about root cause data may not even exist; many transactional processes have evolved over time and have never been formally analyzed at any meaningful depth. The usual fix has been another Band-Aid, another procedure, a new IT (information technology) request, or some other local change that might create issues in other areas. The seasoned mentor must appreciate the integration of enabling technology and improvement because

- Enabling technology drives the organization toward a necessary, single version of the facts based on the integrated enterprise architecture. It is totally inefficient to manage with a kludge of spreadsheets and (now) via opinions and perceptions using iPhones, iPads, Blackberrys, and other devices.
- Enabling technology provides the formal architecture between strategy and execution with standardized and customized information and feedback.
- Enabling technology provides the essence of what is needed for leadership, management, and improvement: accessible information and data.
- Enabling technology provides structured systems, standardized process disciplines, internal controls, and operating data across all transactional streams, which is necessary in analyzing root causes of transactional issues.
- Enabling technology provides the only ability to view the interactions, data flows, and transactions in suspense (defect trails) between key business processes.
- Enabling technology provides the data for the sampling plans of improvement initiatives, which defines the specific data elements necessary to analyze and solve problems. After billions of dollars in IT investments, it is too slow and too costly (and foolish) to collect data via manual checksheets for improvement projects.
- Enabling technology automates and keeps current many of the manual improvement tools that people have implemented in the past, such as kanban cards, schedule boards, quality analysis and resolution, throughput monitoring, routine value stream analytics, and the like.
- Enabling technology provides real-time feedback, real-time visibility into key business process performance, and capabilities for all types of individual process and management performance dashboards.

Enabling technology is definitely accelerating the pendulum swing of continuous improvement and will continue to play a vital role in improving how we improve. I wish to offer one cautionary note about enabling technology. Think about a typical business meeting. There is a PowerPoint presentation flashing in the front of the room. Attendees are either physically in the room or connected remotely via video conference capabilities; all attendees are multiprocessing as they text away or check and respond to e-mails; a few step out for quick cell phone calls. Everyone is easily connected to a spouse, their children's school, their online diet, a honey-do list, and literally thousands of other possibilities on demand. Enabling technology is expanding the ability to multiprocess, and the more one multiprocesses, the less efficient the person becomes at any single activity. Enabling technology is an *enabler of* improvement, not a *replacement for* data-driven improvement and root cause thinking. In addition, improvement is a powerful enabler for the successful integration of enabling technology.

DMAIC THE PROCESS OF CONTINUOUS IMPROVEMENT

As mentioned, continuous improvement is also a process. Variation exists in all processes, including continuous improvement. There is no magic mantra for success; the series of events that happen during a long-term strategic improvement initiative are unpredictable and therefore subject to many course corrections. Things such as legitimate delays in projects due to unforeseen circumstances, a team pulled from another project and assigned to an important customer issue, the departure of an executive or team member from the organization, misunderstandings in project objectives, shifting in priorities, problems with acquiring data and information, workload conflicts, absenteeism, dysfunctional behaviors, poor team performance, a trip to a supplier, unexpected quality or engineering development problems, and thousands of other events introduce variation and disruptions to the implementation process. Successful improvement initiatives require the leadership, DMAIC thinking, and know-how to recognize these detractors and take the right swift actions to reset the course. This is the very essence of DMAIC*ing* the process of improvement: continuously critiquing progress based on actual achievement and making the necessary course corrections to the process.

Think about a complex machine for a moment. When one attempts to manage this operation by intuitive tweaking all of the adjustments in the absence of facts, it actually introduces more variation. If the same machine were producing high scrap levels at $150/hour, our first inclination would be to find out why and then fix the problem. Now, let us consider the process of improvement. What typically happens when organizations are not getting the expected results from their improvement initiatives? The answer is not much. The cost to organizations from not improving is in the millions of dollars, yet we allow the process to remain in waste mode until it fades away. Improvement does not have to work this way because proactive leadership and infrastructure fix its problems. The difference is that continuous improvement as a process is most influenced by individual behaviors, decisions, and actions—influenced by the human behaviors, decisions, and actions of superiors and others around them. Human processes require unwavering leadership, interventions, and reinforcement to remain on a desired course.

How is this accomplished in a real-life improvement initiative? The executive steering team provides the leadership, builds the sustaining infrastructure (e.g., Strategic Leadership and Vision, Deployment Planning, and Execution), and then proactively aligns all elements of sustaining infrastructure to customer and market needs. The team operates on a philosophy of no team left behind; all projects will be successful. This is a dynamic, interactive, and deliberate effort that requires all of the basics of a great process: formal goals and objectives, baseline performance, measurement systems, root causes of problems, feedback and corrective actions, and sustainable change (recognize the DMAIC yet?). There is absolutely nothing wrong with changing the process of improvement to a better state. This is called Improvement Excellence™ or *improving how we improve*. Continuous improvement is not possible unless organizations improve the process of how they improve. Sustaining infrastructure is the formal process that enables organizations to *improve how they improve* successfully.

THE CONTINUOUS PROCESS OF FINANCIAL VALIDATION

Another important factor in a successful improvement initiative is to immerse the financial organization throughout all planned and executed improvement activities. Finance plays a key role in

- **Strategic Leadership and Vision:** Participating in the business diagnostic, Improvement Strategy and Vision, and policy deployment efforts; providing financial and operational information; validating all findings, conclusions, assumptions, and improvement opportunities.
- **Deployment Planning:** Participating in the macrocharter development, particularly in individual project baseline performance, and improvement goal assumptions and benefits. Occasionally, a perceived issue identified during the business diagnostic is either smaller or larger than anticipated or possibly dated due to informal and less-visible improvement efforts.
- **Execution:** Assisting individual teams with improvement and savings assumptions, classification of savings, providing standard methods and rates for savings calculations, preventing double counting savings, validating claimed savings achievements, and pegging improvements back to financial statement accounts. A financial representative should be a member or extended resource for every improvement project.

Some organizations view the financial impact too narrowly and attempt to limit improvement efforts only to projects that directly affect profit and loss (P&L). Successful improvement initiatives recognize the *very real* hidden costs and associated waste in their business (usually classified through a formal cost-of-poor-quality or COPQ framework). There is a big difference between improving financial performance and improving financial statements. As we are all well aware, the latter promotes short-term thinking and Band-Aid improvements (or no improvement at all), while the former promotes root cause problem solving, creativity, and innovative improvement. The real purpose of finance is to provide a consistent and standardized approach to identifying, evaluating, and calculating project savings whether they are visible or hidden. Visible costs such as labor, scrap, premium freight, returns and allowances, operating supplies, and many others are straightforward in terms of baselining current performance, calculating savings, and pegging the savings to a particular account in the P&L. These are the typical "main effects" cost and operating income improvements. Costs such as excess/obsolete or missing inventory, a horrible patient experience, product development process inefficiencies, cost of compliance, the impact of work-arounds on other areas, supply chain synchronization, or advertising effectiveness are much more complex in terms of isolating root causes of waste, defining value-added versus non-value-added costs, estimating improvement opportunities, and pegging savings to a particular chart of accounts. These are the "interaction effects" improvements such as revenue growth, cash flow, variance reduction, cost avoidance, and restructuring of priorities that are difficult but not impossible to quantify. However, these savings are *very real savings* and should not be overlooked or excluded in a deployment. Sometimes, the benefits are more strategic investments; however, the benefits down the road should be quantified. To the extent possible, we are fanatical advocates of tying everything back to financial performance as much as possible. Successful improvement initiatives begin and end with financial performance, one project at a time. Keep in mind that financial performance improves directly and indirectly with the right actions.

ACCELERATE INDIVIDUAL PROJECT PATHS

The purpose of this element of Execution infrastructure is to manage the interaction of all accelerators proactively to positive levels of performance. The sustaining infrastructure as a whole is a systematic network of connected subprocesses. The inner workings of a single accelerator directly or indirectly influence the performance of one or more of the other accelerators. For example, the following is a short list of common implementation problems:

- Falling down on the continued maintenance of the Improvement Strategy and Vision
- Making mountains out of molehills and vice versa (inappropriate application of various improvement methodologies and tools)
- Selection of pet projects that are not strategically important
- Poorly defined and scoped projects
- Boilerplate Lean Six Sigma education
- People running around with a bag of tools looking for a problem to solve
- Disengaged and disconnected leadership
- Ineffective communication, awareness, and reinforcement
- Staffing improvement initiatives with the undesirable, freed-up resources
- Failure to deal head-on with controversy and conflicts

Improvement Excellence™ requires that every element of sustaining infrastructure is working well and systematically with all other elements. This element of infrastructure allows executives and their organizations to view the larger picture of their strategic improvement initiatives and highlight potential negative trends, detractors, and barriers to continued success. Proactively managing the accelerators is a deliberate and systematic process. Why? The accelerators create strong interactions with each other in practice—positive, neutral, and negative interactions. An organization cannot be great at one or two accelerators and expect to achieve sustainable strategic success. Allowing the dynamics of improvement to evolve without recognizing the power and influence of these accelerators is a sure way to railroad success. One of the practices encouraged by the executive steering team is to seek actual known or potential deployment detractors continuously, whether they are particular strategic issues or the performance of an individual on a team. Next, it is useful to associate these detractors with the most related accelerator. Finally, the executive steering team further probes into the current situation and discusses corrective actions around the best practices guidelines of each accelerator. Frequent open discussions about detractors followed by the right corrective actions provide a healthy process of improvement. Within a short time, it promotes interest and attention to the human dynamics and key factors that really matter in a successful change initiative.

INTEGRATION OF IMPROVEMENT METHODOLOGIES

The other side of accelerating individual projects is to develop teams to deploy the right improvement methodologies to the highest-impact opportunities. Too often, continuous improvement initiatives have followed the route of generic training followed by a force fitting of tools to a problem. One of the largest goals of strategic improvement is to create a talent pool with the right understanding and skills about various improvement methodologies and tools. At one point, many organizations had their own silo departments for Six Sigma, Lean, Kaizen, and other initiatives. No single-point improvement is all inclusive and all encompassing, and the parade of buzzwords and jargon has confused many people in organizations. Since the 1980s, continuous improvement has been more tools focused versus a leadership-driven cultural standard of excellence. However, the execution part of creating this cultural standard requires success through the application of the right methodologies to the right improvement opportunities.

In 2000, we recognized the need in our practice to integrate various improvement methodologies into a single powerhouse initiative. The result was the birth of our Scalable Lean Six Sigma™ methodology, a simplified, rapid deployment and rapid results improvement model designed for smaller and midsize organizations that could not afford the time, resources, and investment of a large, top-down, train-the-masses approach. It is a simplified approach to Lean Six Sigma based on the 80/20 principle. The original goal was to improve the *process* of improvement and the original birth of improving how we improve. Over the years, we have demonstrated many successes with Scalable Lean Six Sigma™ in a variety of industries and organizations, ranging from Fortune 500 corporations to smaller, privately owned businesses, hospitals, and other service organizations. During this time, we worked with our clients to develop what we referred to as a "master craftsman toolbox mindset" around continuous improvement. We encouraged people not to get hung up on the brand or use of every tool of improvement and instead focus on the process of improvement. The purpose of this approach was to develop their competencies through the right application of the right methodologies and tools to the right improvement situations. Our toolboxes at home have several drawers and several different tools. In one drawer are the screwdrivers, in another drawer are the wrenches, in another drawer are the different hammers, in another drawer are the power tools, in another drawer are the fasteners and hardware, and so on. Our selection of tools is dependent on the home repair. If we choose to limit our capability to a hammer, everything looks like a nail. The same holds true for strategic improvement. If an organization embraces just Lean, just theory of constraints (TOC), just benchmarking, just 5S, just Six Sigma, or just enabling IT, it misses the boat of strategic improvement big time. In fact, there exists a wide spectrum of different types of improvement opportunities in organizations that require a multidisciplinary approach for success.

Figure 6.4 provides the integrated methodologies of Improvement Excellence™ and Scalable Lean Six Sigma™. All improvement methodologies and tools (even ones not shown) fall under the house of Improvement Excellence™. On the left side of this house are the simple Kaizen, just-do-it improvements that require little to no analysis. These are the small, incremental improvements with widespread involvement. To practitioners, this is referred

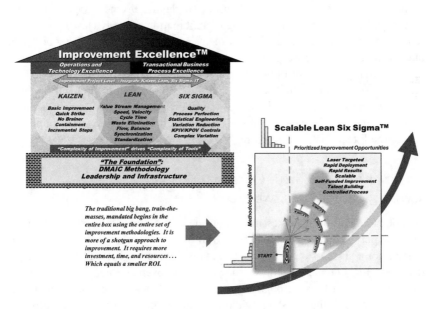

FIGURE 6.4 Improvement Excellence™ and Scalable Lean Six Sigma™. Key Process Input Variables (KPIV); Key Process Output Variables (KPOV); (ROI, return on investment. © Copyright 2011 by The Center for Excellence in Operations, Inc. [CEO].)

to as the low-hanging fruit or fruit on the ground that people trip over every day. In the middle of the house are the Lean opportunities; simple analytics such as value stream mapping are used to segment value-added from non-value-added activities in processes. Much of Lean focuses on basic flow, quality, and throughput issues that improve asset management. The primary goal of Lean is to eliminate waste. Practitioners refer to this as the fruit in the middle of the tree. Moving to the right are the Six Sigma opportunities. These are more complex improvements that require more complex analytics and statistical tools. Six Sigma is about chasing down and reducing or eliminating variation in processes. We classify Six Sigma opportunities into two levels: opportunities requiring the basic "blocking-and-tackling" tools (e.g., basic statistics and graphical analysis, Pareto analysis, measurement system analysis, capability studies, etc.) and the more advanced statistical tools (e.g., hypothesis testing, screening experiments, analysis of variance [ANOVA], design of experiments (DOE), etc.). Practitioners refer to these opportunities as the fruit at the top of the tree. These improvements usually create breakthroughs in performance.

The foundation of Improvement Excellence™ is leadership and sustaining infrastructure. The common language of improvement (DMAIC) is also part of the foundation. There are several powerful messages behind this diagram. First, the methodologies and tools themselves are either the right means or the wrong means to successful continuous improvement. The tools are the means, not the ends. Second, continuous improvement is never continuous without the right foundation for sustainable success. Third, a single improvement opportunity may require either a single tool or the right combination of tools (just like a home repair job). Fourth, having the tools by themselves at one's disposal does not make one an improvement guru. Just like a master finish carpenter, it takes years to become highly skilled at improvement, and it requires many skills beyond the tools themselves. Fifth, the specific requirements of the improvement opportunity drive the seasoned practitioner to the selection of the right combination of improvement tools. The methodologies and tools themselves are a very important part of the Execution infrastructure.

APPRECIATE THE SIMPLE STUFF: CHECKLISTS, TEMPLATES, VISUALS, FLAGS, AND PAEANS

One of the common mistakes in improvement initiatives is to go for the home run. Inexperienced people return from a training session on the tools and begin looking for a place to apply the most complex Six Sigma tools. They were taught that these tools create the breakthroughs in improvement, and they want to be associated with a breakthrough from the get-go. These individuals cannot see the forest through the trees yet, while they are stepping all over great improvement opportunities. One of the basic fundamentals of continuous improvement is to discover an appreciation of what we nickname the simple stuff: checklists, templates, visuals, flags, and paeans. These simple improvement methods are the foundation of the Toyota Production System (TPS) and have widespread use, especially in professional and knowledge processes. Production operators, pilots, and several surgical units in hospitals routinely use checklists and templates to maintain process quality and service levels. Visuals are effective because they communicate real-time performance and current conditions. Flags are effective to create immediate awareness of a process problem. Flags may be physical or embedded in software applications. Toyota and many other companies have used "green-yellow-red" management practices for years. One of our clients has used all of these simple techniques in the client's automated new product development tracking system. Everyone has a real-time, up-to-the-minute picture of the status of all projects in development, performance to schedules, bottlenecks, insufficient or missing tasks, and individual accountability. There is a certain peer motivation when one's name shows up next to a problem that has shut down the process. Finally, it is important not to overlook the paeans for great performance on the simple stuff. Sometimes, these simple methods are viewed as insignificant, even though they save the day in many situations.

COMPLETE THE C IN CONTROL

The *C,* which stands for Control, is the most important phase of the DMAIC cycle. It is also the most important component of the Execution infrastructure. This is the actual point of implementation, the realization of improvement, and process owner handoff for sustainability. Over the past several years, we have observed some organizations that make their way through the DMAI phases of Lean Six Sigma and then fall down on *C.* It almost appears as if their continuous improvement efforts end with the PowerPoint presentation of *what they are going to do.*

Control includes the following six major elements:

1. *Validation of improvement:* This element verifies that the recommended actions have actually improved the process. For some organizations, their approach is sufficient if someone says, "Oh yeah, things are much better now." That is simply not good enough. Validation occurs through measurement of the key process metrics before and after the changes. Sometimes, validation is achieved by positive and negative replication of results (shifts back and forth from old to new processes, demonstrating oscillations in performance). Improvement should be demonstrated by a positive movement in the metrics. Finally, the benefits derived by improvement must be validated by the financial organization.
2. *Sustaining measurement systems:* This element defines performance ownership, which metrics will be monitored by the process owner, corrective action guidelines for slippage in improvement, periodic audit and validation plans, and integration into the overall performance measurement process. This includes tracking of both primary metrics

and critical root cause metrics, and practices to expose and prioritize ongoing root causes.

3. *Process owner transition:* This element includes all activities that must take place (e.g., new procedures, checklists, templates, visuals, education, IT modifications, knowledge transfer, etc.) to transfer ownership of the improvement initiative to the process owner. This element addresses all questions related to transfer and continuation of improvement, dismantling of the improvement project team, and freeing up resources for new improvement initiatives. Process owner transition includes both the hard process improvement details and the emotional, interpersonal, or human drama issues of improvement and change.

4. *New improvement opportunities:* This element has to do with defining additional improvement opportunities that are either directly or indirectly related to the current improvement project. The team is in a great position to comment on further improvements to the existing project or other unrelated project opportunities that may inhibit further improvements. These ideas go into the macrocharter hopper for further investigation and prioritization against the existing content of planned improvement projects. Some of these may also go directly to a functional manager or supervisor for additional Kaizen-type improvements. The other piece of this element is asking each team member to identify and commit to an improvement activity in his or her immediate areas, using the methodology and knowledge gained in the member's project.

5. *Knowledge repository:* This element is twofold. First, the executive deployment team officially closes out an improvement project in a formal team meeting. The purpose of this meeting is to capture any additional lessons learned firsthand and integrate them into the overall deployment. Second, the executive deployment team must build a formal process to archive the knowledge, experiences, analysis, and other relevant information for future teams. This repository of knowledge is available and accessible for future improvement initiatives as both living and learning examples and to reduce redundancy in improvements (e.g., using value stream maps, analytics, or failure mode and effects analysis (FMEAs) from previous improvement activities).

6. *Celebration:* The final element of control is celebration, which incorporates much more than a few token pats on the back for the team members. One important aspect of celebration is organizational reinforcement through the showcasing of success. The other aspect is recognition and reward for the team and extended participants. Celebration must also become a deliberate formal process because this is an opportunity to leverage Lean Six Sigma and strategic improvement.

Control is the most critical part of DMAIC. Treating the tasks of Control casually and haphazardly is a sure way to fail at improvement. In the short term, process owners and their people will have difficulty repeating and sustaining the results of the team, and they will slide back into business as usual when leadership becomes focused on another issue. In the long term, infrastructure and talent development are not in place to sustain gains and improve the process further. The consequence of wavering leadership and lack of sustaining infrastructure is that there will be a gradual backsliding in gains until people are back to their original routines as they existed before improvement. The journey of improvement is difficult because people are human and are susceptible to human error and variations in consistency, perceived expectations, and performance.

CONCURRENT CONTINUOUS IMPROVEMENT

This final element of Execution infrastructure is the continuous development of people and completion of improvement projects and is based on current critical needs. Organizations have pursued continuous improvement in batch mode; deployment begins with mass education followed by teams and projects leaving the same starting gate. Subsequent activities are also managed in batches of waves. Concurrent continuous deployment embraces projects, priorities, and resources that are always ready to go; individual project launches are staggered based on resource availability, and improvement capacity is managed. Concurrent continuous improvement optimizes the opportunities for improvement by *overlapping* improvement activities and reducing aggregate cycle time for the overall completion of multiple streams of projects. This significantly reduces the traditional wave wait time and resource conflicts of a *batch* deployment and increases the capacity of improvement by as much as 30% in the same window of opportunity. Simply stated, concurrent continuous deployment enables organizations to achieve more with less.

IMPROVING HOW WE IMPROVE

Concurrent continuous deployment has evolved by borrowing a few Lean improvement methods from the past, such as continuous flow, throughput management, quick changeover, dynamic finite scheduling, and standardized work. These methods are integrated with best project management and concurrent engineering practices in an attempt to optimize resources and results. The following section provides a brief review of these concepts.

> *Continuous Flow:* The notion of continuous flow production promotes the practices of small lot sizes (e.g., scoping improvement projects into many smaller manageable chunks) and continuous progressive activity (e.g., by eliminating wait time, overloading and wasted resources, and other inefficiencies). In a continuous flow production environment, each part is pulled through at an ideal rate of one piece at a time, and this greatly reduces the manufacturing lead time. In a project environment, continuous flow promotes the overlapping of projects based on

improvement pull and availability of the right resources. This improvement pull is the voice of the executive deployment team and is based on their identification and prioritization of strategic improvement needs via the macrocharter process.

Throughput Management: This concept strives for getting the most throughput and results in the shortest amount of time. Leveraged mentoring plays the most critical role in this process by giving the appropriate attention to projects where it is needed the most. The objective here is to help teams eliminate or reduce the bottlenecks and dependencies in their improvement projects. Another objective of throughput management is to search for and eliminate the broader deployment barriers and bottlenecks and recognize the leverage points to achieve a desired rate of improvement in the deployment. Achieving a desired rate of savings by a given time is directly correlated to the type, quantity, and velocity of improvement activity. Throughput is achieved by exploiting all of the bottlenecks of improvement (pulling out all of the stops and proactively managing all the barriers to success).

Quick Changeover: Quick changeover promotes the elimination of any wastes between ending one improvement project and launching another improvement project. In a production environment, the goal is to keep the bottleneck operation available. In strategic improvement, quick changeover promotes the constant redeployment of improvement resources to additional improvement activities so the larger dynamic of continuous improvement becomes internalized.

Dynamic Forward Scheduling: This is a practice that requires constant attention by the executive steering committee. The objective here is to look ahead and anticipate completion of improvement projects. The official launch date for new projects is a formal process, similar to scheduling production based on need dates and equipment availability. The other side of this is taking the projects that are ready to go in the macrocharter and resourcing them based on the availability of the right people and other talent development goals. Dynamic forward scheduling is a deliberate activity that not only improves the rate of improvement but also allows the executive steering team to project the results of improvement. If an organization has the ability to project its improvements, there is no reason why these projections should not be built into operating plans and personal goals and objectives. This closes the loop on continuous improvement by providing strong incentives for engagement and success.

Standardized Work: The architecture of strategic leadership and vision, deployment planning, and execution provide the standardized process of successfully deploying Lean Six Sigma or any other strategic improvement initiative. The DMAIC methodology is the common language of improvement throughout the organization. The infrastructure provides a disciplined and structured process that the organization eventually marches to and understands. However, this infrastructure is not so rigid that it kills the opportunity to be innovative.

Best Practices Project Management: There are many books available on this topic alone. Another great resource is the Project Management Institute (PMI), which offers certification courses on this topic. At the risk of oversimplifying this topic, the objective here is to make sure that all deployment activities (from executive deployment team activities to individual improvement project tasks) are broken down and managed in a Gantt format. At any moment, it should be easy to review the status of projects or other deployment activities in terms of current position, detailed definition of next steps, timing of next steps, responsibilities and assignments, and specific deliverables. Project management provides the opportunity to develop, load, and manage critical resources realistically while getting everything done that needs to be done. Projects are much more nebulous than a production line is. It is much easier to walk out to a production line and estimate status than it is to walk into an engineering organization and put one's hands around the portfolio of new development projects. The only hope of managing a Lean Six Sigma deployment or any other strategic initiative is by incorporating best project management practices into the equation.

Concurrent Engineering: In a Lean Six Sigma deployment, concurrent engineering promotes the idea of moving away from improvement projects scheduled as independent waves toward improvement projects scheduled based on need and resources. In effect, it is the overlapping and parallel processing of waves of improvement projects. To do this well, the executive steering committee needs to know the status of all in-process and planned activities in the deployment. This is a deliberate and proactive leadership process by which executives manage the deployment to optimize results, resources, and learning. Applying concurrent engineering to the deployment establishes a formal sustaining process of improvement by setting the expectation verbally and visually that improvement is a continuous process. Improvement is a condition of successful employment, and everyone is expected to develop personal expertise with improvement.

TRANSLATE THE SYSTEMATIC PROCESS
INTO BREAKTHROUGH RESULTS

Chapters 4, 5, and 6 have provided a proven roadmap for planning and executing strategic improvement initiatives successfully. Formal education and literature have focused to a large extent on the strategy and planning aspects of improvement. Execution of improvement is not nearly as clear and well understood as the flashier front-end launches and mass training exercises. Hence, it should be no surprise that this chapter was so comprehensive. The purpose of Chapters 4, 5, and 6 is to build stronger competencies around the execution and sustainability of improvement by setting all of the critical success factors in place. Let us briefly review the major generic root causes of continuous improvement failures:

- Wavering leadership through visible behaviors, decisions, and actions
- Lack of a solid improvement strategy and vision
- Failure to establish the unquestionable recognition of the need throughout the organization
- Introducing a strategic improvement initiative with a primary focus on plain vanilla, train-the-masses education
- Reluctance to deal with resistance to change positively and head-on
- Failure to step down the improvement strategy and vision into more manageable and prioritized chunks for the organization
- Inability to communicate effectively to build stakeholder engagement, showcase successes, and reinforce the need to change
- Failure to implement efficiently and methodically and continue to put the money on the table
- Not paying constant attention to all the details of improvement and making the right corrective actions via visible formal processes
- Failure to identify and deal with the unpredictable situations that arise with major change
- Failure to align strategic improvement with individual performance and reward systems
- Lack of the magic rhythm or cadence that keeps the process of continuous improvement alive and transforming culture

Execution is the most difficult phase of continuous improvement and the phase in which the life cycle changes to a negative direction. Execution requires fuzzy reasoning because this is the point at which the unknown, unplanned, and unpredictable situations come out of the woodwork. Believe me—after decades in this business, there are still so many leadership, technical, process, and human drama situations that jump out at you during implementation. The accelerators embedded within sustaining infrastructure are the multiconditional propositions that get organizations through the maze and haze of execution.

There are a few more ugly facts about execution that have been downplayed through the history of continuous improvement. First, the entire sustaining infrastructure is a process, and the elements of Strategic Leadership and Vision, Deployment Planning, and Execution are integrated and ongoing subprocesses. This is how organizations keep the word *continuous* in continuous improvement. This systematic process has been missing in most organizations, causing continuous, disappointing results with improvement. Second, no organization possesses all of the required skills for success internally. So, the organizations have chosen to work with an outside consulting firm (usually a large, prestigious firm) to fill this void. It turns out that most of these firms (some with 20% to 30% turnover rates) also do not possess all of the required skills for success—especially the competencies of execution. This is not meant to discredit the intellectually brilliant consultants because they are applying what they believe to be the right approaches from their MBA or Black Belt backgrounds. In all fairness, many of these folks also have myriad leadership and organizational issues restraining their success, and they do not have the savvy and depth of experience to overcome these obstacles. However, the fact remains that there is much more known about strategy and conceptual improvement than the "how-to-do's" of execution. Third, the introduction of improvement and training are the easy parts of strategic improvement. Organizational reception is always positive because nothing is changing yet. People are off from their daily routines, enjoying training and pizza. This approach usually creates a large, unstructured, temporary improvement feeding frenzy. Execution has been viewed more as a series of mediocre detail tasks to be left to the "grunts" of the organization because it is beneath the perceived priorities of leadership. True execution and follow-through in organizations are generally weak because the sense of urgency and priorities moves around. It becomes a game of "close enough is good enough" as people move on to the next crisis. These people work in organizations where mediocre execution is reinforced by leadership and culture. In the case of improvement, Execution is the only bridge between planning and results. If leadership does not get everyone across this bridge, leadership fails at improvement. Strategic Leadership and Vision, Deployment Planning, and Execution are equally as important when one views this sustaining infrastructure as an integrated systematic process. People have debated this topic for years, expressing their invalid opinions about developing a great strategy or their preferences of mediocre planning and great execution. Keep in mind that with continuous improvement, both sides of this argument result in failure.

BIBLIOGRAPHY

Burton, T. 2011. *Accelerating Lean Six Sigma Results: How to Achieve Improvement Excellence™ in the New Economy.* Ross, Ft. Lauderdale, FL.

Burton, T. T., and Sams, J. 2005. *Six Sigma for Small and Mid-Sized Companies*, Ross, Ft. Lauderdale, FL.

Ringo, T., Schweyer, A., DeMarco, M., Jones, R., and Lesser, E. 2009. *Integrated Talent Management: Turning Talent Management into a Competitive Advantage.* IBM Institute for Business Value, Somers, NY.

SAP. 2009. *Time to Change: New Thoughts on Supporting Business Change Fast and Flexibly.* White paper. SAP AG, Newtown Square, PA.

Senge, P. M. 1990. *The Fifth Discipline: The Art and Practice of the Learning Organization.* Doubleday, New York, NY.

Sullivan, J. 2005. The top 25 benchmark firms in recruiting and talent management. http://www.ere.net (accessed August 17, 2011).

7 Transforming Culture through Internalization

INTRODUCTION

Every organization has its own unique culture—its values, vision, mission, and expected codes and standards of conduct. Culture is the personality of the organization. No single individual is responsible for culture, but some individuals have more influence than others do. The characteristics of culture are shaped by the collective behaviors, decisions, and actions by many different leaders and organizational events over time. Many of these leaders have come and gone with their different styles, agendas, personal goals, and organizational expectations. Culture plays out in a variety of ways. One can observe characteristics of culture from how information is communicated, if and how feedback is given, how performance is defined and managed, and how key business process activities are cocoordinated within the organization. Culture is reflected in the way the organization is structured, whether work is conducted cross-functionally or within individual silos, how the hierarchical levels are set up, and how the chain of command and span of control work. Culture is often defined by the type of industry, the backgrounds of the executives, the discipline of systems and processes, and the less-formal rituals, symbols, and rumor mills in the organization. Culture is even reflected in how and why meetings are held in an organization. Often, there is a big difference in culture between the mission statement on the lobby wall and the actual behaviors and practices behind the lobby doors.

From a practical perspective, culture is what it is, and we cannot flip a switch and change it overnight. As strategic and continuous improvement experts, we must recognize that culture may be the largest enabler or obstacle to change. Most of the time, culture is an obstacle when introducing change and a legitimate obstacle requiring strong, competent, and unwavering leadership. Why? This is because people do not want to change, especially if they do not recognize the need for change and ultimately internalize the benefits of change. Culture is simply about individuals in a group sharing expected patterns of behavior. There is no cultural absolute because culture is both relative and dynamic to the organization's strategy and mission. Left on its own, culture is not sustainable. Culture is not some natural evolution in business; it is formed by the right intentional behaviors, decisions, and actions. Executives have the power and responsibility to create and nurture a culture that is the best fit for an organization's future direction.

THE CULTURAL CHECKUP

In terms of strategic and continuous improvement, what is the difference between an improvement-dysfunctional culture and a great improvement culture? If we look back at the last three decades, almost every organization is guilty of temporarily embracing flavor-of-the-month improvement programs. Let us answer this question based on the Lean Six Sigma initiatives of the past dozen years or so. First, great cultures do not view improvement as a quick, emergency response to changing business conditions or as a whim program that everyone else is implementing. Executives with high anxieties to make their numbers launch these programs based on *wishes and hopes*: They are wishing for a home run from a single-point program, and they hope everyone in the organization embraces their strategy of change without asking questions about all of the unknowns. These overhyped and shoehorned improvement programs ultimately fail because they lack accountability, they fail to achieve widespread organizational credibility, they have no authenticity in terms of substance, and they are undermined by ongoing executive behaviors, decisions, and actions.

Second, great improvement cultures adapt a rapid but practical, pragmatic, committed-to-excellence *process* of improvement. Their process is similar to the formal sustaining infrastructure of Strategic Leadership and Vision, Deployment, and Execution. Their process has succeeded in keeping the organization, its leaders, and its people on the improvement track for the long haul.

Third, the hype in the name of their improvement initiative is not there in great improvement cultures. There are no fancy acronyms, baseball caps and tee shirts, mugs, and other meaningless banners and slogans—just great and continuous efforts followed by superior performance in a balanced scorecard of all metrics. Improvement is a living best practice because it is a critical enabler of strategic and operating performance. Executives and their organizations focus on improvement every minute of every day intuitively, without even thinking about a buzzword or a tool. They have formal metrics for their efforts, such as rate of improvement; aggregate improvement; improvement by key business process, executive, area, and individual; and other measures of success. Improvement is built into performance via recognition and rewards and direct compensation. In these organizations, it is difficult to tell the difference between executives, managers, and the workforce because great ideas for improvement are coming from everywhere. Everyone is engaged and empowered to make decisions about improvement and corrective actions, and they understand the dynamics of getting the right people involved. The organizational hierarchy and silos are replaced by interactive networks of people working together. Improvement is not viewed as a fad program; it is an unquestionable standard of excellence woven into the fabric of their culture.

The Broken Moral Compass

There are many disturbing trends and practices that tend to break the moral compass of leadership and work against continuous improvement. One is performance and reward systems. American capitalism, our free market system, and Wall Street are not going away. That being said, organizations must focus on hitting their numbers; that is just the way it is. Executives must focus on hitting their numbers if they wish to remain in their chairs. Everyone else in organizations must focus on hitting their numbers if they wish to remain employed. Hitting the numbers produces immediate success, but improvement is the sure bet that sustains this success. The problem with a single obsessive focus on hitting the numbers consists of the following:

- Success is accomplished at the expense of other important organizational and cultural needs.
- Success is not predictable or sustainable because much of the actual performance is generated by random acts of heroic effort in the last week of the month or quarter.
- Success is all based on short-term financial statement results, which are subject to various practices in putting these documents together to achieve the desired results.
- Performance driven by financial statement results compresses leadership and management time frames, perspectives, and interests.
- Financial success pays inadequate attention to the human capital and talent development capabilities that drive continued success in organizations.
- This month's or this quarter's financial statements by themselves do not provide a representative sample of the overall longer-term health and well-being of the organization.
- Numbers have promoted illegal accounting practices and scandals in many highly publicized organizations and government agencies.

Another trend is the urgent need for rapid and sustainable improvement—a given in the new economy. Management systems in organizations tend to force choices, but what is needed is a more balanced hybrid process that drives to optimize options and trade-offs. Executives cannot choose between A or B; they must go beyond the monthly and quarterly numbers and create a great improvement culture. In other words, they must figure out how to do both successfully and not one at the expense of the other. Brute force works only for so long; eventually, organizations must improve and *improve how they improve* to keep hitting the numbers with any consistency. If executives want to transform culture, they cannot remove hitting the numbers; they need to add in the other ingredients for success. Many organizations are in a cultural quagmire at the moment. Our economic collapse has certainly shifted the needle to numbers and away from the human elements of culture. As the needle shifts, the focus tends to change from

"What's in it for us?" to "What's in it for me?" because people are operating in the immediate "whack-a-mole" space. For executives, performance is reduced to either a bonus or termination. What everyone perceives as greed is the by-product of this unbalanced measurement system. These forces are shifting executive behaviors, decisions, and actions around but always in the direction of immediate results. In some organizations, these forces have driven culture backward and away from where organizations need to be to compete in the future.

In addition, corporate governance processes in U.S. corporations have allowed executive salaries to become incredibly disproportionate to those of the rest of the workforce. In the 1980s, executive salaries were 42 times the average worker's salary, and today they are over 400 times as much. This is insatiable. What was once future investment in infrastructure is now executive compensation. One of the basic practices of production incentive system design is to offer a balanced opportunity in which an individual has the opportunity to make significantly more compensation and motivate others around him or her. The design is capped at a fair maximum that is unquestionably fair for the incentivized worker, but its magnitude does not incite decreased morale in others around the worker. Why does this same practice not work for executive compensation? No one is worth a $50 or $100 million bonus regardless of what the person does. Plowing trillions into individuals' pockets instead of future investment in infrastructure supports the case for outsourcing. Another factor at play here is that the intensity of global competition is tipping the scales of typical research and development, new product and/or services development, and general infrastructure investments in organizations. Competing with the likes of China and other emerging third world countries requires a higher ratio of long term investment to compete, yet organizations have cut back in the interest of short term results. The answer by no means is government intervention but a more moral compass perspective of compensation.

By contrast, the ratio of chief executive officer (CEO) pay to that of the average employee has remained around 22 in Britain, 20 in Canada, 11 in Japan, and substantially less in China. The delta in executive compensation is going back into their organizations as investments in their futures. Today, when executives hit the numbers, they are paid extravagant bonuses, and when they fail, they are also paid extravagant exit bonuses and simply move on to another organization to repeat the performance. This is a measurement system in which executives are overcome by their own sense of importance; leadership becomes more about "me" than the moral obligation to the rest of the organization.

In either case, the real casualties are the average worker and organizational culture. In every *Fortune* magazine, there are several stories about executives who are paid bonuses in the tens of millions of dollars for their turnaround numbers, but nothing about the people who helped these executives achieve these numbers—no coverage and no compensation. Some executives have departed a failed organization with huge exit bonuses while breaking the pension bank for the remaining employees.

Numbers can also encourage and compensate people for doing the wrong things. Ineffective outsourcing practices are a great example of this. The savings from improvement are translated into rewards for a few individuals and sunk costs for the rest of the organization. The unbalanced measurement system is incomplete and rewards forfeiting the future of the whole for immediate personal gain. Understand that it is the broader corporate governance processes, not individual executive motivations, that are broken. You get what you measure; it is human nature. You cannot invest these sunk costs (bonuses) into investments that improve domestic competitiveness because they are gone. Now, it can only be invested in an individual's investments, another Ferrari, or another home in Palm Beach or Aspen. As a result, fear and insecurity abound for most working people today because they do not know if they will be outsourced tomorrow.

Decades ago, one of Deming's original points was "drive out fear." These practices have driven a huge wedge in culture, creating an "us-versus-them" environment. Finally, broken governance processes are not limited to corporations; they are also broken in banks and financial institutions, healthcare, and especially in federal, state, and local governments (with a few exceptions). In the future, all leaders must extend their time frames and perspectives and develop more holistic measurement and reward systems for the whole.

The basic fundamentals of continuous improvement are like the Gospel; they do not change. This is why many successful executives make analogies between continuous improvement and religion. Yet many executives and organizations are stuck in a mode of doing the wrong things based on the wrong metrics while losing religion of doing what is right. This is a leadership problem, and leadership has a moral responsibility to step up and break this vicious cycle. Many are questioning where these enlightened leaders will come from and when they will show up to save the day.

Executives have their work cut out for them in the new economy. At the very core of culture is character and best practice leadership behaviors. Rebuilding the core virtues and values of honesty, vision, integrity, candor, courage, teamwork and empowerment, dignity, respect, commitment, passion, discipline, empathy, listening, and talent expansion of, with, and through others is an enormous and extremely necessary challenge for executives in many organizations. Executives will need to become more social system architects and push innovation, collaboration, empowerment, the means of control, and shared recognition and rewards to new levels of excellence.

THE DYNAMICS OF CULTURE CHANGE

True cultural transformation is the continuous improvement of culture. As mentioned, culture is what it is, but it may not be what it needs to be to plan, deploy, execute, and sustain continuous improvement. Over the years, culture has been given more lip service than attention to the very things that trip up strategic improvement initiatives. The mechanics, methodologies, and tools of improvement are the easy part of improvement. There has been this expectation that if organizations casually kick the improvement can down the road long enough, the culture will automatically change. Unfortunately, this is not the case.

Cultural transformation is the most difficult aspect of change. The majority of organizations pursuing strategic improvement initiatives never realize this level of excellence. The major reason for failure is Deming's first point: constancy of purpose. In Chapters 2, 3, and 4, we discussed the elements of the Strategic Leadership and Vision part of sustaining infrastructure. This is the point at which executives must put culture under the microscope and identify the human gaps and barriers to success. This is also the point at which executives begin cultural transformation efforts. Cultural transformation is a deliberate effort that requires momentum, just like other improvement initiatives. We refer to this as the momentum of cultural transformation.

The momentum of cultural transformation can be expressed by a spin of Sir Isaac Newton's three classical laws of motion:

1. An organization improving in the positive direction possesses this momentum, and it remains in the positive direction unless acted on by some unbalanced force;
2. The rate of improvement and cultural transformation of an organization is directly proportional to the best practices leadership behaviors, decisions, and actions implied on it; and
3. In improvement-dysfunctional organizations, every effort to change is met by an equal or greater and opposite effort to remain the same.

Culture does not have a steady state. Culture is always transforming itself, although not intentionally and deliberately in most cases. There is positive momentum from the right executive behaviors, decisions, and actions, and there is negative momentum from the wrong executive behaviors, decisions, and actions. There is also negative momentum from lack of action because many people in the organization have great ideas about change and want to play a proactive role in change. Today, the majority of working people in all organizations are unhappy because the environment is not allowing them to realize their full potential. Why do we think generation Y people have held four or five jobs or more by age thirty? The "wait and see, do nothing" executives not only frustrate the hell out of their organizations but also are the root cause of organizational casualties down the road. Procrastination and complacency are the largest wastes because they multiply existing waste, delay dealing with the inevitable, increase the size and complexity of problems, and negatively impact the organization. Some of these executives wait until they have more problems than a sumo wrestler on the top of Mount Washington* in a January blizzard. In the future, executives must find

---

* Mount Washington, located in North Conway, New Hampshire, is known as the home of the world's worst weather. During a wild April snowstorm in 1934, a wind gust of 231 miles per hour (372 kilometers per hour) pushed across the summit. This wind speed still stands as the all-time observed surface wind speed record.

new ways of unleashing the tremendous human imagination and improvement capabilities that exist in every organization.

Let us leave Sir Isaac behind and discuss cultural transformation in a more pragmatic sense. Leadership is the engine that drives this momentum—that is, the *right* best practices leadership behaviors, decisions, and actions. This journey requires enlightened leadership with a higher moral compass for improvement and views the risk of doing nothing as a deliberate action to fail. Although the formula appears to be simple and straightforward, the details behind it are not so easy. The following is a brief discussion of each component.

VELOCITY OF IMPROVEMENT

Velocity is important because it validates improvement quickly and enables organizations to deliver more results by more people in a shorter period of time. The best way to create the value proposition for improvement is results. This raises the interest level with improvement and the desire to become associated with a positive strategy.

MAGNITUDE OF IMPROVEMENT

The magnitude of improvement relates to the precise targeting of highest-impact improvement opportunities and the best use of limited time and resources to achieve success. Magnitude also validates improvement because teams achieve a level of improvement that was thought to be unreachable or even impossible. Magnitude also creates the personal discovery moments that people need to become true believers in continuous improvement.

SUSTAINABILITY AND ADAPTABILITY OF IMPROVEMENT PROCESS

This component may sound a bit contradictory, but both words are synergistic. *Sustainability* refers to the capacity to endure over time, while *adaptability* is the power of a systematized process to adjust and transform quickly to changing circumstances. The first three components of the formula (e.g., velocity, magnitude, sustainability and adaptability) are covered by Strategic Leadership and Vision, Deployment Planning, and Execution—the leadership best practices, the formal sustaining infrastructure, and the specific accelerators of strategic improvement.

CRITICAL MASS ACCEPTANCE

Critical mass acceptance is the enlightenment stage of strategic improvement, a deliberate process that occurs through "internalization." Executives and their organizations understand the greater philosophical reasoning for improving how we improve. The shared beliefs, values, and assumptions about improvement are evident in the behaviors of groups or individuals and are visible in how people think and work every day. Improvement becomes embedded in culture, and executive behaviors, decisions, and actions amplify the importance of improvement. The process of internalization not only represents superiority but also ensures the longevity of improvement through cultural transformation.

In terms of the formula, most organizations create only a small amount of momentum with their improvement initiatives and for a relatively short period of time. Hence, most organizations cut their journey short and never experience cultural transformation intentionally through improvement. Internalization is the space where organizations reach sustainable continuous improvement.

WHAT IS INTERNALIZATION?

In short, internalization is a process of transforming culture through critical mass acceptance. Internalization is the deliberate, human-focused process of instilling shared beliefs, values, assumptions, attitudes, and organizational best practices about improvement into the egos of individuals, groups, and the organization as a whole. Over time, internalization becomes the acceptance of a set of norms, strategies, and expectations established by, and maintained by, leadership. The process starts with learning what the norms are, and then the individual goes through a process of understanding why they are of value or why they make sense, until finally the individual accepts the norm as a personal created viewpoint.

With continuous improvement, internalization begins with individual egos in a manner that is integral to one's sense of self, usually through personal discovery moments. It is one thing to believe in improvement conceptually or intellectually. Individual beliefs become much more powerful through engagement, empowerment, and the success of eureka moments. When this happens repeatedly, the external world of improvement as a corporate operating philosophy is brought into the internal belief systems of individuals, thus creating individual ownership for improvement and at the same time filling in the separation anxiety of improvement (from "in addition to" daily work to a "normal integral part of" daily work). Internalization always begins with individuals or individual improvement teams. One important lesson about improvement in organizations is that nothing changes until people are willing and ready to change.

Figure 7.1 provides an overview of the internalization of improvement. This deliberate and longer-term process is achieved through proactive management of four subprocesses:

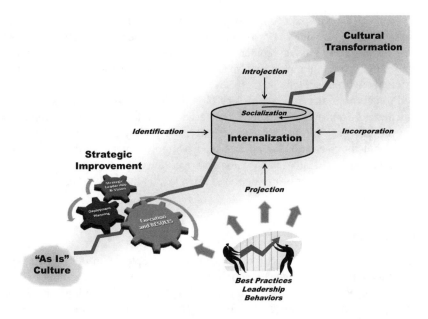

FIGURE 7.1 The internalization of improvement. (© Copyright 2011 by The Center for Excellence in Operations, Inc. [CEO].)

- Projection
- Introjection
- Identification
- Incorporation

These subprocesses are continuous; they require continuous attention and management to keep transforming culture in a positive direction. When Deming, Juran, Crosby, Feigenbaum, and other gurus talked about continuous improvement as a relentless, never-ending process, they meant what they said. Continuous improvement is not easy, but like everything else, it becomes more of a routine at the mastery stage. The remainder of this section provides additional information about each subprocess of internalization.

Projection

Projection is the initial defense mechanisms in response to improvement and change. Fear is the major driver of projection because individuals are afraid of all the perceived loss, effort, commitment, discipline, sacrifice, risk of failure, and disruption to their established norms. When the individual does not understand the why, what, when, where, and how of improvement, the individual fabricates an illusion of negative thoughts. The more a person thinks about change, the perceived losses, and unanswered questions, the larger the person's initial barriers grow. The signs of resistance are obvious: silence, deflection, criticism, confusion, denial, easy agreement, pocket vetoes, excuses, or "whatabout-itis." Projection is the attempt to put space between the inner self (norms) and the external environment (change).

Projection is also positive. Every organization has the initiators and early enlistees of improvement. These people generally have positive attitudes and see the glass as half full instead of half empty. They may have similar concerns, but they see more good than bad in improvement. Communication of the improvement strategy and vision and overview education are two effective methods of dealing with projection. This phase is the early stage of the next subprocess, introjection.

INTROJECTION

Introjection is a group version of projection. As people begin talking with each other about their individual perceptions of change, the exchange (positive or negative) becomes a collection of data points that shape the perceptions and visions of improvement and change. People are drawn into beliefs or are influenced by others internally by the communication that they are receiving from the external space. Through this subprocess, individuals replicate in themselves the behaviors, decisions, actions, attributes, or other fragments of people around them, especially leadership. Introjection occurs through rumors, political motives, the stronger personalities of others, or the real data and facts. People cannot decide whether to jump on the train or hang around and get run over by the train. If the perception of the messages is negative, it creates pockets of naysayers and dogmatic cults, but a great improvement initiative exposes these folks rather quickly. Introjection is a dynamic process that continues to be influenced and shaped by the communication and direct engagement in the improvement process. The shared beliefs, values, and assumptions about improvement are influenced by inconsistent versions of improvement, wavering leadership, a perceived or actual change in commitment, and other leadership behaviors, decisions, and actions. This in turn can change the behaviors of groups or individuals positively or negatively and the organization's ultimate commitment to improvement. Constancy of purpose, effective communication strategies, and "walk-the-talk" leadership are the best methods to manage introjection.

IDENTIFICATION

Identification is the subprocess in which individuals seek to become an integral part of the larger group in terms of shared beliefs, values, and assumptions about improvement. Many of these people are the show-me people. Once they either experience or understand improvement, they jump on the continuous improvement train. Through this subprocess, internalization occurs through the transformation of individuals, groups, and the organization, wholly or partially, after the role models of leadership and other champions of change. It is in this phase that the new personalities of individuals, groups, and the organization are formed. This is the phase in which, with enough participation, cultural transformation is visible in the way people think and work every day.

INCORPORATION

The final subprocess of internalization is incorporation. This is the psychological and social ingestion of the philosophy of improvement as well as the systemized process of improvement. Incorporation is undeniably a cultural standard of excellence—in individual behaviors, decisions, and actions in their own daily work and in the daily work of the entire organization. Cultural transformation is extremely visible in the way people think and work and how they are intolerable of mediocrity of those around them. Incorporation implies permanence in shared beliefs, values, and assumptions about improvement that are superglued into culture—and lead to the rhapsody level of continuous improvement.

SOCIALIZATION: THE OPERATING SYSTEM OF INTERNALIZATION

Socialization is not a subprocess, but it is an important part of every subprocess of internalization. Socialization is the continuous process of transferring and nurturing the organization's mission, vision, shared beliefs, values, expectations, and standard code of conduct. The goal is to establish unity of purpose between the organization and its people. Socialization develops the knowledge, skills, and personality characteristics within individuals so they can function successfully within the broader context of the organization. This occurs through many directions: from leadership or organizational development to employees, from older employees to newer employees, exchanges between individuals in a department, exchanges between functional areas, from an experienced improvement resource to a new team, from champion employees, and from many other directions. With continuous improvement, one area to include is orientation of new employees. Many of our clients include an overview of their improvement initiative as part of orientation. This will become increasingly important in our new "job-hopping" economy. Socialization is the operating system of cultural transformation and alignment because it grows people to internalize and conform to organizational norms, values, and practices.

Cultural transformation requires the continuous human process of internalization. Picture the dynamics of internalization. At any given moment, an individual might shift to a different phase, there may be an increase or decrease in shared beliefs, or one may doubt leadership's commitment to improvement. This might occur from an actual or perceived change in leadership behaviors, decisions, and actions—or it might be the result of an informal comment from a coworker. Now, multiply this by 1,000 or the number of people in your organization and the challenge of internalization becomes evident.

Another point about internalization is that perception is reality. Since people are human, they need assurance and reinforcement because there is a natural tendency to drift or slide back into old habits. Executives must keep their eyes and ears open to the negative signs of internalization and respond immediately and frequently with great awareness, communications, visibility of successes and positive progress, and recognition and reward practices.

MEASURING THE SUCCESS OF CONTINUOUS IMPROVEMENT

How does an organization know if it is achieving success with continuous improvement? I have lost count of the number of organizations I have visited over the years that were involved in various improvement initiatives and not formally measuring progress. When asked how they knew they were succeeding, I have heard comments like, "We just know" or "People are happier" or "Everyone likes it better." In other organizations, there is the spectrum of outdated charts to actively measuring everything under the sun. In one organization, I noticed a chart in the lobby that had not been updated in 4 months. When no one was looking, I wrote "Update Me" on the chart. During a return visit a few days later, I noticed that the same chart was replaced but without my handwriting.

One of the familiar scenes in organizations is this tendency to measure and post everything in the organization. Many organizations have their familiar war room or performance binders full of charts on just about everything imaginable. We refer to this as "metric mania"—the need to cover one's backside by measuring everything. This practice creates the perception that there is an understanding of what is going on because it is quantified and tracked. It must be a balanced scorecard because it includes metrics for everything. Certainly, it is data driven. There are several problems associated with metric-mania practices:

- It is unactionable because there is no distinction between outcomes, root causes, and dependencies. Further, it probably does not measure true root causes or include the right metrics.
- These war room metrics are usually updated well after the path of the problem has turned cold. It becomes more of an administrative task rather than a proactive management tool.
- It confuses the organization because it cannot decide what to do or where to begin to improve performance, so the metrics practice becomes a pure information-sharing process with no conclusions, action items, or improvement plans.
- It encourages opinionated and perception-based conclusions by attempting to explain relationships between metrics. Charts may go up or down, but the explanation of *why* is subjective. Therefore, the corrective actions are usually subjective (firefighting).
- It encourages finger-pointing, justification of poor performance, lack of ownership, and lack of accountability.

- It is a monumental task to update and take the right corrective actions with a repeatable and reliable process.
- It clearly demonstrates that the wrong metrics drive the wrong behaviors and achieve the wrong results.

The last point is a strong conviction. Two things become clear after significant experience with improvement: All organizations measure many of the wrong things and fail at measuring the true root causes of process performance. Several improvement projects with our clients have focused on identifying the factors that are most influential in achieving growth and profitability, and a residual finding is always a mismatch in performance metrics. In other projects, it becomes clear that existing metrics are measures of symptomatic issues rather than of root causes. In our Scalable Lean Six Sigma™ model, one of the most interesting factors has been this identification and ongoing measurement of root cause metrics. This represents a major enhancement to the balanced scorecard approach because it makes a formal distinction between root cause metrics (factors or inputs) and effect metrics (responses or outcomes).

STRATEGIC LEADERSHIP AND VISION METRICS

Like all other processes, the strategic progress of continuous improvement can and should be measured with a formal process. A good approach is to agree on five or six key, top-level business metrics to gauge the effectiveness of Lean Six Sigma and other strategic initiatives. Per the business plan and the improvement strategy, these metrics follow the balanced scorecard rules and have a baseline level and a goal by which success is achieved. Although the specific calculations may differ from organization to organization, these metrics usually include the following categories:

- Customer satisfaction
- Market and revenue growth
- Profitability
- Balance sheet and cash flow
- Economic value added (EVA)
- Human capital improvement

To the extent possible, organizations should be pegging and measuring the influence of their specific improvement initiatives on the continued well-being of these metrics.

DEPLOYMENT PLANNING METRICS

Like any other process, deployment planning requires metrics and performance measurement. To gauge the effectiveness of the deployment, several formal metrics are used:

- Planned and completed improvement activities (improvement projects, quick strikes) by organizational area with time-phased benefits
- Current and projected rate of improvement based on completed and planned improvement activities
- Showcasing of best projects and sharing attributes of success with others in the organization
- Depth and breadth of improvement by organizational area and confirmation of activity levels to the right strategic areas
- Inventory of assigned and available improvement resources and plans for developing improvement talent across the organization
- Ongoing dialog with deployment participants about what is working well, where people need additional help, and what aspects of the deployment can be improved (this is literally a continuous improvement initiative on the deployment and execution process by the direct participants with speedy corrective actions)

One challenging bullet point is in measuring the rate of improvement. Idealistically, executives would like to see their organizations increase their rate of improvement. The reality is that the rate of improvement goes through life cycles, even in benchmark Lean Six Sigma deployments. In the beginning, there are usually so many opportunities identified from the business diagnostic that the rate of improvement can be increased for 1 or 2 years. Once the initial improvement opportunities are implemented, it becomes increasingly difficult to mine new opportunities and implement new improvements that are of the same magnitude of savings as the initial stream of projects. The rate of improvement may crest or begin to descend, but this is initially not an indication of a bad thing. Every organization has its own maturity rate of improvement, but it must figure out how to keep the process of improvement going. The only way to increase the maturity rate of improvement at this stage is by a paradigm shift, such as

- Expanding improvement initiatives throughout the entire enterprise or institution;
- Expanding improvement initiatives externally in the extended enterprise to customers, suppliers, and other related stakeholders;
- Revisiting business strategy to see if any competitive opportunities are either emerging or changing that might require improvement attention;
- Evaluating the end-to-end systematic processes of improvement and improving how we improve;
- Innovation in improvement applied to areas such as research and development, new product planning and brand management, standardization of surgical procedures and equipment, consolidation of supply chains, technology development, advertising and promotions, competitive analysis, and so on.

The rate of improvement is an excellent metric for sustainability and continuous improvement. The key to successful deployment planning is not in waiting for something to fail. It is the proactive shaking of the bushes (using the sustaining infrastructure and the ten accelerators of Improvement Excellence™) to anticipate and prevent deployment planning activities from failing and simply to improve the deployment planning process continuously. It is one facet of Improvement Excellence™ or improving how an organization improves.

EXECUTION METRICS

Execution is a more focused process with the intent being success—one project at a time. If this is done effectively, the whole is also successful. The execution process includes two types of metrics:

1. *Informal action-oriented metrics:* These may be informal but they include the Sense-Interpret-Decide-Act-Monitor (SIDAM) behaviors of a seasoned mentor. The common informal action-oriented metrics include
   - Daily check-ins with the executive deployment core team leader
   - Frequent dialogue and feedback with team leaders, executive sponsors, and process owners
   - Open sharing of events of the day and communication of heads-up topics
   - Daily interactive and interference mentoring on topics such as team performance, lack of executive mentoring and commitment, coaching on executive behaviors, functional or political conflicts, clarification of expectations, and so on

2. *Formal measurement practices:* These are deliberate metrics describing the effectiveness of individual projects and deployment progress to plan. These metrics lead to more formalized actions to a particular team or to the deployment in general. Some of the common formal measurement practices include
   - Green-yellow-red (GYR) deployment management; projects and teams are slotted into their appropriate color based on progress. Green is good shape, yellow is okay but potential danger, red needs improvement immediately. These charts are generated every 1 to 2 weeks and shared with the CEO and the CEO's staff, the executive deployment core team, executive sponsors, process owners, and the team.
   - Weekly formal executive deployment team reviews. Ideally, these meetings are limited to 1 hour—30 minutes for reviewing GYR project status and team performance issues and 30 minutes for discussing new business or how to improve the deployment process and further integrate improvement throughout the organization. This might involve one 2 to 4-hour working session with a "red team" or

"yellow team" to get back on track, and a simple 30-minute review session with a "green team."

- Weekly 15-minute update to CEO and executives in their staff meeting. Improvement progress is a formal agenda item at the CEO's staff meeting. This update is provided by the executive deployment core team leader and is a short version of the executive deployment team review mentioned. Members of the executive deployment core team are also on the CEO's staff.
- Financial validation of results for each improvement project and a structured project close process (Control phase of DMAIC [Define-Measure-Analyze-Improve-Control]).
- Cumulative benefits mapping or mapping the cumulative verified results by project, functional area, location or site, key business process, or other improvement categories.

Figure 7.2 provides an overview of these planning, deployment, and execution metrics. The key to success lies in proactively managing these metrics to successful conclusions. Organizations have focused more on the projects themselves while allowing their deployment processes to take on a life of their own. Success with Lean Six Sigma cannot be allowed to happen based on chance or perception. Success is a choice that is achieved by deliberate management of the critical deployment success factors.

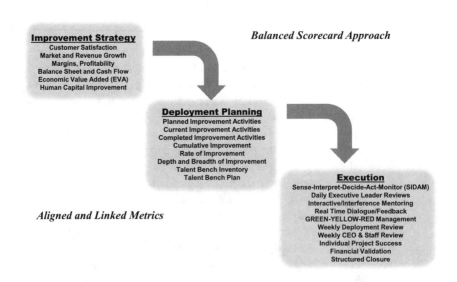

FIGURE 7.2   Critical improvement metrics. Strategy, deployment, and execution infrastructure. (© Copyright 2011 by The Center for Excellence in Operations, Inc. [CEO].)

GREAT CULTURES ATTRACT SUCCESS

Most of this chapter discussed culture in terms of continuous improvement. Great cultures are like a huge magnet to success. There is no question that organizations with strong adaptive cultures enjoy competitive success and superior financial performance. Not surprisingly, these organizations become the best places to work and most admired by their customers. A great culture fosters innovation, performance, diversity, pride of ownership—and outlasts any individual charismatic leader.

Beyond improvement, great cultures attract the best people and keep the succession planning pipeline strong. When people value and are passionate about their workplace, it shows up in the products and services it delivers to customers. Great cultures amplify the response to the voice of the customer in a very audible and visible way. Customers and suppliers also enjoy working with these organizations. Cultural transformation and alignment are an investment in infrastructure.

Culture can drift off course on its own through poor communication, inconsistent and mixed signals, loss of interest, a new focus on more important priorities, the failure of executives to reinforce desired behaviors and shared values, and dozens of other reasons. The recent meltdown and slow recovery without a doubt have had their toll on organizational culture. None of this is intentional; it happens by well-intended people under pressure, with wrong responses to extremely complex situations, and in the absence of time, resources, and facts. As one learns in Six Sigma, a process with complex variation and hidden root causes cannot be improved through an instant "quick-strike" effort. In fact, reactionary responses usually increase variation and the size of the problem. If one does not improve this process correctly, they will deal with recurring problems or turn them into larger problems. They will also create additional problems for others upstream or downstream in the organization. Firefighting is the equivalent of grasping at symptoms. People can neither see nor deal correctly with the root causes of these issues when they are deep in the quicksand of firefighting.

Unhealthy cultures can become magnets to failure as they create a death spiral around improvement, innovation, and employee commitment and loyalty. Strategic, continuous improvement is the best strategy to achieve competitive success and cultural transformation, namely:

1. Enlightened leadership that proactively demonstrates best practice behaviors by their actions
2. The formal sustaining infrastructure of Strategic Leadership and Vision, Deployment Planning, and Execution
3. Internalization and continuous alignment of strategy and culture

In the new economy, every executive has the opportunity to create and nurture a great culture within his or her organization. However, it is not possible by staying in the mode of "batten down the hatches." Let us face it: Many of the wastes in organizations have nothing to do with President Obama and other external forces. Much of this waste existed before the meltdown, and the across-the-board freezes, the resultant firefighting, and leadership choices to "wait and see" have exacerbated the hidden costs of waste and negative forces on culture. Today is a great opportunity to turn these situations around. Injecting and gaining back the positive attributes of a great culture are well within the domain of executive control. Improvement enables organizations to hit the numbers *and* achieve longer term success—especially the latter. Executives and organizations have all the improvement methodologies and tools available to them—it all comes down to the choice of becoming a great organization with great competitive success, great financial performance, great people, and a great culture.

BIBLIOGRAPHY

Harvard Business Review. HBR's 10 Must Reads on Change. 2001. Harvard Business School, Boston.
Klein, M. 1932. *The Writings of Melanie Klein.* Free Press, New York.
Mitchell, S., and Black, M. 1995. *A History of Modern Psychoanalytic Thought.* Basic Books, New York.
Window to Wall Street. 2009, March 22. Give CEO pay the pink slip. http://windowtowall-street.com/managementpayperks.aspx (accessed September 12, 2011).

8 The Role of Technology in Strategic Improvement

INTRODUCTION

It is mind boggling to think how organizations like IBM, SAP, Oracle, Microsoft, Google, Yahoo, Apple, LinkedIn, and many others are reinventing the landscape and models of business. In the new economy, technology is enabling the warp-speed transformation of organizations into global, multilevel networks of transactional enterprises. Unlike manufacturing improvement, transactional improvement is transparent and comprised of key business processes, information flows, knowledge, and decisions. Further, there are literally hundreds of people managing thousands of dynamic process touch points, a continuous churn in changing requirements, specific country needs, time constraints, communications issues, and exponentially greater opportunities for waste, variation, and bad decisions. This chapter is about two fronts of strategic improvement:

1. Getting the most out of existing technology and integrated enterprise architectures, and
2. Assimilating emerging technologies such as mobility, real-time enterprises, cloud computing, and other capabilities as a strategic weapon of global competitiveness.

Emerging technology is rapidly becoming a major enabler of the next generations of strategic and continuous improvement. The powerful combination of technology and business process knowledge has become much more important to the success of the next levels of Lean Six Sigma and strategic improvement in general. No longer is the notion of enabling technology and process improvement mutually exclusive, sequential, or left totally undone. Technology and improvement are inseparable and vice versa. Technology is the critical enabler of transactional enterprise improvement in this rapidly developing global environment. Strategic improvement includes the correct deployment of technology to reinvent business models, produce global competitiveness, achieve superior financial performance, and transform culture. Technology plus improvement is clearly a two-way street.

THE CHANGING ROLE OF CIOs

The chief information officer (CIO) role is one of the most challenging positions in the organization. CIOs have evolved to a role in which they must

Senior Executive   Business Model Innovator   Technology Expert   Process Improvement Guru   Vendor Relationship Manager   Financial Value Creator   Change Agent   **The New CIO**   Security Officer

be part senior executive, part improvement guru, part technology expert, part business model innovator, part security officer, part change agent, part vendor relationship manager, and part financial value creation. This used to be a much easier role as a management information systems (MIS) director when information technology (IT) was centralized organizationally and physically in the data center. Most of the IT business content was centered on localized finance and operations, and the office operations were relatively simple or informally managed. Much of this new CIO role has evolved from the emergence of transactional enterprises and the need to integrate the entire customer-to-supplier value stream. Existing and emerging technology have grown to become the largest enabler of connectivity, integration, information exchange, strategic and tactical improvement, business controls, and performance management. However, the path to success in these areas has become increasingly complex.

CIOs, their IT organizations, and the large software providers are constantly blamed for wasteful process issues and the extreme and growing costs of IT expenditures. This is also one of the first areas executives look to cut operating costs. Since 2010, almost 50% of organizations have reduced IT spending and head count. The problem with this strategy is that we are no longer building factories—we are building transactional enterprises that require infrastructure just as a manufacturing plant requires floor and office layouts, equipment, power, maintenance, and facilities management. Cell phones, videoconferencing, and e-mail are helpful, but not enough.

THE EMERGENCE OF TRANSACTIONAL ENTERPRISES

The new economy is accelerating the transformation of organizations into a complex global network of interdependent transactional enterprises. The physical content of work is being replaced with knowledge processes. For example, what was once a well-established stand-alone manufacturing plant in North Carolina is now a complex global supply chain with several contractors in China, India, and Brazil. In healthcare, the combination of consolidations, a focus on preventive medicine, IT, ambulatory surgical centers (ASUs), and Internet clinics are also moving hospitals in the direction of interconnected transactional processes. In many government activities, well, the complete understanding of objectives, business processes, inputs, outputs, and controls does not even exist. Complexity in business processes is growing but so is the need for improvement. This renaissance in improvement through technology is creating the greatest opportunities for forward-thinking organizations to improve, leapfrog competitors, and dominate global markets in the new economy. The future of improvement is definitely in the transactional enterprise and extended enterprise space of organizations.

Transactional processes continue to become enhanced by technology. Since transactional processes are integrated and interdependent, major improvements in one area provide residual improvements in other areas. The real challenges with improvement are in working one's way through the transactional maze and in defining and scoping out legitimate, data-driven transactional improvement opportunities. This process relies more heavily on IT than it ever has before. With transactional processes, one cannot pick up a part and measure dimensional characteristics to determine defects and quality levels. The improvement expert uses the organization's integrated enterprise architecture and other applications to trace transaction streams like a detective conducting transactional forensics as they reconstruct the waste crime scene of the process. These are not your father's Lean or Six Sigma tools at work here. The challenges of harvesting these large-scale opportunities lie in an organization's ability to evolve toward a state of Improvement Excellence™: *improving how they improve* through the correct integration of enabling technology. Organizations cannot harvest these large transactional improvement opportunities without the correct assimilation of technology because

- Technology provides a single version of the true facts. It replaces the kludge of spreadsheets and informal practices with a uniform standard of structured systems, internal controls, and operating data across all transactional streams.
- Technology provides the means to automate many previous improvement activities such as electronic kanbans, readily accessible performance dashboards and business analytics, flow coordination and control, real-time quality and reliability tracking, maintenance and facilities planning/management, critical resource and equipment utilization, supplier performance tracking, and the like.
- Technology provides the only ability to analyze transactional processes, view the interactions, data flows, and transactions in suspense (defect trails) between key business processes.

- Technology provides data for sampling plans in improvement projects and the ability to receive real-time feedback (collecting data manually consumes most of the elapsed time in improvement projects).
- Technology enables the opportunity to set and monitor the correct metrics and productivity indices and make the necessary corrective actions in real or near-real time.

Leadership must drive their organizations away from informal decision making toward more structured and formalized fact-based and data-driven decision making. Despite the billions of dollars in IT investment, there are too many executives and organizations managing by perception, opinion, or egos. My favorite example is the typical morning operations status meetings at which most of what is presented, discussed, and decided happens in the absence of the facts. In the future, successful organizations will need to embrace root cause problem solving via enabling technology. Technology is already available to allow people to view what is actually happening in their organizations. Well-designed performance dashboards are the glass windows to actual processes. With technology, it unquestionably takes significantly less time to do the right things right the first time than it does to do things wrong and then do them over to correcct the problem. Another word of caution is that the opposite is true: Technology overlaid on bad processes also produces the capability to create more waste than ever before. Today, many organizations are stuck in this last state and do not know how to turn things around. The only road out is improvement.

TECHNOLOGY IS NOT STOPPING FOR COMPLACENCY

Technology is moving faster than most people and organizations can digest it. There is a definite trend of increasing numbers of traditional organizations transforming themselves into transactional organizations through software technology. All of this technology is available and these emerging technologies can be widely delivered on a global scale. In the future, many resident transactional processes will rise to the cloud of computing. Success will still hinge on how organizations assimilate and choose to use technology. A few market-leading organizations have figured this out. Apple is the largest music company and poster child of this transformation. Amazon is the largest bookseller via technology, while Borders files bankruptcy. LinkedIn is the largest recruiting company, and Google is the largest direct-marketing platform. Today's leading real-world retailer, Wal-Mart, uses software technology to power its logistics and distribution capabilities, which it has used to crush its competition. Ditto for FedEx and UPS, which are best thought of as the greatest supply chain software networks that happen to have trucks, planes, and distribution hubs attached to their infrastructures. More and more organizations like Costco, AT&T, Comcast, Bank of America, and many others are following suit.

How will this shape the future of improvement? There must be continued physical improvements in manufacturing domestically and in regions where organizations have outsourced their products. In many situations, organizations have outsourced their product or software development, manufacturing, and quality problems alongside their products and services: They "moved" versus improved. These improvements will need to be sponsored or cosponsored by the customers of these contractors and suppliers because any customer problems are ultimately owned by the organization whose name is on the box. This is evident today as more people commute regularly (or temporarily locate) to Shanghai, Vietnam, India, Kenya, Venezuela, Brazil, and other global locations. By the way, these costs were never figured into the majority of the original outsourcing decisions. Much of these costs were unpredictable but are now opportunities for improvement.

Transactional processes are rapidly becoming the dominant form of processes in all organizations. This is as true in the world of business as it is in the world of healthcare, personal banking, or parent-teacher communication. Many transactional processes have just evolved over time, but not intentionally by a specific design. Some transactional processes are the equivalent of a patchwork quilt, designed over time around whatever requirements were deemed necessary at the time. There is much more "gold" in transactional process improvement than there is in beating another 0.010% yield out of a mature product. For example, think about the millions of dollars in warranty and returns, miscellaneous variances, or obsolete inventory. Allocating reserves to cover these problems is not fixing these problems, right? They are back next month, next year—as institutionalized waste. Manufacturing organizations are well into this transformation of transactional process improvement with the management of complex global supply chains; Internet sales and marketing in twenty different countries; global invoicing and electronic cash management; global new product, software, and service development; management of global quality and reliability standards; and many other transaction-based processes. Financial institutions have also been early adapters of transactional process technology (when is the last time you talked to a bank teller?). Intelligence agencies have replaced many of the physical processes of their investigative work with large-scale data mining using software and transactional processes to uncover and track potential terrorist plots. Many industry structures will change significantly from software technology, and the slowpokes will be gobbled up. There will be more Amazon versus Borders in the future for organizations that fail to recognize and reengineer their transactional processes for new market needs. The success or failure of commercial airlines today and in the future hinges on their ability to price tickets, maintain equipment and spare parts, and optimize routes and yields correctly—with software technology. Using the FedEx and UPS analogy, hospitals can benefit by viewing themselves as complex distribution and logistics networks with clinical services, equipment and facilities, administrative functions, and patients attached to them. Their goal is very similar to FedEx and UPS: optimize patient-centered care as they move through their complex processes at maximum velocity and minimum cost. In the near future, hospitals, governments, retail, transportation, and many other industry sectors will transform themselves via transactional process improvement through integrated software technology.

AVOIDING TECHNOLOGY ENTRAPMENT

The evolution of technology since the mid-1980s has been unbelievable. Most people cannot figure out how they worked without their laptops, e-mail, iPhones, iPods, Blackberrys, iPads, and other personal devices. Back then, a pager and an executive assistant familiar with Microsoft Office were technology blessings, and now 10-year-olds are doing their homework with Word, PowerPoint, and Excel. Today, technology is an embedded skill in every individual of the organization. There are more cell phones than bank accounts in the world. Technology has also become an accepted part of our personal life with the routine presence of onboard computers and GPS in automobiles, Bluetooth technology, smart toasters, networked home and automotive security systems, communicating gauge clusters for utilization and maintenance planning in off-road construction equipment, home theaters, massaging shower stalls, and a variety of other developments. Now, it is possible to view a video that continuously reports about your 16-year-old son's driving performance. Some people spend the entire day with their cyberfriends on various social networking sites.

Technology is beginning to manifest itself in every part of our lives, not just at work or the home office, but in religion, politics, social events, parent-teacher conferences, new friendships, our love lives, and how we keep our secrets. Generation Y people have already replaced much of the face-to-face or telephone communication with technology. Their tolerable problem-solving window is shrinking to the time it takes to receive an e-mail, text, or Google response to their question. Much of the social content of work has been replaced by cyberspace. Recently, a teen from Brooklyn, New York, received an award for the most text messaging: over 6,000 per month on average. LG now sponsors an annual U.S. texting championship with a $50,000 prize. This velocity will only increase with generation Z children, who now ride their bicycles and play sports on their Xbox 360 and then text their parents good-night from their upstairs bedroom. We are in the infancy of this technology evolution as people connect and choose how they will be changed.

There is an emerging trend that causes some concern, and people hope that it is just part of the learning process. But, as stated, technology and process must go hand in hand. Technology is an enabler of process, and it should not be confused with a replacement for process. Improvement is not as easy as buying new technology. Technology devices and applications are significantly impacting how people work in organizations and in their personal lives. However, technology is only as good as the person using it. In other words, people must still use their brain, draw the right fact-based conclusions from information, and initiate the right actions. Think about a typical day at the office. People attend a meeting and are guided through a PowerPoint presentation while reading and responding to e-mails on their laptop, texting on their Blackberry, and answering their cell phone. A few attendees are videoconferenced into the meeting and sometimes forget that others can view what they are doing. Sometimes, there are groups of people in a conference room totally silent but busy e-mailing and texting other associates. Later, as one meeting attendee takes the family out for a relaxing dinner, they find the restaurant is loaded with people conversing at their tables while communicating with other people via cell phones, e-mails, and texts. These same activities occur inside business conference rooms every day. No matter where we are these days (work, the mall, freeway, grocery store, your son's karate class, Sunday mass, etc.), we are likely to either observe others communicating or hear a digital ring or vibration of a cell phone or alert for an e-mail or text message.

Technology entrapment is the use of technology in a manner that creates a perception of productivity, improvement, and accomplishment. Technology has increased the ability to multitask, which has increased the practice of multitasking. This is also promoting question-answer behaviors that are not always based on the facts. Another way of saying this is that this multitasking may be replacing some level of root cause thinking with an instant gratification game of opinions and perceptions. Numerous studies from the Massachusetts Institute of Technology (MIT) and other institutions are indicating that the more people multitask, the less effective they are on every single task, and the less effective they are overall. Multitasking provides a false sense of productivity because many activities are accomplished, but the process promotes an intuitive, self-confident, reactionary mode of behaviors, decisions, and actions.

The answer by no means is to stop the evolution of technology, but to marry technology with process (for real), as it should be to produce the most successful results. When technology and process are allowed to diverge, waste and non-value-added effort emerge as false productivity from processes. With more people using technology, organizations are actually introducing the opportunity for more work-arounds and variation in core business processes. These are not technology issues. These issues revolve around the lack of fusion of technology and process and the choices about how to integrate and use technology as an enabler of strategic success.

The solution is simple: Technology is creating many other changes that have an impact on the workplace. People come to work today (but not necessarily physically) and plug into their own detached cyberspaces. Instead of getting up and walking to the next cubicle, people are communicating through e-mail. Technology as it exists today has done great things but is reducing the interpersonal and social content of work. Some claim that these relationships are no different in cyberspace, but they are for sure. For example, IBM's Westchester office was built in 1988 to house thousands of employees, and today on any given day, it is a ghost town. The people are still employees, but they are working from their homes, automobiles, a customer's or vendor's site, Starbucks, a son's soccer game, or Panera Bread. People are also connected to work much longer than they were 20 years ago.

This is the new norm for IBMers, and they openly admit to the loss of interpersonal and social content of the office. Future technologies at IBM and other places are already working on improving these relationships through cybertechnology, and IBM and MIT are developing simulated cyberconference capabilities by which participants can digitally gain back the human interaction element of communication. Developers are forecasting the future and discussing the ability to talk and translate different languages in real time. Early signs of this evolving capability demonstrate that people will be able to meet face to face in cyberspace regardless of geography, language, and other constraints.

Imagine six people in a cybermeeting, all talking in their native language; everyone can interact with each other, share exhibits and other documents, and fully understand the conversation. There already has been initial feedback on this developing technology regarding perceptions of how people are viewed by others in cyberspace, much as it would matter if they were in the same room. It is hoped that "Watson" will advance from the Jeopardy game to solve many future issues of "improvement through technology."

The transition to cybertechnology is easy for 5- to 18-year-olds, who according to recent studies, spend more than 50 hours per week in digital space. This continuation of technology changes not only the way people work but also the way people live. Think about the typical middle-class household: The husband or wife returns home from a day of work only to find the spouse on the Internet looking for a recipe while texting a friend, and the children are at the kitchen table—also on the Internet—doing their homework (their homework assignments are e-mailed daily to mom's iPhone by the teachers). Most parents make the effort to monitor and control where their children go on the Internet because it is like a large city. It has good safe neighborhoods and bad neighborhoods or good people and bad people. Later, they all go out for ice cream, and the husband checks on the dog with his iPhone via the Web-enabled audio/video home security system. The following Saturday, the husband goes deer hunting using his handheld GPS to locate the tree stand and digital scouting cameras and checks the memory stick for any recent sightings in the area. The opportunities for technology are unlimited.

Technology always requires the balance of good and bad. In Asia, for example, there is an epidemic of teens skipping school and spending 8–24 hours in digital cafés playing cyberspace war and other violent games. They are playing these games with the seriousness of a real war, competing against other players that they never met or have no idea where they live in the world. These teens have become cyberjunkies—the technology has become as addictive as alcohol and drugs. Some teens have died in the café chairs from playing games so long without food and water. There are even rehabilitation clinics where some of these teens are sent to break their addiction to cybergames. Many believe that technology is modifying behaviors in younger people so they demand and expect instant gratification. The tough work of research and analytics is being replaced by the question-answer process via the Web, texts, e-mails, or other digital media. These embedded technology norms will significantly impact the future behaviors, thought processes, and expectations of our young people.

Taking available technology for granted without thinking may have the most harmful behavior changes for children. We are creating a society in which people think they can do anything with the sole effort of Google, Twitter, or direct texting. Technology in education has replaced Sir William Curtis's basic skills (the three *R*s, which stand for *r*eading, w*r*iting, and a*r*ithmetic) with e-books, spell-checkers, and pull-down menu calculators. Children are using technology in many cases as an *end* rather than a *means* (or enabler) to the end. Just because something shows up on a display, it does not mean it is the truth or a fact. Regardless of what technology is available, people must not forget that they still need to *think* and go through the basics of listening to and synthesizing information, drawing the right conclusions from fact-based information, making the right data-driven decisions, taking the right actions with technology, and making sure that technology is working well as an enabler of whatever they are trying to accomplish. They still need to do this through the basic skills of reading (proficiency), writing (especially spelling), and math (especially multiplication tables). When children become helpless if you remove their laptops and iPhones, it is a much more serious problem than a generation gap.

TECHNOLOGY ENABLES RAPID DEPLOYMENT, RAPID RESULTS

The new economy is driving the need for more immediate attention and more immediate response. The combination of technology and improvement is enabling organizations to build real-time, interactive value streams by which they manage by a process nicknamed SIDAM, which stands for Sense-Interpret-Decide-Act-Monitor. This will replace some of the traditional discrete Kaizen events with near-real-time improvement. Another capability that many organizations have already embraced is real-time, event-driven metrics, walk-around metrics, or good-day-bad-day metrics. This is the upgrading of manually maintained story-boards and charts, which are now embedded within technology as performance dashboards. The objective of these real-time performance dashboards is to communicate performance and potential issues in real time so that organizations can SIDAM in more of a prevention mode. SIDAM creates the "in-flight center" mindset of daily management and improvement with the true facts. The shared visibility keeps a lot of peer pressure on the process owners of those dashboards. Executives can no longer lead successfully without the full integration of technology and improvement. In the new economy, improvement is ineffective without strong leadership and technology to enable its success, and technology investments result in questionable value without being accompanied by a business case, business process improvement, and strong leadership. This is the present and future of strategic improvement.

Technology is a lot like Lean Six Sigma and improvement in general: It can either produce great results or increase overhead spending. Technology must be introduced as a justifiable investment, not as a cost of doing business. Organizations do not have the best track records in deploying IT expenditures correctly so they produce profitable and justifiable results. In the past, IT organizations always talked about *enabling technology,* which suggests technology to improve the business via its key business processes. Enabling technology also embraced conceptually that technology and process are inseparable. The way that technology has typically been introduced in organizations has not always been *enabling* from a competitiveness and profit-and-loss (P&L) perspective. This is not a technology issue; it is a leadership, planning, deployment, and execution issue.

SCRUBBING AND REMOVING THE BLACK-AND-WHITE SPACES

There is an age-old problem with IT, and traditionally it has not been the fault of the IT organization (although it is evolving in that direction). In organizational structures, there is a phenomenon called "managing the white spaces." White spaces are the conceptual spaces between the boxes of an organization chart where responsibility and accountability may become unclear. Leadership inserts and allows these white spaces to exist via silo management practices, wavering direction, weak talent development, a low interest in and commitment to process improvement, the structural design itself, and other possible reasons. These spaces have a high potential for improvement (by looking outside the silo at key end-to-end business processes). Improvement scrubs and removes the white spaces of organizations.

In technology, there is a similar phenomenon that we refer to as "managing the black spaces." The introduction of technology creates these black spaces. These are voids that compromise the cohesiveness, continuity, standardization, integrity, and overall success of technology. They occur through planning, implementation, and ongoing choices about how technology is used on a day-to-day basis. For example, implementing and using an extensive integrated enterprise architecture such as SAP has the potential of achieving significant business process improvements, culture change, and enterprise and extended enterprise excellence. SAP's technology is involved in over 60% of the world's transactions. Every 0.7 seconds, over three billion transactions are processed through SAP's cloud, so the influence of this technology on enterprise success is enormous. However, its implementation has created many black spaces in organizations.

Let me reiterate that this is not an SAP problem; it is a technology introduction, planning, implementation, and user processes and practices problem. IBM, Microsoft, Oracle, IDC, Sage, Siemens, and all other software vendor implementations have created black spaces. Again, the problem is not the software. Like white spaces, leadership determines the magnitude, length of stay, and return of these black spaces. Black spaces are dynamic: They appear or grow with changing circumstances, and they disappear or shrink with the right business process improvement responses. In the planning stages, an organization may not have done the due diligence to define requirements properly and instead opt for standard templates or failure to determine and turn on necessary features. During implementation, many failed to make the investment in concurrent business process reengineering or improvement and instead overlaid SAP on a network of inefficient or missing processes. Master data cleanup during conversion may have been determined to be close enough and therefore postponed. Education and training on basic supply chain processes, best practices, plus SAP features, functions, transactions, standard reports, inquiry capabilities, and so on might have also been cut short. Historically, leadership and implementation teams under unreasonable deadlines have postponed process improvement and education because they are perceived to add cost and slow the implementation process.

This sets the organization up with a lack of appreciation and knowledge of the basic disciplines required of a formal integrated architecture, therefore creating black spaces (e.g., data integrity, timeliness and accuracy of transactions, incorrect or skipped transactions, unawareness about planning parameters, perpetual inventory and bill-of-material accuracy, incorrect master or customer data, contracts and pricing accuracy [and sales overrides], order configuration control to global specifications, realistic sales and operations planning [S&OP], immediate task/silo focus, insensitivity to problems created on upstream and downstream operations, information overload and noise, and many other common issues). In daily use, people are doing the best they can through tribal knowledge, workarounds, meetings, e-mails, off-line spreadsheets, and other informal practices. They (and their IT representatives) are unaware of the embedded features, functionality, standard reports, or inquiries in the SAP architecture, so the technology is enabling black spaces instead of removing them. In many organizations, this is their process—and their performance is directly correlated to the capability of this process. The behaviors, decisions, and actions in each of these three phases create the black spaces in technology. Over 25 years ago, subject matter experts like Oliver Wight, Jim Burlingame, Walter Goddard, and George Plossl were talking about the same basic Enterprise Resource Planning (ERP) issues at American Production and Inventory Control Society (APICS) conferences. With more people using technology, organizations must accept that they are actually introducing the opportunity for more variation in core business processes. Finally, let me underscore that our example is not an SAP problem; it is a technology introduction, planning, implementation, and user processes and practices problem.

Accepting and managing in the presence of black spaces require wasted time, cost, poor use of resources, and unnecessary IT requests and *consume* value rather than adding value. Black spaces also foster a culture of reactionary behaviors and firefighting, an environment that is too busy and adverse to improvement. No organization is completely without technology black spaces. Although it has been more than a decade since Y2K, many organizations are sitting on several user-created business process improvement opportunities within their integrated enterprise architectures.

The assimilation of technology correctly is a preventive measure against black spaces. Strategic and continuous improvement scrubs and removes the black spaces of technology. Organizations that allow technology by itself to drive people and processes ultimately become victims of technology. The root cause is that process improvement and continuous improvement keep falling out of the technology implementation picture. Most of this is driven by leadership's perception of saving time and money or a plan to implement the hardware and software portion of the project first and return to the process improvement needs at a later date. The process improvement portion is usually the first casualty and postponed indefinitely, while users blame IT and the vendor for their inefficiencies. Many of these kludge, black space *patches* have become institutionalized as "the process" in organizations. Organizations spend billions on technology investments, and a large part of daily work is handled through disconnected Excel spreadsheets, Access databases, and dozens of daily hot list meetings. The resulting black spaces add up to millions of dollars of hidden waste in most organizations.

In the future, organizations must view and actually implement their IT investments as *improvement through enabling technology.* Many CIOs believe that their organizations are already acting in this manner. A closer look at the true technology return-on-investment (ROI) numbers reveals that they are not. CIOs embrace improvement through enabling technology in concept, but the rest of the organization does not evaluate and deploy technology in a deliberate value enhancement manner. The issues around the success of enabling technology are the same as the issues around successful strategic and sustainable improvement: Organizations can never find the time to do the right things right the first time, but they always find the time to do things over or discover work-arounds in their avoidable waste environments.

Organizations such as IBM, Oracle, SAP, and other IT consulting firms are providing implementation support services, but these services are too tilted toward *acquiring technology* instead of *total enterprise improvement and financial well-being.* Actual "hands-on" business process improvement experience and expertise are weak in many applications software firms. Overlaying technology on bad processes may produce some structural benefits, but it usually automates the ability to create business problems faster. This may also create friction and controversy between the organization and its technology vendor, which does not solve the business process improvement issues. Technology may be marketed as a productivity tool, and in many cases, specific applications combined with the implementation approach accomplish this objective. The added value of technology comes down to how people and organizations choose to introduce and use it.

Organizations have not taken the time, patience, and the efforts to plan and implement their IT investments in a value-enhancing manner. Of the problems with IT, 99% involve people and how they choose to implement and use the technology. Only a tiny portion is due to hardware or software problems. If organizations hope to get better at ROI on their present and future IT investments, they need to make the component of strategic process improvement a major factor in the requirements definition, evaluation, feasibility, and implementation of technology.

THE FUSION OF TECHNOLOGY AND IMPROVEMENT

The new economy is driving the critical fusion of technology and improvement, which are indeed inseparable if an organization wishes to erase the black spaces of technology and achieve best practices and benchmark performance. Figure 8.1 provides an overview of this fusion process. Leadership is always the engine of

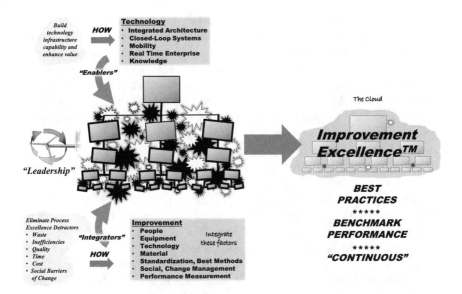

FIGURE 8.1 The fusion of improvement and technology. (© Copyright 2011 by The Center for Excellence in Operations, Inc. [CEO].)

Improvement Excellence™: Executive behaviors, decisions, and action determine how the combined forces of technology and improvement are deployed throughout the organization. Leadership provides the means of defining, creating, and managing processes—and ultimately determines the capability of these processes for the organization. The performance of the organization is only as good as the processes that leadership has provided for them. This is Deming 101, Continuous Improvement 101.

Technology is the front door, the touch points, and all entry and exit points of these transactional processes. Technology provides the *enablers* of process in the form of the integrated enterprise architecture and other fully integrated applications. These are enablers because they are the means of adding in and building IT infrastructure and value, not the ends. The trouble with many technology-based deployments is that hasty and overanxious people treat technology as the ends—the quick cure-all and end-all to the organization's problems. These technology issues are represented by the black spaces discussed. Improvement provides the *integrators* of process, including people, best methods, standardized procedures and policies, change management, and performance management. Improvement defines a vision for process excellence (including the integration of enabling IT) and then removes the detractors of process excellence. The detractors are represented by the white spaces discussed. These may include inefficiencies, waste, process defects, time, cost, and organizational or social barriers to change.

By themselves, technology and improvement are suboptimized attempts to drive business process improvement. Technology without improvement enables people to automate bad processes and make more mistakes more quickly, thereby adding to the waste and non-value-added work-around activities. Improvement without technology creates a perception of improvement, but the results are merely a snapshot of a moment that lacks flexibility, responsiveness, and sustainability. For example, this is why most Lean efforts that involve manual kanbans, fixed cell designs, perfectly balanced progressive assembly stations, static work instructions, manual storyboards, and defined build rates fall apart as soon as new products are introduced or the mix or volume of customer requirements change.

Most antiquated, mechanically managed Lean efforts cannot be reengineered quickly enough to address ever-changing design requirements evolving from the new economy. Lean, Six Sigma, and other improvement initiatives need to transform themselves into more targeted on-demand improvement activities driven by customers and markets via the technology infrastructure. It is this correct fusion and deployment of technology and improvement that drive process excellence and achieve best practices and benchmark performance. There really is no justification to implement technology and improvement in some phased sequence, eliminate improvement to save technology implementation time and costs, or implement improvement to save on IT investments. Separating technology is a *pay now, pay more later* decision. Nobody has documented the negative effects of digging out of poorly executed Y2K implementations (some organizations are still digging), but these hidden overhead costs have resulted in poor customer service, inefficient operations, multiple versions of the facts, a kludge of isolated spreadsheets—other non-value-added costs are in the millions for most individual organizations. The fusion of technology and improvement is the best way to optimize IT value, avoid these hidden costs, and actually achieve best practices and benchmark performance.

TECHNOLOGY: THE SUPERACCELERATOR TO CLOUD IMPROVEMENT

Like many topics in this book, it is time to return to the basics and connect the dots of improvement and technology. People multi-tasking with their handheld devices is reminiscent of the pre-Lean Six Sigma days where mechanics would tinker and make multiple adjustments to equipment. Subjecting this practice to the Lean Six Sigma microscope demonstrated that these practices actually added more defects and variation to processes. Technology provides access to information . . . tons of information. Technology also tends to feed intuitive decision making by keeping people overfed with information but undernourished with analysis. A key take-away is that technology does not remove the need to use one's brain to assimilate information correctly and better understand the cause and effect relationships in processes.

Integration of improvement methodologies (Kaizen, Lean, Six Sigma, and all other improvement techniques) and enabling technology are the roadmap of future improvement and competitiveness. Technology often adds the "hot stove" attribute to improvement, where process infractions can be followed by quick disciplined responses to the root causes, and near real-time improvement. The more an organization chooses to integrate Lean Six Sigma and IT (while focusing on the highest impact opportunities), the sooner they will achieve larger and faster returns on their efforts. Although the recent meltdown has taken its toll on organizations, it has also changed how people and organizations will work in the future—and for the better. It has also changed how people and organizations *improve how they improve*. One should not be disappointed by all of the great improvement and technology work that has been accomplished up to this point.

Some critics claim that formal improvement initiatives are no longer necessary as the world transitions from hardware to software, clouds, and mobile digital devices. Presently, information on mobile devices is limited by the available internet Operatiing System (iOS) applications. This technology provides information in real time that enables the right leadership decisions; technology does not automatically think, draw the right data-driven conclusions, and take the right actions. This is why the devices are called personal pocket "assistants." Organizations still require leadership and standard processes and practices that can always be improved. Everything occurs within the context of process. Therefore, technology is not a replacement for improvement; however, it will make improvement much quicker in the future.

Others claim that people intuitively use the logic of formal improvement when they use their laptops and handheld devices. We covered this topic in the section about technology entrapment. Two relevant thoughts come to mind. First, relative to DMAIC (Define-Measure-Analyze-Improve-Control, the standard problem-solving methodology of Lean Six Sigma), most people multiprocessing on overload with handheld devices and other available technology are skipping D, A, and C and just performing M and I. This is a symptomatic, hit-or-miss approach to improvement that generates both real and hidden costs. Technology is being used as an enabler of firefighting, not improvement. This leads to the second thought about the subject of rolled throughput yield. This is a statistic to calculate actual process yield, netting out all rework and repair activities. If twenty people in a department are multiprocessing with their handhelds today, and each makes correct decisions 98% of the time, how effective is the group as a whole? On a first thought, this might sound good, but it is not. The answer is 0.98^{20} or $98 \times 98 \times 98 \times 98 \times 98 \times \ldots$ (20 times) or about 66.67% of the time—and it is even less when one adds in the normal sigma shift in all processes. The remainder is waste, and the only way to permanently eliminate waste is through process improvement and root cause thinking. Yelling and scolding these people will not improve performance because their performance is process dependent and process limited. This example also explains why close enough is no longer good enough.

Technology is raising the bar of possibilities that people and organizations never dreamed of—especially Improvement Excellence™—*the mastery of developing and implementing successful strategic and continuous business improvement initiatives, transforming culture, and enabling organizations to improve* *how they improve.* What does the future of work hold? Soon, we will have moonshot mission control capabilities on personal devices yet to be developed. Instead of "going to the Gemba,"* we will be walking around "in the Gemba" with accessible, cloud-enabled applications and information all around us. One cannot help but technology forecast the future, which might include medical care or automobile maintenance in the cloud, new versions of cybershopping that might include digitally trying on and customizing clothes for fit and look, individually interconnected cyberenterprises, and many other possibilities that are *not that far* out there.

The CIO role, as mentioned, is becoming more improvement guru focused, so the integration of strategic improvement and technology makes logical sense. Technology and improvement have always been compatible, but leadership has kept the two separate and distinct.

Successful organizations will integrate strategic improvement and technology and improve the financial and value-enhancing results of their IT investments. These organizations will also accelerate their strategic improvement initiatives through the integration of IT information and data capabilities, analytics, and real-time performance dashboards. Technology has changed the face of traditional continuous improvement tools and is enabling the magnitude, scope, velocity, sustainability potential, and *continuous* attributes of strategic improvement more than any other time in history. Yet there are still many consultants and trainers out there who are stuck in an improvement time warp, conducting their tools-focused business as usual, and who still do not get it. The folks who continue to insist on unplugging IT while promoting manual kanban cards, maintaining symbolic storyboards, and hyping up the beautification exercises and oversimplified Lean by teaching about tools for the shop floor are the improvement dinosaurs of this new economy.

BIBLIOGRAPHY

The Center for Excellence in Operations, Inc. (CEO), and SAP. 2004. Building the Lean Extended Enterprise: a special SAP/CEO research report. *Breakthrough! Newsletter.* http://ceobreakthrough.com/pdf_files/LeanExtendedEnt_Special0411.pdf.
IBM Global Services. 2011. Taking end user services to the next level with IBM's Right-to-Left strategy. http://public.dhe.ibm.com/common/ssi/ecm/en/enw03003usen/ENW03003USEN.PDF.

---

* Gemba is the Americanized version of *Genba*, a Japanese word meaning "the real place." Japanese detectives refer to a crime scene as the Genba; a Japanese production manager calls the Genba the shop floor where people are engaged in problem solving, and information is gathered at the source.

9 The Multimillion-Dollar List of Improvement Opportunities in Manufacturing, Distribution, and Service Corporations

INTRODUCTION

This chapter provides an aggressive list of transactional and knowledge process improvement opportunities in typical manufacturing, distributor, and service industries. All of these opportunities are based on actual, real-world improvement projects in many diverse types of industries: high technology, automotive, consumer goods, traditional manufacturing, aerospace and defense, process industries, capital equipment manufacturer, papermaking, pharmaceutical, medical instruments, clean room microscopic assembly operations, and dozens of other environments. The improvement opportunities presented in this chapter are also relevant to many industries outside manufacturing with very similar transactional processes, such as communications, mining, building construction, energy, transportation, insurance, healthcare, financial services, utilities, retail, and professional services organizations. For those who may be thinking "we are different," this excuse no longer holds water in the new economy.

Many organizations do not fully appreciate the magnitude of these opportunities because they are viewed as institutionalized, hallowed processes. In addition, the costs and benefits are "hidden" and therefore unknown. For most of the suggested improvements in this chapter, the initial challenge is akin to "boiling the ocean." Accordingly, my advice is not to improve these areas with a single effort. Each of these areas may consist of several individual improvement projects. Based on our firm's diverse consulting experiences, a single project in many of the examples to follow achieves as much as hundreds of thousands to millions of dollars in benefits.

The remainder of this chapter provides the multimillion-dollar list of improvement opportunities.

STRATEGIC MANAGEMENT

STRATEGIC PLANNING PROCESS

This is a great opportunity for many organizations. The emerging windows of opportunity and windows of change are much shorter than the traditional 1- to 5-year planning horizon of strategic planning. The stagnant *update-the-binder* approach to strategic planning tends to be more of a financial and numbers exercise and does not integrate the rapidly emerging challenges and opportunities of the new economy. Traditional strategic planning processes tend to view business strategy as a discrete (annual) process instead of a continuous one. The risk is that many strategic opportunities may be identified too late in the window of opportunity.

Several organizations have modified their strategic planning horizon by applying Lean Six Sigma (e.g., Pareto analysis, value stream mapping, regression analysis, etc.) to their strategic planning process. A few organizations we are familiar with have shifted to a 1- to 3-year strategic plan with quarterly planning updates on an exception basis. This exception basis is a *tall-pole* analysis of opportunities with existing and new product and service opportunities. Lean Six Sigma techniques help executives better understand the strategic levers of their business and how to best influence strategic and financial success. Strategic planning processes must become more responsive and must be guided or influenced by strategic improvement initiatives. The described improvements are driving the convergence of an organization's strategic planning and annual operating plan activities.

ACQUISITION AND INTEGRATION

The area of acquisition and integration is yet another that most may not associate readily with Lean Six Sigma and strategic improvement. A successful acquisition requires a lot more effort than analyzing financial statements, looking at customer lists, and conducting pro forma Excel spreadsheet analysis. Organizations that limit themselves to this kind of thinking end up missing opportunities or end up with an acquisition loaded with unanticipated problems. Many times, we are invited to participate in due diligence activities to define the current state of the business, confirm strategic fit both qualitatively and quantitatively, identify potential improvement opportunities, and develop the implementation and integration plan, which is ready to go directly after the acquisition is consummated. In addition, this additional information is critical for conducting a more robust feasibility analysis of the proposed acquisition. Acquisition decisions are not reversible, so the value of doing things right the first time is critical to success.

Another vital improvement in this area is the development and standardization of a robust acquisition evaluation process. In many organizations, this high-risk initiative is backed up by informal ad hoc processes or lack of process. A well-structured and disciplined acquisition and integration process avoids millions of dollars in unexpected costs and pays for itself in the first few minutes of the acquisition.

GLOBAL OUTSOURCING STRATEGY

Executives are constantly faced with achieving goals at less cost. During the past several years, outsourcing has become the latest in-vogue strategy to reduce operating costs and internal manufacturing complexity and content. The primary fundamental behind outsourcing was to set up a national presence in other countries, such as China, Brazil, India, and others with high-growth potential for goods and services. Over 50% of revenues in many corporations come from international markets. Many of the high-growth areas overseas are in products that are either mature or in the decline in U.S. markets. China, with its population of 1.3 billion people, represents an enormous opportunity for incremental revenue growth. Also, labor costs there are significantly less than for U.S. manufacturing, and people are better educated. Therefore, it made sense to move everything to China. Outsourcing is not some deliberate anti-America business strategy. It is a global growth, market share, and profitability strategy. Outsourcing decisions have also been influenced by poor government policies around trade, regulatory, healthcare, labor union, and other areas that tip the cost scale away from U.S. manufacturing. China is the new manufacturing power of the universe, today and for many years in the future. That is just the way the world works. One can only hope that future government policy decisions will facilitate the rebuilding of a competitive manufacturing base in America.

Many organizations have hastily outsourced operations based on some corporate directive and spreadsheet and bandwagon mentality. In their journey, many became confused with the difference between price and cost—and believe me, there is a big difference when it comes to outsourcing. Many organizations simply moved their manufacturing problems elsewhere, which have grown exponentially in magnitude, cost, and complexity across oceans and country borders. From a profit-and-loss perspective, over 50% of outsourcing decisions need significant improvement to achieve valid long-term feasibility. This is not insinuating that outsourcing decisions be reversed because the upside revenue potential in China, India, and other emerging third world markets is too enormous to overlook. However, outsourcing is a dynamic process, and many of these initial decisions need to be revised. There are significant opportunities to reduce the hidden costs of outsourcing in most organizations. Based on recent benchmarking data and looking at fully loaded costs, these hidden costs are usually in the range of 14% to 53% of purchase prices.

Many companies use the slot machine approach to managing their outsourced supply base: try one supplier—if problems are found, try another supplier, and on and on. This supplier-to-supplier hopscotching creates variation in the supply chain that is extremely costly. A small amount of variation and waste at the front end of the supply chain only grows exponentially (along with costs) as it is measured further down the value stream and into the hands of customers. Worse yet, buyers might be paid bonuses for favorable purchase price variances (PPVs) when the product quality and total ownership costs are in horrible shape. The problem is not so much with outsourcing, but with the details of an organization's outsourcing process itself. The improvement is not in reversing outsourcing decisions, but in filling the holes in deficient outsourcing strategies, processes, and evaluation metrics.

Many outsourcing process improvement projects involve the use of value stream mapping, formal analysis and evaluation of strategic opportunities in other countries, and ongoing analysis of total cost of ownership. In the future, outsourcing must resemble a chess game in which the eggs are capable of being removed from one large basket and strategically placed in many smaller baskets around the globe. In other words, organizations must continuously seek to optimize country opportunities and minimize total cost of ownership. Since many of these costs are hidden, they must be dug out and allocated based on valid statistical assumptions. Total cost of ownership includes excess and obsolete inventory, material overhead, coordination and third-party costs, corrective action costs for quality issues, turnover, lost opportunities from intellectual property theft, lost sales due to mismatches in distribution stock, competitive knock-off products using the same supplier, scrap and rework, significantly higher planning costs, higher forecast and delivery variation, incorrect documentation, loss of flexibility to schedule changes, theft and inventory shrinkage, product and packaging damage, training and development, incremental medical and disability costs, premium air freight, employee travel, security, and a multitude of other factors that are not considered in outsourcing decisions. Some of these factors are controllable, and some are environmentally driven and noncontrollable. Nevertheless, they are real costs of outsourcing and conducting business in another country, and improvements geared to reducing these costs are in the millions of dollars.

NEW PRODUCT DEVELOPMENT

CONCEPT DEVELOPMENT

Concept development refers to the translation of an idea into a workable design concept and eventually a solid product specification. The detracting dynamics here are the decisions that result in the continuous churning and changing of new product specifications and *feature creep* well into the development process. This causes significant hidden engineering waste and costs, delays in time to market, or huge risks in quality and reliability by pushing and expediting designs through the shrinking back-end time horizons in the development process. The goal is to freeze the specification early on in the development process to prevent feature, cost, and time creep later in the development cycle. Granted, the world is not perfect. However, when an engineering organization routinely practices drive-by engineering and adds features as the product is due to be released, there is definitely something broken in upstream processes. These activities can often be improved significantly via many simple quick-strike improvements that include standardized templates, checklists, guidelines, and standardized information requirements for a functional specification.

Often, the development of new product ideas is emotional and informal and influenced by those with the most political clout in the organization. Something as simple as developing a standardized product concept template ("business case") creates enormous benefits on the front end of the product development process. This process allows a larger group of new product people to evaluate the feasibility of new product ideas and proposed functions and features relative to market potential, technical feasibility, development cost, target cost, and time-to-market considerations. This standardized business case template can be carried through the development process and used to reaffirm market opportunities, hold people accountable for projected assumptions, and reprioritize projects in the development pipeline.

NEW PRODUCT AND SERVICES DEVELOPMENT PROCESS

The new product and services development process refers to the typical five-stage gate product development process found in most organizations (e.g., idea or concept, functional specification and business case, product and process development, validation and test, and new product commercialization). Every organization claims to have a formal product development process, but the reality is that many organizations do not follow a formal and disciplined process on a daily basis. The more engineering and technical talent becomes overloaded, the more they seek work-arounds and shortcuts.

There are dozens of improvement opportunities in this lengthy and complicated set of technical business processes. Potential product development improvements must be defined, scoped, and prioritized based on total impact (e.g., Where are the top Pareto pole improvement opportunities in product development? Where are the largest pain points in the development process?). Since development cycles are lengthy and difficult to study in real time, the best way to flush out these opportunities is by historical benchmarking and re-creations of things that went wrong in other projects. The right group of engineers in a room, pulled away from their latest crisis, can be very revealing in terms of product development improvement opportunities. Like Benny in Chapter 1, they know more about their roles and their chronic problems than anyone else in the organization.

Engineering vice presidents may not think of their organizations in terms of complex, interconnected knowledge processes. New product development is one of the highest opportunities for improvement in organizations. For example, the lost opportunity and cost of each design verification cycle is $10,000 to $100,000 per spin in some organizations. Reducing time to market by 50% to 75% by eliminating non-value-added elapsed time, wait times, and hidden waste of resources might result in an additional 10% to 30% market share. The cost of engineering changes and development after product release can easily add up to millions of hidden dollars and lost or wasted engineering capacity in many other development projects. Another interesting set of questions to ponder: How many development projects are released on time? On budget? With minimal to no post-engineering for field quality and reliability, technical issues related to warranty and returns, customer service support, and other postrelease activities? One of our clients, a $1.5-billion high-technology company, racked up $13 million in savings on their first five improvement projects in new product development.

Product development processes are similar in concept to manufacturing processes. The stage-gate and phase review process is analogous to routings; there are tasks and critical paths, rework and quality problems, work backlogs, standards and inefficiencies, bottlenecks, changes in schedules and priorities, and difficulties determining the true status of projects. The big difference is that equipment is replaced by talented engineering and technical people. Intelligent people are less likely to follow standardized processes because they are smart enough to work around them and get things done. Often, process and standardization are viewed as deterrents to creativity and innovation. The challenge with new product development is to install standardization and data-driven development that actually enables (vs. stifles) more creativity and innovation.

SOFTWARE DEVELOPMENT PROCESS

Software development is an interesting improvement opportunity. Many of these professionals are developing software that will be integrated with hardware, but the full requirements are still in an evolving state and are unknown. It is a bit like driving to a new location without the GPS: Some of the destination may be known, but it usually involves getting lost, asking for directions, and making several detours before arrival. This becomes complicated by outsourcing decisions in which software applications are developed in different locations around the globe (e.g., operating systems, software languages, Web-supported applications, utilities and libraries, interfaces, remote team development, and dozens of other complex combinations of choices). Coordination of all of the pieces is a complex, wicked problem; the variation increases proportionally with the complexity of the requirements and the number of people involved, regardless of development standards and practices.

This often leads to software that does not work, software with duplicate efforts, or software that exposes unexpected bugs and glitches some time after release. Although software development is confusing and complicated to most, the improvement of software development is more common sense than rocket science. Lean Six Sigma and DMAIC (Define-Measure-Analyze-Improve-Control) as concepts of fact-based improvement are still applicable, but not in typical linear form. Improvements in software development are similar to improving the innovation process and are also best accomplished by a more free-wheeling, open collaboration approach. Some of the methodologies and practices include voice of the market, constant communication, use of integrated software development teams, visualization and information sharing, morphological and matrix analysis, Teoriya Resheniya Izobreatatelskikh Zadatch (*TRIZ, Russian for Theory of Inventive Problem Solving*) techniques, risk and worth factor analysis, modeling, and the like. A combination of process standardization, requirements standardization, bug and Bugzilla root cause analysis, the right corrective actions, and frequent formal hardware or software integration updates goes a long way toward improving software development.

GLOBAL COMMERCIALIZATION

Many elements of product global commercialization are an afterthought with many organizations. Commercialization includes all the necessary activities that will create a smooth new product launch and a smoother postlaunch evaluation. As products reach the launch phase, organizations discover that they do not have the packaging ready; the packaging was produced with an older die cut specification; the Asian color and corrugated specifications are different from the U.S. specifications; operator manuals are not printed in all the required international languages; some of the language versions are either incomplete, misspelled, or accidently (by the choice of words) insulting to potential customers; the manuals are printed in all the correct internal languages but they do not fit into the box and have caused $84,000 in packaging damage in the international containers; the software is full of bugs and not ready for release; the service, supplies, and spare parts have not been planned and staged in distribution centers and repair depots; or the mix between domestic and international power requirements is off—the list goes on and on. These problems are not only costly but also negatively affect brand image. There are also many improvement opportunities in this area, ranging from more data and fact-based decision making, to prevention of these events with well-defined proactive subprocesses within the stage gate process. Many of these problems can be avoided by the creation of standard templates and decision matrices that are embedded in the development process. The cost of preventing these problems in the first place is much lower than the cost and lost customer goodwill of dealing with these problems after they are out there and visible.

GLOBAL SUPPLY CHAIN MANAGEMENT

SALES AND OPERATIONS PLANNING (SINGLE-PLAN CONCEPT SALES, OPERATIONS, FINANCE)

Sales and operations planning is often referred to as SOP, S&OP, or SIOP (sales, inventory, and operations planning). This key business process is the turbine of the organization because the performance in this area has far-reaching implications into other areas of the organization. The S&OP process influences all other key business processes and is one of the highest-impact opportunities for improvement. S&OP performance has a direct impact on inventory pipeline performance, product availability, customer satisfaction, and financial performance. Although there are dozens of improvement opportunities in S&OP, some of the major issues include

- *Unrealistic Planning Assumptions:* These occur when the S&OP reflects what management "wishes" it could make and sell versus what is a realistic balanced plan based on the known data and facts.
- *Overplanning or Underplanning:* Driving demand and supply plans that when planned units are extended to planned dollars are totally out of synch with operating and financial plans. This creates backlogs, lost sales and customer confidence, low on-time delivery, and poor inventory performance. Removal of excess demand at this point prevents a significant level of non-value-added activities in the manufacturing execution and supplier management areas downstream.
- *Unplanned Demand and Supply:* Although the S&OP was developed based on what sales projected it would sell, there is a mismatch of available versus needed product due to forecast error. Many sales organizations make their revenue goals every month by discounting and selling what is available, and this masks deep-rooted customer service level issues.
- *Never Right Trap:* The S&OP process requires executive leadership capable of balancing conflicting requirements. Otherwise, S&OP becomes a low-priority "damned if you do, damned if you don't" role in the organization driven by the highest authority at the moment. If the plan is too high, sales is happy, but manufacturing complains about lack of capacity, and finance complains about excess inventory. If the plan is on the money, sales complains because there is not enough "buffer stock" to sell to meet their revenue goals (and cover their forecast error). If the plan is too low, sales loses, manufacturing is happy with a build schedule well within capacity, and the company misses the operating plan, although finance is happy about inventory performance.

Forward-thinking organizations are using the Lean Six Sigma methodology to track down, Paretoize, and eliminate root causes of problems in the major pieces of their S&OP process: forecasting, demand and supply management, configuration planning and planning bill of materials (BOMs), integration of S&OP and operating plan ("one-plan" best practice), planned hedge strategies, information integrity, customer collaboration, and segmented planning practices. In addition, organizations are developing the capability of measuring S&OP performance by customer, product families, product groupings, sales territories and regions, time and seasonal factors, and new or existing products.

In a typical S&OP process, all products receive equal planning treatment and are planned once per month. A new improvement strategy in S&OP is called *segmented* or *hybrid S&OP management*—replacing a one-size-fits-all S&OP process with a segmented S&OP process that recognizes the dynamics and attributes of different discrete groups of customers, markets, and products. A cluster analysis enables the management, policy deployment, and performance of these segments in different ways with different S&OP practices, policies, and review frequencies. A segmented S&OP process keeps limited resources focused on the most critical products (the A products) versus equal treatment of all products (A, B, C, D, E products). The goal of a segmented S&OP process is to manage the segments with appropriate planning policies, keep supply and demand streams synchronized and fact-based, and micromanage the tall poles. Segmented S&OP management provides visibility into the highest priorities, enables planning by strategic groupings of products and services, measures segment-level performance, and identifies more specific and actionable root causes. Some organizations are able to monitor and peg their tall-pole S&OP performance at the territory-sales representative-individual customer location.

GLOBAL PLANNING, LOGISTICS, AND CONTROL

Global planning, logistics, and control are the execution side of planning; the S&OP is translated into global, multiplant manufacturing schedules and purchase requirements. The most common issue in this area is schedule linearity or the hockey stick effect. In many organizations, 80% of execution happens in the last week of the month or quarter. For the remainder of the month, everyone sits around blind, either biting their nails or expediting like maniacs. People also sit in suspense until the final hour of closing the books before they know if they made the plan or not. This is not a criticism of those who somehow do whatever it takes to deliver the goods each month. I relate to these folks because I have lived in their shoes: climbing stockroom fences to get needed parts out of stock, shipping product without circuit boards (and telling customer service to get to the customer before the customer opens the box), stealing common parts from kits in other manufacturing areas, rounding up and shipping computer peripherals sourced from the office area, ordering parts from a Chinese supplier without purchase authorization, and many more heroics. Remember—it is the process and the measurement systems that drive these behaviors, and it is just the way it is in many manufacturing environments.

A common mistake organizations make is assigning a single team to improve supply chain management with a one-shot improvement project. This is called "boiling the ocean," and it is ineffective. The first logical step (from an improvement perspective only) is to split planning and execution and then break these areas into smaller chunks of improvement opportunities. There are literally dozens of individual improvement initiatives in this area, such as rightsizing safety stock, schedule leveling, removing the planning factor fluff, improving inventory performance, eliminating bottlenecks, reducing back orders and backlog, implementing buyer/planners, aligning planning resources to major customers, using in-plant planning (co-location at the customer's or supplier's site), improving a premier customer's delivery performance, reducing product and packaging damage, reducing premium freight, short-interval scheduling and review practices, green/yellow/red management, buyer/planners assigned to new product development, consigned shipping strategies, visual daily and month-to-date performance dashboards, and literally dozens of other opportunities.

Actual improvement efforts in these areas have generated millions of dollars very quickly for our clients.

Supplier Development and Management

With the increased trend toward outsourcing, organizations must leverage their supply base for competitive advantage. The attributes of velocity, flexibility, perfection, responsiveness, value, and flawless execution are more dependent on global supplier networks. Supplier development and management are important because the performance of the supply chain is highly dependent on the collective performance of individual suppliers and contractors. Some benchmark studies have placed the competitive dependency due to suppliers in the total supply chain as high as 70% to 90%.

There are dozens of improvement opportunities worth millions of dollars in this area. Previously, I discussed outsourcing process improvement. Other improvement opportunities include supplier sourcing and evaluation, supplier selection based on capability, supplier quality and delivery improvement, collaborative and short-interval S&OP, spend management, targeted cost reduction and collaborative improvement programs, formal information sharing and performance dashboards, supplier certification, direct ship strategies, collaborative product development, supplier performance management, and supplier conferences.

One recurring conflict in this area is the metrics of product development versus manufacturing and procurement. New product development organizations that are measured on the basis of lowest unit price design may be motivated to select inferior suppliers with the cheapest price or select through-hole versus surface-mount technology (SMT) components due to lower cost (and not considering the larger picture). Then, the organization finds out after new product launch that the supplier or contractor of choice does not have the capacity or process capability to meet specifications. In the case of component selection, this may result in a significant amount of hidden rework, repair, and scrap with internal and external manufacturing. Purchasing is measured by PPV, which motivates them to find lower-price suppliers who may also introduce new manufacturing and design issues. The deeper and farther away these sources are from the customer, the higher the hidden costs. Most organizations have an incredible opportunity to harvest millions of dollars in improvement and competitive advantage in the area of supplier development and management.

QUALITY, COMPLIANCE, AND REGULATORY MANAGEMENT

Quality Management Systems

The issue with quality management systems is how to create a nimble, best practices quality system. Within quality systems are a variety of subsystems, such as process verification and control, inspection and test procedures, quality audits, selection and calibration of measurement equipment, standard operating procedures, International Organization for Standardization (ISO) and documentation control, supplier quality, material review board (MRB) and disposition of defective materials and products, product acceptance standards, warrantee and returns, quality laboratory operations, labeling and packaging controls, compliance and regulatory requirements, and several other duties and responsibilities. Many of these quality management systems have evolved over time and under different managers with different ideas and perceptions about how to verify and validate quality. In the case of compliance, many practices are designed around the perceived requirements to meet customer compliance and not the customer's specific compliance instructions. Many of these subprocesses are bureaucratic and inefficient or include non-value-added activities and test procedures. Many test procedures may not validate process capability and control at all; however, the choice to use them is locked in. In automotive and aerospace and defense industries, there is a reluctance to improve these subprocesses because of the lengthy and complex recertification process. In the automotive industry, for example, different customers require different production part approval processes (PPAPs). The same holds true with multiple military standards in the aerospace and defense industry. I have heard many people make comments like, "We cannot change this; it is the certified practice in our ISO manual," or "We want to avoid going through the PPAP all over." Just because a practice is ISO documented or has gone through the PPAP, it does not make it a best practice. It is only a documented and approved standard practice.

There are many opportunities in this area that provide residual value to the rest of the organization. Often, a quality management system may provide a barrier to change. The goal is to transform quality management systems into enablers of improvement by streamlining and eliminating waste in the subprocesses. Many improvement projects have been completed in areas such as reducing test and burn-in cycles, measurement system analysis, MRB and scrap reduction, elimination of incoming inspection, elimination of in-process inspection, reduction of hidden waste and cost of poor quality (COPQ), reduction in cost of compliance (e.g., Sorbane's Oxley, GMP, etc.) quality at the source, improving laboratory productivity and throughput, and many other improvements.

WARRANTY AND RETURNS

The warranty and returns area is complicated but a significant improvement opportunity for many organizations. The way that most organizations deal with warranty and returns is to allocate financial reserves to cover the cost. Does this uncover root causes? No. Does this solve the problem? No. But, this is the generally accepted financial practice of dealing with this problem. Some organizations do not even view warranty and returns as a problem or improvement opportunity but as an accepted cost of being in their business.

Another problem with warranty and returns is that these processes are weak in terms of usable feedback. Most warranty data are recorded based on nonstandardized customer comments or a technician's opinion, and many warranty and return transactions are posted with a "no problem found" comment. This type of sketchy feedback to engineering does not improve much of anything. This also makes it increasingly difficult to conduct effective root cause problem solving in this area of the business without accurate and timely data.

Like other large, key business processes, warranty and returns usually include many different improvement opportunities around specific customers, product families, a common design issue across many products, specific root causes, and so on. One method of digging to root cause data is to audit trace the individual return transactions and categorize nonstandardized data into standardized root cause categories. This can be augmented with a few phone calls to the customer to learn more about the customer's particular experience and the reason for the return. The 5-whys thinking is useful in projects such as these. Remember, we do not need to study and explain the universe. All it takes is a relevant sample that tells the story about what is going on inside the larger process with data and facts. A single improvement project in this area can easily yield millions of dollars in financial benefits. One of our clients racked up $18 million in annual savings through ten different warranty and return improvement projects.

SALES AND MARKETING

INNOVATION AND MARKET RESEARCH

With innovation, strategic improvement requires leadership and practitioner judgment in terms of how to translate the ideological qualities of Lean Six Sigma into meaningful, value-added improvements. Reducing innovation to a rigid, linear DMAIC process is a sure way to choke the idea generation and innovation process. Improving innovation is best accomplished by establishing the free-wheeling, open collaboration environment and culture for innovation. Conceptually, the evidenced-based philosophy of Lean Six Sigma is valid, but actual improvements require different means (e.g., voice of the market, constant communication, use of innovation teams, visualization and information sharing, TRIZ analysis, function deployment and other open concept evaluation methods, nonlinear mapping techniques, risk and worth factor analysis, modeling, etc.).

Organizations can benefit more from Lean Six Sigma on the execution side of innovation: How are new product ideas translated into commercialized products? There are several high-impact transactional opportunities in this area. Organizations are challenged with defining the right new products and their associated features, functions, and other specification data. A large part of these decisions is based on emotion and the gotta-have-it mindset of the sales and engineering organizations. Many are also challenged by defining new product architectures in the next 3–5 years with people stuck in the mindset of today's technology. In many cases, product definition and compromises are left up to interpretation by individuals downstream, where it becomes incrementally costly. Other weaknesses typically include the failure to analyze and directly relate the importance of product features and functions to time to market impact, additional costs, quality and reliability risks, supplier capabilities, incremental market share, and updated profit-and-loss impact. Product and market strategy can benefit greatly by having a disciplined and formal fact-driven process, standardization of product definition and evaluation activities, front-loaded risk assessment, pro forma financials and modeling, and metrics for these activities.

Another improvement opportunity involves the application of Lean Six Sigma and other data-driven analytics for ongoing processes to better understand the multiple voices of the customer. The new economy is driving the need to conduct more segmented and targeted customer analysis (e.g., size, region, sales history and trends, solution opportunities, etc.), real-time point-of-sale (POS) analysis, and other ongoing analytics that enable a better understanding of customers, customer segments, and their different requirements.

Organizations are also using Lean Six Sigma to transition from an all-things-to-all-customers business model to a more focused and targeted customer relationship management model driven by different segments with different requirements. Several independent improvement opportunities exist in this area to develop more robust customer and market analysis processes that provide additional facts about specific data-driven requirements, competitive profiles and offerings, customers and market share, drivers of customer and market loyalty, and future business opportunities. Many organizations are inundated with customer and market research data and related information, but they do not have standardized methodologies and robust processes to synthesize this information and draw the right data-driven conclusions about market and new products and services opportunities.

REQUEST FOR QUOTATIONS

One of the most interesting efforts is value stream mapping the request-for-quotation (RFQ) process. Several common findings usually surface. It should not be a surprise that 80% to 90% of the elapsed time is wait time and waste. Many organizations attempt to treat every RFQ as a unique quote and fail to use leverage from the knowledge base of previous quotes. In many situations, the confidence limit on the quote might be 60% to 70% despite 2 to 4 weeks of sales, applications, engineering, and financial analysis. When everything needs to be quoted, the RFQ backlog and lead times stretch out. By the time organizations turn around the quotation, the customer has placed a purchase order with a competitor.

Think about the power of instantaneous quotes. This saves the time of many people in the organization, and it communicates efficiency and responsiveness to the customer. The key here is reducing cycle time and improving quality through a complete redesign of the quotation process. One of our clients accomplished this by creating a series of standard attribute and features tables. The team created an order entry matrix of product and service attributes, such as material, size, color, quantity, finishes, packaging, and so on. The design was a menu-driven approach, and the new process eliminated 70% to 80% of the RFQ activity. Their order entry associates could now quote in real time, provide delivery commitments based on true available capacity, and then ask for the order. The remaining quotes went through the traditional process for deeper analysis. The benefit of this one project was millions in incremental sales and a reduction of $140,000 in non-value-added hidden costs.

PRODUCT MANAGEMENT AND RATIONALIZATION

Product management and rationalization involve a formal life cycle management process for the product portfolio. Many organizations are great at adding new products and SKU (stock-keeping unit) variations to their product portfolio, but it becomes a major emotional process of discontinuing old products from the portfolio. The sales organization wants anything it can possibly sell to remain in the portfolio and points out the risk of potential lost revenue. The problem with this thinking is that, over time, old products generate maintenance, selling, and service costs that far exceed gross margins. Furthermore, the risks are imaginary and based on sales perceptions and opinions. A fully loaded and Pareto-ordered cost analysis demonstrates that many of these products may have negative margins that subtract from total profitability. In addition, turning the organization on its head to build and ship the trivial many, short-pole SKUs dilutes its capabilities to nurture and grow the core business—the tall-pole, high-potential customer and product SKUs. Sometimes, there are rational reasons for continuing with loss leaders.

Several benchmarking studies have pointed out that over 80% of an organization's resources are focused on the trivial short-pole space of the Pareto analysis. Many organizations have the ability to grow by achieving superior value and service performance with their premier segment of customers and high-selling SKUs. There are always the emotional arguments such as, "What if this small customer grows" or "We can't sell X unless we have Y." There is a wealth of opportunity here by taking care of the legitimate exceptions and routinely rationalizing the entire product portfolio with facts rather than emotions.

Here is a good example of what happens: Executives in a specialty paper manufacturer in a shrinking industry pressured their sales organization to get whatever orders they could, no matter what they had to do. The sales organization decided to promote a mass customization strategy, allowing customers to choose the color, volume, and other product features above and beyond the standard product line. This seemed to make sense because once they landed new business, the company would be the sole supplier for repeat business. The sales organization also allowed customers to order products in much smaller lot sizes without any regard to the implications on their business model of large capital equipment and high-volume/low-mix production.

The number of SKUs increased almost overnight. Customers were attracted to their own branded choice of product, but the color, texture, and weight differences between product groups were almost unrecognizable. Although their "Burger King: Have it your way" strategy was unique in their industry, there were good reasons why the rest of the industry had not transitioned in this direction. A dilemma unfolded: The more they sold of their mass customized SKUs, the less capable manufacturing became at delivery. As always, the first reaction was to finger point and scream at manufacturing, which was already running 24/7.

A Lean Six Sigma project was kicked off to solve the problem. Four different teams came up with quick improvements in scrap and setup reduction, but not enough to fix the problem. Next, another team analyzed capacity and profit contribution analysis on the entire product line. The factory load from current and planned orders exceeded demonstrated capacity by more than 60%. The company was also manufacturing many new, lower-volume products at much higher scrap rates. In this industry, changeovers generate scrap: the more changeovers, the higher the scrap rate. They were literally *wrapping $100 bills* around each shipment. The analysis pointed out that over 90% of their revenues and profitability was derived from just 118 products. Worse yet, servicing these customers became a severe drain on their ability to take care of their premier customers and markets. So, the result was continued shrinking of revenues, canceled orders, and many more unhappy customers.

The team provided recommendations on how to reconfigure the business back into standard and custom products and pruned several other negative-margin product offerings. The standard offerings were offered at competitive prices with smaller lot quantities. The custom products were offered at premium prices. The number of SKUs was reduced by almost 36%, and the company reestablished its positive profitability position while increasing revenues from its tall-pole premier customers. There were also residual improvements from improved forecast accuracy to higher yields and reductions in premium freight. These improvement projects are interesting because they result in significant benefits and challenge people to find the right balance between mass customization and variety reduction based on true data and facts.

THE SELLING PROCESS

The selling process has been exempt from improvement initiatives because marketing and selling products and services has a higher perceived priority to some executives than that of improving how the organization markets and sells products and services. Many have not viewed sales and marketing as a process. The terms *selling* and *improvement* have been commonly viewed as two distinct and conflicting business activities. In reality, organizations are capable of selling more by improving the marketing and selling process.

One of the most effective analytical approaches in sales and marketing organizations is worth factor and value analysis. Basically, this is an inventory of how sales and marketing organizations spent their time and resources versus the value contribution to revenues. This reveals much more about the process than just concentrating on the aggregate sales numbers. Not surprisingly, sales and marketing people often spend the most time and resources on customers, prospects, market opportunities, and other activities that are non-value-added activities. We remind you again: It is not a criticism of sales and marketing; it is the process. Much of this process is driven by the emotion of "if we don't do this, we will lose the sale."

Again, this area is an emotional roller coaster; unfortunately, emotion wins over facts (because the real facts are unknown). However, when one looks at these activities and outcomes with data and facts—including the *all-in* hidden costs—there are several improvement opportunities through realignment and reprioritization of activities. The facts demonstrate that it is not always the best use of time and resources to drive out to Timbuktu in the last few days of the month to sell any short-pole product to a one-time customer at a deep discount and an unrealistic delivery commitment just to get an order. When the selling process becomes more of emptying out the warehouse by selling anything to anyone, profitability suffers. Today, hitting dollarized sales targets followed by washing-the-hands gestures are not enough.

The end of the month drives a lot of frenzied behaviors that might generate additional sales but not always the accompanying additional profits. There are significant opportunities to improve sales and marketing efforts by realigning resources and metrics on the activities that matter the most. Think about when the deepest discounts are offered. When are customers going to buy product? Customers have been well trained to wait until the end of the month to get the best deal, and in the process it creates the hockey stick (and the associated real and hidden waste) effect on manufacturing schedules. How about discounting policies that level the schedule through the month and quarter? Another fact that sales and marketing must pay attention to is technology, which is rapidly changing their role from outbound to inbound mode.

The right improvements to the selling and marketing process draw focus away from getting an order (any order) to strategic selling and landing profitable business. The analytics of improvement in this area are also applicable to other complex knowledge areas, such as research and development, materials planning and purchasing, engineering and new product development, quality management, and finance, to name a few.

ADVERTISING AND PROMOTION EFFECTIVENESS

The area of advertising and promotion effectiveness causes a high-ticket emotional cost in many organizations, especially within consumer products companies. Many organizations do not have formal processes for identifying and developing advertising strategies, designing and running promotions, and measuring the effectiveness of these efforts. Often, these activities are driven by creative emotions and perceived needs. Many people who work in this field view process and measurement as foreign concepts that do not apply to their operations. Instead, things are often done without any order, out of order, with missing information, and with many changes and rework swirls—all in the name of creativity. Sometimes, campaigns might be driven by other people, like the vice president of sales or vice president of engineering, who may have the influence and convincing opinions about knowing what is needed to promote with customers. The effectiveness of advertising and promotions is not formally measured, so organizations never know if their campaigns succeeded or met the initial objectives.

Most people do not think about the hidden costs of an ad campaign, a direct mail catalog, or a failed promotional program. Often, the analysis reveals that it requires two or three times the effort to produce and execute on a particular advertising or promotional plan, which could easily generate non-value-adding costs in the range of six or seven figures. Improvements in these areas often involve facilitating the creative process visually and with open collaboration and facts but supplementing these activities with standardization of execution processes, formal milestones, and measurement criteria. It is not about passing or failing, like it is for product quality. It is more about innovation followed by solid program management, objective feedback, learning, and knowledge development. Usually, the initial improvement projects in advertising are not about traditional cost reduction or reducing advertising budgets. Rather, these projects are about enabling organizations to accomplish *more with less*: more advertising with less resources, which is equal to more advertising and more effective advertising per dollar spent. Over time, improvements in this area may drive down advertising and promotion costs. The other side of these improvement initiatives is to develop formal processes to measure incremental revenues that are directly attributable to advertising and promotion efforts.

CUSTOMER SERVICE

Many best-in-class customer service organizations are beginning to resemble the floor on Wall Street. For others, it is a frustrating customer experience as calls are tossed around the organization, and people become increasingly frustrated with the number of transfers, automated greetings, and inconsistent information. The key to great customer service is knowledge and talent development, access to the right information, and attention to the right details that solve the customer's problem. Some of these include standardization of best practices, visual measurement and widespread awareness of call-handling volumes, call wait times, length of calls, time to solve the customer's problem, ability to solve the customer's problem on the spot, and integration of help desk processes.

Many improvements in customer service are in the quick-strike category: the use of standardized templates and checklists, standardization of processes and practices, formal buddy system and call escalation procedures, or installation of formal measurement systems. Multiple flash improvement meetings are also helpful (e.g., What types of issues are we experiencing? What needs more attention? How can we move staff around to better balance workloads? etc.). Analytics are also useful in customer service, such as understanding arrival rate and call queues for optimizing schedule coverage; workload balancing via staggered work schedules; analysis of calls by number of contacts required to solve a problem; categorization of customer services calls and complaints; call mix and performance by representative; and allocated cost of customer service by customer, product family, and type of call. Improvement projects in this area are similar to advertising: more quality customer service value at less cost per incident.

FINANCIAL MANAGEMENT

FINANCIAL CLOSE PROCESS

The monthly financial close activities are is another area that most may not associate readily with Lean Six Sigma and strategic improvement. Financial reporting and analysis are critical business and legal requirements of all enterprises. In terms of improvement, there are several common problems with the monthly reporting of financial data, such as reporting at an aggregate and consolidated level (e.g., variances), performance information after the path is cold, conflicting and confusing data relative to cause or effect, or incorrect metrics that drive the wrong behaviors and results.

From a Lean Six Sigma perspective, finance is riddled with defects, which are not viewed as defects in their processes caused by others in the organization outside finance. These defects are in the form of journal entries, trial balance adjustments, and other transactions that were not processed right the first time. Think about this: If finance had defect-free internal suppliers, it could prevent resources from being buried in the process and instantly close the books with the push of a button. Of course, this is not reality. The challenge to making financial information more improvement friendly is to simplify and improve transactional quality, reduce the cycle time of reporting, report the right metrics, and expand reporting to include activity-based and hidden cost information.

A popular improvement project in finance is to reduce the monthly close cycle and other reporting cycles. It is an interesting analysis to group and Paretoize monthly close transactions by transaction type, root cause category, source of problem (process and responsible individual), cost of transaction, and time to correct transaction. One will find that 80% of the effort, time, and cost is consumed by a small grouping of transaction types that are assignable to root causes and therefore are correctable.

Every month, it might require a dozen valuable financial resources, several other resources outside finance, and several days to chase down and correct problems that occurred throughout the month. Usually, there is no data-driven root cause analysis and therefore no corrective actions—so the process and the defects repeat themselves every month. In the mind's eye of the improvement practitioner, this is institutionalized rework. Well-paid financial resources could be put to better use than fixing everyone else's defective transactions and looking for the rest of the financial picture. Many projects in this area reveal that with the right data-driven analysis, correcting 20% of the transactional problems gets an organization 80% of the benefits. These defects are typically workmanship issues that are correctable through quick-strike improvements such as training and education, work discipline and attention to details, transaction templates and checklists, visual performance dashboards, and performance consequences for nonperformance. Many of these issues are caused by an attitude of "I don't have time, or I don't know how—and someone else will catch it anyway." The problem with this attitude is that by the time the problem is discovered, it has created a dozen other problems in the organization, and the effort and cost to fix the problem have grown exponentially. Using this analysis, it is not unusual to reduce the close process from a week to days or hours. When these hidden costs are quantified, they are unbelievable—in the neighborhood of $160,000 to millions of dollars in hidden costs, depending on the size and structure of the organization.

EXCESS AND OBSOLETE INVENTORY

The issue of excess and obsolete inventory is usually handled similarly to warranty and returns. Rather than deep diving and eliminating root causes, organizations tend to allocate reserves to cover the write-down cost of their excess or obsolete inventory. On the excess side, this practice might be paired with stock promotions and fire sales to move finished goods inventory or possible vendor returns at 20¢ on the dollar for raw materials. None of these practices fixes the problem because organizations go through these motions month after month. The hidden cost of these administrative motions is usually in the millions of dollars.

In several client situations, the root cause of excess/obsolete inventory can be pegged to continued optimistic forecasts for new products, an optimistic region's sales forecast, buyers who are under pressure to manipulate PPV, a particular customer or product family, or some other logical grouping and root cause category. The data and the right analysis always tell an interesting story. A large amount of excess or obsolete inventory is assignable to specific root causes and can therefore be reduced or eliminated. Successful projects in this area have reduced the financial reserve rate and significantly boosted profitability.

INVOICING AND COLLECTIONS

Many organizations overlook the invoicing process because the percentage of billing errors is low, and everything is fine. This is an area that often generates significant cash flow improvements. A good root cause analysis reveals several interesting conclusions in this area—conclusions that have surfaced multiple times in different client deployments:

- Customers are not proactive in communicating overbilled situations and instead sit on the total accounts payable amount due. Then, the problem is identified when it is close to the term date or past due. Overbilling creates payment delays and hundreds of thousands to millions of dollars in hidden corrective action costs and disruptions in cash flow.
- Customers are less proactive in communicating the underbilled invoicing errors because it produces a favorable PPV, which flows directly to their bottom line. Even though it is dead wrong, it also sets the wrong expectation for what customers want to pay for products and services.

Like overbilling, the result is payment delays and hundreds of thousands to millions of dollars in hidden corrective action costs and disruptions in cash flow.

- Statistically, invoicing processes create both overbilling and underbilling problems (e.g., the normal curve, where the mean discrepancy is 0). Both underbilling and overbilling require proactive audit, discovery, and resolution on the part of the organization that generates the invoice.

Improving the invoicing process requires basic analytical tools such as value stream analysis and basic data analysis. The corrective actions are usually simple quick-strike activities such as checklists and templates, cross-checking practices, and other basic controls to prevent billing errors.

REAL ESTATE AND FACILITIES MANAGEMENT

GLOBAL SPACE MANAGEMENT

The area of global space management has usually evolved piecemeal according to the requirements of the business. Again, most may not associate this readily with Lean Six Sigma and strategic improvement. Outsourcing, downsizing and consolidations, and technology are driving major changes in corporate real estate requirements, namely, a significant amount of vacant, costly space. In most cases, the total cost of real estate and space management (including support, maintenance and repair, overhead, and utilities costs) is not readily available or known. Since many of these costs are either hidden or unknown, quantifying these costs is usually received as a big surprise to executives. Sale and leaseback based on needs might reduce costs. Some organizations have changed their office philosophy from a private office mindset to a reserved "bullpen" mindset in which much less open space is available on a first-come, first-served basis, and people have their own plug-and-play, rollaway modules. There are always emotion and debates regarding space, geography, proximity to amenities or other departments, furnishings, status, physical appearance, and perceptions of change by others. Nevertheless, there are millions of dollars in opportunity for many organizations that commit data-driven and fact-based improvements in real estate management.

STRATEGIC UTILITIES, RECLAMATION, AND WASTE MANAGEMENT

Traditionally, organizations view these areas as fixed costs. When one has a true improvement mindset, there is no such thing as fixed costs. The largest reason why fixed costs remain fixed is due to lack of root cause thinking and the availability of real facts. Technology is also making it possible for organizations to translate fixed costs into variable, controllable costs.

For example, a utilities improvement team used the Lean Six Sigma methodology and tools to analyze major utilities usage and costs (e.g., electricity, fuel oil, propane, oils and lubricants, maintenance cleaning supplies, etc.) and their associated cost drivers. Within weeks, they developed many basic recommendations to reduce peak electricity costs by developing a standardized equipment startup sequence, moving selected production runs to second and third shifts, using variable heating and air conditioning practices, installing motion switches and timers in less-used areas of the plant and office, changing preventive maintance (PM) procedures, changing to a supplier-managed consigned maintenance, repairs, and operating (MRO) inventory system, and several other simple changes. Within 90 days, the team identified over $2 million in annual utilities savings. The team also created a visual awareness program that compared utility costs to dollarized pictures, such as a Cadillac Escalade, a Fleetwood recreational vehicle, a new home, a Hawaiian vacation for 15 people, and other comparisons with great visual impact.

There are unlimited opportunities in this area. Another client sold its different scrap metal filings based on weight. The client weighed its scrap on antiquated scales that were calibrated annually. One good load drop by a forklift could send these scales out of calibration. An improvement team performed gage repeatability and reproducibility (gage R&R) studies of the scales and found serious underweight problems, resulting in lost revenue from scrap vendor purchases (the scrap vendor never noticed any problem). The team developed a quick-and-simple calibration procedure and implemented a weekly calibration schedule. The monthly scrap revenues shot up by an annualized rate of $5 million.

Another client implemented a waste reduction effort on their disposal of trash and other hazardous materials. When people are unaware of their actions and mix regular trash in with hazardous waste, it takes up space in the container. Although it is not hazardous, the cost of disposal is at the hazardous waste rate. An improvement team conducted a quick 2-week study of trash flow, types of waste, and associated disposal frequencies and costs. The team implemented a new practice: Waste was characterized and segregated at the point of generation, followed by a designated, labeled container program for different types of waste. The goal was to separate and minimize regulated waste with higher disposal costs. Also implemented was a new procedure for handling and crushing corrugated and other bulk waste. This effort was more to reduce the requirements of trash pickup. The team's combined quick-strike efforts saved the organization over $170,000 per year.

HUMAN RESOURCE MANAGEMENT

Talent Acquisition and Management Process

Most may not readily associate the area of talent acquisition and management readily with Lean Six Sigma and strategic improvement. When one considers areas such as talent development, the hiring process, or benefits, the hidden costs of poor performance are massive because it has an impact on the productivity and well-being of large sections of the organization. For example, the cost of hiring and terminating the wrong manager includes hidden costs equal to 40% or more of their compensation, especially if hiring and exit bonuses are involved. Many worker's compensation claims could have been prevented through a proactive process and safety improvement. There are many improvement opportunities in organizational development and human resource management worth millions of dollars to the organization. Areas such as absenteeism, executive search, hiring and termination, education and training, succession planning and development, employee compensation and benefits, performance review processes, communication and change management, talent and career development, workplace safety, wellness initiatives, diversity planning, legal reporting and compliance, security management, and team-based work present major opportunities for fact-based analysis and improvement. These opportunities also include both direct and indirect benefits to the organization, both of which are quantifiable and measurable.

BENEFITS PACKAGE VALUE ANALYSIS

Many of our clients have conducted improvement initiatives in the area of benefits package value analysis. Using the data-driven methodology of Lean Six Sigma, an interesting exercise is to break the benefits down into elemental services and costs. It is a good idea to include the benefits provider on the improvement team, and sometimes the provider is reluctant to participate. Benefits providers bundle their packages with what they believe to be the best offerings, and organizations have grown accustomed to purchasing the entire content of the shopping cart. Employee data provide insight into the most useful offerings and the offerings not used but paid for. In many organizations, only 20% to 40% of the benefits package is used by employees, and insurance providers are very flexible with negotiating policy portfolio changes when it comes down to keeping the business.

INFORMATION TECHNOLOGY

ENTERPRISE ARCHITECTURE PROCESS IMPROVEMENT

The enterprise architecture and information technology (IT), in general, are areas that often get caught up in insatiable demands, a bombarding of questions and complaints about applications, an unending backlog of projects, the proliferation of server networks and other equipment, and large requests for additional IT expenditures. Executives complain about rising IT expenditures, yet many costs are driven by the operating choices of key business process owners external to IT. The costs of IT are usually known, but the benefits of IT can sometimes be fuzzy. Some of the areas in which Lean Six Sigma has generated substantial benefits are the areas of requirements definition and justification, IT value analysis, managing IT backlog and priorities, software development and release, user collaboration and development, IT project management, server and network uptime, and IT performance.

A good improvement opportunity lies in analyzing IT requests for enhancements and modifications. One recurring trend in this area is that when there is an

IT problem, a closer look reveals that there is really a business process problem. Often, users do not understand or are not aware of the full functionality, features, standard reports, and so on in their enterprise architecture. In addition, users often create self-serving work-arounds that add more waste and IT glitches than value to the organization. Many IT people (and the solution provider resources) are also unfamiliar with the full functionality and features of their enterprise systemsdue to its sheer scope and complexity. Many of these IT requests are generated because users have a perceived issue with the software and do not take the time to drive to root causes. It is easier to throw an IT request over the wall than it is to conduct true root cause problem solving. Although users may disagree, many of their IT requests are pure non-value-added requests—generators of more waste. If more users used the Five Whys and took the time to understand *why* they are having problems, they would find that the corrective actions often have nothing to do with the need for another IT request. Often, the problems are related to discipline, nonstandard practices and procedures, inefficient business processes, lack of applications knowledge, and data integrity—which are all correctable through continuous improvement.

IT VALUE ANALYSIS

Another useful analysis in IT is value analysis. This is the inventory of current and proposed projects quantified by objectives, benefits, resource requirements, costs, time, and risks. Usually, the IT group is stuck in a continuous overload state with everything the user community is demanding of them. It is not much different from manufacturing: When input is significantly higher than capacity, the process is constrained, and output happens at a much slower rate. Many IT organizations lack a formal management process of routinely reviewing, reprioritizing, or canceling IT projects. Worth factor and value analysis replaces the subjectivity and emotions in these decisions with quantified time, costs, risks, priorities, and dependencies. This management process is helpful in resetting priorities, expectations, and realistic deliverables—and in redirecting limited resources to execute on the most critical issues. The problem with IT is similar to the catch-22 problem with engineering organizations: There are never enough time and resources to complete all the changing requirements in the pipeline, and it is not feasible to consume all of the time and hire all the resources that are necessary to complete the changing requirements in the pipeline. So, what does the chief information officer (CIO) and his or her organization do? A great first step is optimizing the process around the true operating constraints with data and facts.

BALANCED PERFORMANCE MANAGEMENT SYSTEMS

Performance measurement system analysis represents a major opportunity across all transactional processes. Many organizations are unaware of the hidden costs associated with inadequate measurement systems, whether it is a dial indicator or a metric for a territory sales manager. These may include inadequate granularity in the metrics, emphasis on the wrong metrics, too many conflicting metrics, or metrics created by informal or overspecified measurement processes. The value of this information is often much less than the effort it takes to measure performance. As mentioned previously, the right metrics drive the right enabling behaviors to achieve the right results—and the inverse is also true. The remainder of this section provides four examples of improving performance measurement processes.

1. One organization that was overly conscious about product costs developed extremely detailed routings, BOMs, and tracking requirements in their Enterprise Resource Planning (ERP) system. An improvement team was tasked with simplifying transaction flows to increase manufacturing throughput. The team learned that operators spent more time processing completion and move transactions than in building the product. The associated costs and controls of assigning a part number, maintaining, cycle counting, and looking for many low C-level inventory items exceeded the value of the part. The accounting department rejected the team's conclusions. The hidden costs of "cost accounting" equated to fifteen full-time equivalent (FTE) people employed to process and correct accounting transactions. The accountants complained about labor and material variances that were less than the hidden $450,000 cost of processing transactions. In addition, the individual variances were incorrect because operators batch processed their transactions to save walking-around time, making one product appear to be way off standard while another required near-zero time. This is a great example of good intentions with failed results. The accounting department was trying to track labor accuracy to four decimal places and material movement to the nearest square foot.

   In short, the benefits from this project were about $600,000. Routings and tracking requirements were simplified, individual transactions were replaced by back flushing, and many items in BOMs were expensed and maintained as floor stock. Manufacturing throughput improved substantially, and the accuracy of product costs and BOMs also improved with much less overhead cost.

2. A high-tech company designed its quality system to collect detailed information about defects and root causes. Its quality system included eighty-four defect codes and hundreds of secondary root cause codes. When a defect occurred, dozens of operators across all shifts were instructed to enter the correct defect code and root cause code in the system. Quality engineers had the greatest of intentions, but their system incorporated too much discrimination. Individual operators had little consistency in repeating their own correct codes, and different operators across shifts had even less consistency in reproducing the correct codes. In a sample, even the quality engineers showed little consistency in repeating and reproducing the correct defect codes. Over time, their

quality data were contaminated by noise, and the Pareto charts set quality engineers down the wrong trail. Therefore, there was not much success in improving yields. More time was spent analyzing and presenting data than actions of improvement. An improvement team redesigned the quality system with fewer defect codes, and potential root causes were discussed in person with operators before summarizing data into categories. The team knocked down the walls prohibiting improvement. The Pareto charts began to show the true tall-pole problems, and yields were improved significantly. Within 4 months, the annualized cost of scrap and rework was reduced by over $2 million.

3. A new product development organization prided itself on getting new products released on time and at target design cost. Many engineers were rewarded for their performance. An improvement team began looking into the cost of commercialization after release (e.g., engineering change notice (ECN) activities, engineering support to manufacturing, rework and repair due to design for manufacturability problems, supplier and contractor quality and delivery performance, field quality and reliability, warranty and repair, inventory performance, lost revenue, etc., by each new product released). The team demonstrated that the root causes of these recurring inefficiencies were due to specific decisions and issues in the product development process to get the product released on time and on *their* lowest design cost targets. This project elevated many hidden product life cycle costs, and many simple changes were implemented in the product development process. The company saved millions in the commercialization and postrelease cost categories mentioned.

4. Many organizations have their performance war rooms. With one of our clients, two walls were covered with monthly performance charts on everything about the organization. These charts were also bound and distributed to operating managers throughout the company. The walls were like huge two-stereogram posters, staring long enough at the individual charts and hoping to see other images emerge. Again, a well-intentioned initiative created more confusion, emotional interpretation, intellectual debates, rationalizations, and finger pointing than improvement. A big problem with this effort is that it is difficult to differentiate causes from effects, and by the time the charts are available, the data are unactionable. One executive's favorite saying was, "What gets measured gets attention." That is true, but if an organization attempts to measure everything, it dilutes their focus and results.

An improvement team was charged with developing a better process. The team conducted several regression analyses to understand better the factors that influence top-level success. One important conclusion from these analytics is that organizations learn that they spend lots of time and effort measuring activities that are insignificant to success. The team used their new knowledge in redesigning the right set of cascading and aligning metrics based on data and facts, causes and effects.

The war room was replaced by a smaller set of critical, real-time, event-driven metrics in automated dashboard formats. Within 6 months people now had the ability to Sense-Interpret-Decide-Act-Monitor (SIDAM) on a daily basis (and with real facts) and prevent potential performance issues before they occurred. Because performance was now automated, it was easy to increase awareness through additional monitors in strategically located areas of the facility. There was much more focus, discussion, and actions on fewer measurements. What are the savings from organizational alignment? Although it is difficult to quantify the savings in these types of projects, it is millions of dollars in terms of executive and organizational time, effort, and operating results. The most important outcome of this project was performance standardization in which everyone was aligned, looking at, and responding to the same facts.

SUMMARY

Our multimillion-dollar list of opportunities is not fictional, but it does represent only a partial list based on our experiences. There is an endless list of opportunities for improvement in organizations, including those that we do not know about and are yet to be discovered. In addition, these improvement opportunities are highly complex and not for the rookie improvement resource. The organizations represented in these case studies are atypical—particularly in their acceptance of improvement as a competitive weapon, their creativity and innovation in flushing out new opportunities, their bench strength and depth of improvement talent, and their enlightened leadership and follow-through every day. Improvement has evolved to a standard of excellence in the way people think, act, and work together. These organizations are the beneficiaries of improving how they improve in the form of superior performance.

The purpose of sharing these cases is to encourage a new beginning to improvement for many different types of organizations that are either just beginning their journey or need a helpful jump start. These opportunities are common in organizations, but they are not being cultivated and turned into new successes. Improvement is a choice, and there are no shortcuts, only excuses. The book provides the proven path for organizing, identifying, accelerating, harvesting, and sustaining these opportunities. Moving off the dime requires enlightened leadership and commitment, and the rest of the improvement journey falls into place.

BIBLIOGRAPHY

The Center for Excellence in Operations, Inc. (CEO). 2011. Improving the outsourcing process. *Breakthrough! Newsletter.* http://ceobreakthrough.com/pdf_files/Breakthrough1005.pdf.
Gordon, S. 2008. *Supplier Evaluation and Performance Excellence: A Guide to Meaningful Metrics and Successful Results.* Ross, Ft. Lauderdale, FL.

10 Strategic Improvement in Hospitals

INTRODUCTION

Hospitals are a special place where God's work is carried out. Patients arrive with a medical problem; they are diagnosed and treated by superstaffs of physicians, nurses, other clinicians, and those in laboratory support resources. They are given levels of care, encouragement, hope, and meaningful and emotional connections. Ideally, they leave the hospital with their problems cured. For anyone who has spent time in a hospital with a life-threatening problem, it is difficult to place a value on that particular superior patient experience and its related costs, especially when the majority of the cost is covered by medical insurance. Unfortunately, many new forces, like changes in reimbursement formulas, changing demographics, and a longer-living and more health conscious society, are disrupting the conventional healthcare model.

The cost of the U.S. healthcare system has reached a critical point and is beginning to have a negative effect on the whole U.S. economy. A report by the Council on Foreign Relations states that some economists say that ballooning healthcare costs place a heavy burden on companies doing business in the United States and can put them at a substantial competitive disadvantage in the international marketplace. Further, a 2010 study commissioned by the Commonwealth Fund found that the United States ranks last of seven nations overall in health system performance, confirming earlier reports from 2004 to 2007. In this study, the United States ranked last on indicators of patient safety, efficiency, and quality. At the same time, the United States spends more than twice the total per capita expenditures of the seven other industrialized nations studied, accounting for 16% of gross domestic product (GDP) (vs. 8% in the United Kingdom). Americans pay 50% more out of pocket than citizens from most other nations.

THE STARVING BEAST

Over the past several decades, healthcare expenditures have risen at a rate significantly higher than the overall growth of the GDP. This has been good news for those organizations and individuals on the other side of the cost equation (i.e., revenue). Every dollar of cost is someone's dollar of revenue, and much of that revenue is paid to healthcare delivery organizations such as hospitals, physicians, and other health service providers. It appears that the time has come to curtail the revenue flow and to begin to "starve the beast." This is a radical shift in that in the past, additional revenue was always found to meet the beast's demands.

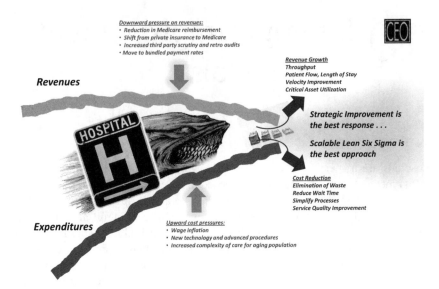

FIGURE 10.1 The healthcare dilemma: "the starving beast." (Copyright 2011 by The Center for Excellence in Operations, Inc. [CEO].)

Figure 10.1 provides a visual overview of the healthcare dilemma. In this analogy, continuing to feed the beast by traditional approaches will only add to its inefficient behaviors. Think about the simple market dynamics at play: a reduction in reimbursements, excess non-revenue-producing capacity, cannibalization of markets, consolidations - it all spells disaster!

More focused tactics are now being implemented by employers, commercial insurance companies, consumers, and state and federal governments to reduce the feed in the trough. How must the beast respond to the reduced flow of revenue? Some hospitals are downsizing, while others are in the midst of legal action with their state government over cuts in reimbursement. Both of these approaches are not sustainable in terms of addressing the deep strategic and structural issues. What is needed is a different operating model driven by strategic improvement. Lean Six Sigma is the most powerful enabler of creating this controlled, systematic innovation needed in hospital operating environments.

There are two basic, nonmutually exclusive responses that are plausible: consolidation and contraction and real operational improvement. In the past, some consolidation has occurred, but for the most part the second part of the dynamic, contraction, has not occurred. Initially, the combined entities simply were added together with no reduction in operational costs, and over time the costs and revenues of the combined entities showed an upward trajectory. This was partially due to the larger entity commanding more market share and control. Some health systems in some markets become "too big to fail," forcing payers to succumb to the increased revenue/cost demands or face dealing with an underserved public. This dynamic took the pressure off the health systems to become serious about process improvement and efficiency. This is no longer possible or sensible.

Given the economic climate in the United States today, available revenues to fund healthcare will be reduced. The time has come for healthcare to employ successful private industry approaches to improvement such as Lean and Six Sigma that have enabled American corporations to be competitive in a global economy. In a nutshell, Lean eliminates non-value-added activities and basic waste that is associated with patient flow, length of stay, wait times, and critical asset utilization. Six Sigma is a more surgical, peel-back-the-onion approach to improvement and focuses on understanding and eliminating deep and often unknown root causes of variation in operational, financial, clinical, laboratory, and administrative processes that improve the patient experience. There are significant overlaps in the improvement methodologies and tools, and both disciplines eliminate waste, improve quality of service delivery, reduce operating costs, increase revenue opportunities, and maximize patient-centered care—hence, the name Lean Six Sigma.

POSTPONING THE OBVIOUS

Healthcare leaders have resisted serious Lean Six Sigma for various reasons, including

- "Industrial process improvement techniques do not apply to service organizations and certainly not healthcare providers."
- "Improvement is less important than patient care services, so it is impossible to get people together to meet and work on improvement."
- "We don't have time and resources to improve and do our regular jobs."
- "We cannot stop what we are doing like other organizations—this would be like changing tires on a moving automobile."

These excuses no longer hold water. Many organizations have learned the painful lesson that the risk of doing nothing is much higher than the risk of improvement. To do nothing but "stay the course" is a path to sure disaster and a clear lack of leadership. Those healthcare leaders who choose this path are inviting continued decline in their organizations to a point at which a turnaround consultant is required to clean up the mess. Unfortunately, this will result in sacrificing the organization's mission for the sake of survival. The only way out of the present healthcare dilemma is through strategic improvement. When executives look at the real facts, improvement is a "low-risk, win-win" value proposition when structured, planned, and executed correctly. It is time to morph the beasts into heroes of healthcare.

REINVENTING HOSPITALS WITH LEAN SIX SIGMA

Lean Six Sigma has made its initial inroads in many healthcare institutions. This is a positive trend because the power of Lean Six Sigma is just what the doctor ordered. Hundreds of hospitals are either evaluating or have begun their Lean Six Sigma journey in hopes of adapting the methodologies to improve their financial challenges. A few hospitals have jumped in with a bold strategy to create a new, more efficient operating model; however, for the most part the initial movement closely resembles the same slow-burn, "tools-based" introduction of Lean Six Sigma in private industry decades ago. There is absolutely no question that a successful Lean Six Sigma initiative can begin a major operating transformation in a hospital that quickly sets the institution apart competitively from other hospitals. Further, the need to move in this direction is being fueled by the coming change in how services will be paid. Currently, most services are paid based on volume. In the future, bundled payments will be predicated on the value of services provided. This move from "volume to value" will drive the dual goals of improving the quality of care delivered and maximizing the efficient use of resources.

Hospital leaders are interested in Lean Six Sigma because it is the right thing to do. However, many of these leaders are missing the critical implementation details that are arrived at through the business diagnostic, improvement strategy and vision, and deployment plan. Many are opting for a slow, casual Lean Six Sigma effort that the hospital will implement over the next 3–5 years due to the present economy and budgetary constraints. Leadership may make mention of Lean Six Sigma in a hospital newsletter and then delegate the kickoff to a quality or organizational development group charged with beginning the process. The typical deployment begins by picking a few random areas and training a small number of people at minimum cost. The entire focus of the training is on the methodology and tools of Lean Six Sigma. The hospital's initial thinking is to go slow, get its feet wet with the Lean Six Sigma concepts, and not be too worried about any initial results. There is the expectation that people will figure out the details as they get deeper into Lean Six Sigma. These efforts produce trivial results, like designing a kanban system for replenishing coffee creamer on the inpatient floor, "5S"ing and labeling the universe, or some other demonstration that is irrelevant to the hospital's strategic challenges. When others observe these trivial pursuit improvements, they lose interest fast. Beginning the journey of improvement because it is the right thing to do is visionless and carries with it a high risk of failure. This is beginning to look like the common entree into Lean Six Sigma in hospitals, and it is not proactive and aggressive enough to make the differences needed in operating performance.

The objective and challenge for hospitals is to design the right departure plan on their improvement journey. The *slow-and-easy* strategy is not a criticism but a familiar experience of all organizations evaluating how they should initially approach improvement. This strategy is most prevalent when an organization has not made the connection between Lean Six Sigma or improvement at the conceptual 50,000-foot level and how to deploy and execute within the complexities and uniqueness of their particular operating environments. Leadership cannot commit emotionally and financially to an initiative with lots of unknowns, risks, and questionable benefits. When people are feeling like "This all sounds great, but we do not assemble automobiles; we save lives," they are not ready to begin the journey successfully. Another way of stating this is that the organization has not taken itself through the formal infrastructure building of Strategic Leadership and Vision, Deployment Planning, and Execution. The result is a large hazy abyss in strategic focus, knowledge, experience, and understanding about how to adapt improvement in the organization, so there are a lot of unknowns and perceived risks and decisions to err on the side of opinionated conservatism. It has been our firm's experience that even within a single hospital, there are many perspectives and characterizations about Lean Six Sigma and even more as one dives deeper into the specifics of waste and value added. In the beginning, there are sharp contrasts between the concepts of improvement and the institutionalized practices of how things are done—and the respective resistance to change. Most organizations need the help of an outside improvement expert to get them through this complex, logical process and prepared for a successful journey that is not radical by any means. In the present economy, organizations are reluctant to pull in external resources to hold the line on costs, and they make the best of their effort internally. Nevertheless, a successful journey must begin with a clarified and embraceable vision of improvement and a solid plan to mitigate or eliminate risk. When organizations remain in this hazy abyss and fail to begin developing their core competency of Improvement Excellence™, the "hard" lost opportunity costs are in the millions of dollars. For some organizations, it is the difference between survival and extinction.

The problem with the slow-and-easy approach has been covered thoroughly throughout the book, in particular at the end of Chapter 3. For hospitals, this approach makes a trifling impact on bending their cost curves at all, never mind swiftly enough. Given the current economic state of hospitals, a bolder accelerated Lean Six Sigma deployment is the right starting point.

ENLIGHTENING HOSPITAL LEADERSHIP

For hospitals, strategic and sustainable improvement is first a surgical procedure on leadership and culture. Candor is an important part of change, and this surgical procedure is one that works best with an external improvement specialist. Some articles about improvement make harsh claims that leadership in hospitals is poor and ill prepared to take on the transformation challenge. The reality of it is that the executive behaviors, decisions, and actions in hospitals are greatly influenced by the past operating model, environment, and measurement systems.

Hospitals have typically been a flagship employer in the community. The healthcare industry has made great strides in technical medical advancements over the years, but it has required double-digit increases in cost to get there. The traditional approach to healthcare has always focused overwhelmingly on the search for cures, with much less emphasis on developing the best processes of patient-centered care. U.S. healthcare costs are the highest in the world, while overall service quality is on par or marginally better. A closer look at the typical hospital model reveals the following facts:

- Service quality and patient care are provided with both value-added and non-value-added activities. From the patient's perspective, a significant amount of time is spent waiting for care. These types of non-value-added activities are hidden and institutionalized as the industry norm, and these costs represent as much as 20¢ to 30¢ of every revenue dollar collected. The cost reduction implications, to say nothing about the customer service improvement, are in the millions of dollars for most hospitals.
- Hospitals are far behind other industries in the area of strategic and sustainable improvement. This includes process improvements that streamline patient flow, increase revenue-producing capacity and throughput, maximize the utilization of key equipment, and eliminate other wastes. This also requires information technology to automate and enable best practices in all of these areas. The concepts of improvement are readily adaptable to hospitals, and the implementation process can be structured with minimal risk. Improvement also brings with it a reduction in complexity and more predictable, controllable, and manageable processes—and accountability for results. Forward-thinking institutions have proven beyond a reasonable doubt that a well-structured and executed Lean Six Sigma initiative can generate benefits equivalent to millions of dollars.
- Since many hospitals are nonprofit, mission-driven enterprises, their leadership can be very similar to leadership in government agencies. Historically, hospitals have not rationalized the rising costs because they have always been able to fund their operations through third-party payments, and most hospitals manage to operate with positive financial reserves for future investments. Since the funding has always been there, it provides little incentive to improve or reduce operating costs. However, with the change in payment moving from volume to value, that is likely to change. As unpopular as this statement may be, the internal politics and inefficiencies in many hospitals have grown to a staggering point. Doctors know it, nurses know it, supply chain directors know it, and everyone else knows it by working with (or around) these inefficiencies on a day-to-day basis. A few improvement pioneers know it firsthand by the millions of dollars in newly discovered revenues and cost reductions their hospitals have harvested.

The largest challenge of Lean Six Sigma in hospitals is changing leadership thinking. Chapter 4 covered the topic and process of enlightened leadership. Most hospitals are currently in the midst of this natural struggle, trying desperately to make the same thinking that got them here carry them through the new challenges of their industry. Hospitals have been on the life support of reimbursement while institutionalizing waste for too long. This is not a criticism of hospital executives as individuals but recognition of their historical operating environment and performance and reward systems. Basic economics is forcing hospitals to think beyond the box and reinvent themselves. Emerging technology is pushing the envelope even further.

How are many hospitals responding? There is the typical downsizing, spending freezes, and litigation against agencies that have reduced reimbursements. Win or lose, where will the money come from? Federal and state government finances are in shambles. It will come from people who already cannot afford insurance or to pay their medical bills. Mandating people to pay for something that they already cannot afford is not the answer. Does this cycle lead to success for hospitals? The answer is no; it leads to greater failures for hospitals and for the healthcare system in general. Strategic improvement can only become an enabler of success if hospital executives transform themselves into enlightened leaders. As mentioned, it usually requires external mentoring to help executives to see their environment and new possibilities in a different light.

RECKONING IMPROVES THE JOURNEY

I mentioned that the internal politics and inefficiencies in many hospitals are staggering. Now, it is time to look at the silver lining. The opportunities for improvement are also staggering. Hospitals are in a great position in terms of adapting Lean Six Sigma and other improvement initiatives. The entire healthcare industry is not much different from the automotive industry in terms of reinventing itself. In the 1950s through the 1960s, Detroit was an oligopoly. There was a handful of auto manufacturers that dominated the market and did not need to pay much attention to customer requirements, quality, and costs. In those days, the Big Three generated enormous profits. There was still plenty left over to pay for grossly inflated union wages and benefits. All of these organizations had the strong "car company" cultures and rarely hired anyone from outside their industry. It was a great run for the U.S. auto industry. The oil embargo in 1973 and the invasion of the Japanese auto industry in the 1980s forced many radical changes to their business model. Since the mid-2000s, the auto industry has undergone another successful transformation; Ford, GM, and Chrysler are all emerging profitably. The successful transformations of these organizations and many other industry transformations are more about reckoning and enlightened leadership than anything else.

Healthcare faces its own need to reinvent itself and transform the industry. For hospitals, reckoning is the prerequisite of enlightened leadership. Most hospitals find themselves staring at an extremely unpleasant and disastrous future. The population is shifting from private insurance to Medicare, and at the same time, Medicare is reducing reimbursement. Hospitals deal with a complete venue of federal, state, and third-party regulatory and compliance requirements. Many of these requirements are redundant, conflicting, or just different enough to create non-value-added work. There is the outside interest to expand requirements because that translates into an increase in job security for the regulatory agency (but additional cost of compliance for the hospital). Then, there are the normal wage inflation, rising operating costs, technology investment, and many other complex challenges.

When someone outside the industry looks at the organization chart, what does the person see? As mentioned, hospitals are organized into functional silos with an underlying administrator-physician divide. However, there is something unique with hospital organization charts. Although the boxes, the names, and the lines are present, the underlying lines of authority and responsibility are very different. Under the chart are relationship-driven processes based on individualism and trust. Power and authority are not straightforward and relative to the positions of the boxes and lines, like organization charts from other industries. People with the most influence may not even show up on the highest-level organization chart. Since hospitals deal with patients and saving lives, the culture is very conservative, parochial, and risk averse for justifiable reasons. This cultural characteristic is carried over into the hospital's executive and administrative functions and reinforced by the continuous availability of funding in the past. We could go on and on with this discussion about the uniqueness and complexities of hospitals. None of this discussion is a criticism; these facts must be integrated into how hospitals *improve how they improve*. These issues are very different from the auto industry, except for one common fact. The purpose of this discussion is to recognize that these issues have a significant impact on the success of Lean Six Sigma or other strategic improvement initiatives. The approach of Lean Six Sigma in hospitals must be tailored to these specific operating and cultural facts. Even from hospital to hospital, there are no uniform improvement strategies, implementation plans, or standard procedures for bringing people together.

Reckoning is the process of dealing with the uniqueness, complexities, and economic challenges head on. Hospitals are facing their own doom and gloom, but it is not the end of the world. Improvement is a choice, and it is a controllable response. On the surface, the realities of a typical hospital environment appear to the uninitiated to be good reasons why "Lean Six Sigma stuff from industry" is not applicable. The most frequent words that I have heard throughout my career are "We're different." As one moves from organizations in the same industry, there is always the "We're different" in the beginning. There is some truth to this term, but there are more unexplained similarities than differences. "We're different" is a customary barrier thrown out there by people who do not understand the why, what, where, when, and how of improvement. They are missing a relatable vision of improvement that is derived from enlightened leadership. This is a normal step in the improvement strategy and deployment process. Quite honestly, no one understands this in actionable implementation detail in the beginning of a Lean Six Sigma deployment. It is the job of the outside improvement expert to cut through this barrier and help the organization develop a credible improvement strategy and deployment plan. Taking the time to incorporate these details up front increases the potential success because it removes the unknowns, barriers, and risks of Lean Six Sigma. The diagnostic also turns on enlightened leadership by creating a shared executive vision of possibilities and by increasing the recognition of the need to change. Enlightened leadership is most often spurred by external influences that challenge the "as-is" outside any political consequences, provide a different perspective and reference points, and present logical fact-based options for change. These are the little details that help organizations rediscover themselves and transform culture.

THINKING PROCESS, NOT SILOS

Hospitals are organized into supersilos of structured functional specialties with very deep knowledge and expertise about each specialty. Clinical staffs and other employees operate with the best of intentions within their own functions, while executing actions that may compete, disrupt, undermine, or create work-arounds in other functional areas. These silos are reinforced by the requirements of regulatory agencies. However, patient care is delivered through a cross-functional logistics process of these specialties (Figure 10.2). Most hospital employees are most concerned with their own specialty area and are not accustomed to thinking across the larger process of patient care. Process thinking is not as obvious as a "cookie-cutter" manufacturing process because the patient care process is unpredictable, complex, and often nonrepetitive. The concepts of waste and non-value-added activity are adaptable to the hospital operating model. Accordingly, improvement opportunities in hospitals exist vertically (functional), horizontally (process), and laterally (cross-functional and at multiple organizational levels). The risk of a silo view is that it may produce small local improvements in one area that are often offset by new inefficiencies in other areas of the broader process.

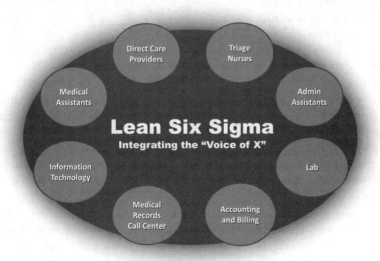

FIGURE 10.2 Engaging the voice of X. (Copyright 2011 by The Center for Excellence in Operations, Inc. [CEO].)

The largest improvement opportunities exist in the horizontal and lateral space and require a broader end-to-end process perspective of improvement and a cross-functional approach.

There is another serious process malfunction in the healthcare industry that is worth mention: Hospitals are inundated by federal, state, and third-party regulatory and compliance requirements. This is not a showstopper to strategic improvement, but it represents even more opportunities for improvement. Many regulatory requirements are redundant, conflicting, or just different enough to create non-value-added work. A hospital's visible and hidden cost of compliance can be millions of dollars. Some compliance and regulatory requirements resemble software development written by individuals who do not understand and have never performed the day-to-day work. In some cases, a lot of work is expended to audit things that have no influence on patient care or other mission-critical activities.

The larger problem is that quality cannot be "inspected or audited" into any process, and this has been proven in private industry since the 1980s. In hospitals, the inspection and auditing approach continues to be done by measuring input activities, such as adhering to clinical standards for screening procedures and reporting blatant adverse outcome. The weakness of compliance and regulatory systems lies in the detection and interpretation of a problem after the root cause path is cold. The typical audit checklist approach lacks the analytics of deep diving for root causes and measuring the relative influence of various process factors on the spot. Conclusions are often left up to the judgment and discretion of the auditor.

With the evolution of Lean Six Sigma, it has been proven statistically repeatedly that inspecting quality into a process is about 85% effective on a good day. Inspection makes a process 85% good and 15% bad. The only way to improve a process through inspection is through a costly strategy called redundancy or inspecting the inspector's results. In our example, doubling the cost of inspection or auditing will achieve a 85% + 0(.85)(0.15) or 97.75% level of process quality. Another layer of redundancy and cost will achieve a 99.67% level of quality. Is this good enough? The answer is no. When we factor in the normal 1.5σ shift in all processes, we are back to the 93% level of quality after tripling the cost of compliance. After all of that expenditure and hard inspection and auditing work, we have improved process quality from 2.25σ to 3σ or from about 85% to 93%. Each incremental investment in inspection and auditing will yield an increasingly smaller gain in quality. Most people do not think in terms of 6σ, but the inspection and auditing approach to quality becomes a costly game of diminishing returns. For industries outside healthcare, the "process police" approach to quality is long outdated. Now ask yourself: Is this approach worth the billions of dollars the healthcare industry spends on compliance?

The preferred industry standard for achieving quality is through prevention. This is the full empowerment and talent development of people who do the daily work. Quality is deliberately built into the robust design of the process up front, whether it is patient care or making a Starbucks frappuccino.* Within Lean Six Sigma, there is a relentless focus on a metric called process capability, and the theoretical goal is to drive process quality to a 6σ level (3.4 defects per million opportunities). Quality is managed at the source in real time, with clear expectations and visible performance. Defects and process variation are proactively eliminated through process analysis, redesign, and improvement. People are empowered to stop the process and eliminate root causes, so they do not have to keep dealing with the same problems repeatedly. This is a difficult concept to get through to people, even with rock-solid financial data: The cost of doing the right things right the first time is much less than the cost of doing things over. Hospitals are no different from other organizations—there is never enough time to do the right things right the first time, but they can always find the time to do things over. Preventive-based quality systems still require skip-level audits and corrective actions but at a much smaller scale of magnitude and cost. The bottom line is that preventive-based systems achieve higher quality at lower costs.

Compliance and regulations have evolved because hospitals operate in a mode that statistical engineers refer to as "out-of-control" processes. Statistically, a process is out of control when its inputs, outputs, and specific work steps are unpredictable and not well understood. The characteristics of out-of-control processes include wide shifts in performance, unknown or unexplainable inefficiencies, unplanned disruptions, work-arounds, poor output quality, schedule changes, wait times, or corrective actions based on opinions and perceptions. Much of this variation comes from nonstandard work and a lack of process thinking, which is also prevalent in hospitals. The point here is that hospitals or regulatory agencies cannot arbitrarily eliminate compliance requirements; they must improve processes so significantly that there is justification for lesser levels of compliance. There is a proven option to the cost of compliance called process excellence. In Lean Six Sigma terms, this means driving up the capability of processes toward the 6σ level. This is the point at which hospitals can justify consistent process quality on their own, and regulatory agencies are adding more waste than value-added activity. Lean Six Sigma initiatives can address these issues and result in significant progress.

One of the attributes of preventive-based quality systems is that individuals are intelligent enough to measure and improve their own quality or escalate quality issues without any consequences. These organizations recognize that problems are caused by the capability of processes, not people—and this is the essence of the Toyota Production System. Higher, prevention-based quality at significantly reduced cost becomes very doable with large-scale strategic improvement initiatives. Aerospace and defense, pharmaceutical, and medical equipment corporations have made significant improvements in simplifying their regulatory and compliance requirements while improving the quality of their products and services. It is time for the healthcare industry to follow in their footsteps. We

---

* Frappuccino is a registered trademarked line of blended frozen beverages sold by Starbucks Corporation.

recognize the strong barriers and resistance from agencies and organizations that make their living in the "quality inspection" business, but many other industries have reduced their cost of compliance. A final thought here is that regulatory and compliance issues are not an excuse to postpone improvement but all the more reason to accelerate improvement.

THE VALUE PROPOSITION OF LEAN SIX SIGMA

At a high level, every organization, including hospitals, has within it the Eight Wastes:

1. *Defects:* Wrong or missing information, out-of-date medicine and supplies, incorrect prescription or dose, repeated or incorrect procedures, preventable death
2. *Overproduction:* Purchasing excess supplies, creating constraints and bottlenecks in throughput by patients in process, scheduling a surgical procedure without knowing availability or capacity, performing activities in excess or too soon
3. *Wait Time:* Having idle time, waiting for signatures, waiting to move patients, waiting for available equipment, waiting for an x-ray, waiting for clinician availability, waiting for surgery, waiting for an inpatient room, waiting for a meeting
4. *Transportation and Movement:* Unnecessary movement and patient flow; unnecessary movement of or unknown location of equipment, materials, and supplies
5. *Extra Processing:* Using work-arounds, doing things over because they were not done right the first time, making exceptions to standard practices, working to make up for the inefficiencies introduced by other people and functions
6. *Inventory:* Excess materials, supplies, equipment that take up space and create other wastes; obsolete or dated stock, allowing materials, equipment, and supplies to be managed outside the supply chain function
7. *Motion:* Activities and tasks in the normal process or practices that do not add value to patient care or other operating needs
8. *Unused Human Talent:* Not fully utilizing the knowledge and skills of the frontline clinicians and other people who have great insights about waste and non-value-added work

These wastes are universal in every organization from General Motors to the local pizza shop. Most people do not realize it, but when these wastes are documented and quantified, they usually represent as much as 25% to 30% of the hospital's capacity and operating costs. This is a great starting point for building the business case and establishing the priorities for Lean Six Sigma. The business diagnostic described in Chapter 4 provides a useful guide for hospitals to work through their reckoning process and identify opportunities, quantify potential benefits, fully understand the driving and restraining forces of change, and develop a hospital-specific implementation plan for Lean Six Sigma.

DEFINING AND QUANTIFYING THE ENTITLED BENEFITS

One of the purposes of the business diagnostic is to define and quantify better the anticipated benefits of Lean Six Sigma. Every executive deserves (and must demand) to see the hard evidence of potential benefits and how best to mitigate the risks of implementation. Without a solid business diagnostic, the risks of Lean Six Sigma are high, and the benefits are questionable at best. No executive should commit resources and funds to Lean Six Sigma because of GE's or another hospital's successes or because it is the right thing to do. Lean Six Sigma is not about what happened somewhere else; it is about what you and your organization are about to accomplish. This is the right mindset for successful improvement.

The word *entitlement* usually conjures up negative perceptions, but in terms of improvement it works well. Entitled benefits are the expected rewards for a successful strategic improvement initiative such as Lean Six Sigma. There is no such thing as a well-planned and executed improvement initiative that has high risks and questionable results. Essentially, this entitled benefits process begins by defining and quantifying a particular problem in terms of quality, cycle time, cost, throughput, or some other key metric. Sometimes, benefits are expressed in larger terms such as length of stay, incremental revenue from additional capacity, or capital or cost avoidance by doing more (of what was planned and in the works) with less. For example, we are trying to answer the question, "How is this process or practice having an impact on the hospital in terms of lost revenue opportunity, length of stay, emergency room or operating room throughput, idle capital and assets, turnaround, process quality, patient care, total patient experience, additional capital requirements, or direct operating costs?" This occurs at a particular process level with a good understanding of the current practices and measure of baseline performance. Engaging the right people up front strengthens this process because they live with the wastes and inefficiencies where they work. Another purpose of the quick diagnostic is to better understand and size up the magnitude, root causes, and priorities for reducing or eliminating waste. The other part of this analysis is to understand and determine how best to deal head on with the barriers and detractors to improvement. The next part of the diagnostic is to develop improvement goals based on hard evidence and facts. These improvement goals should incorporate a balance between stretch goals but believably achievable goals with the right efforts. The difference between current performance and the improvement goals is the benefit. This becomes a logical process of translating the anticipated delta in performance into a financial savings. This process requires assumptions and interpolations but is always validated by the financial organization for authenticity. It is difficult to summarize this process into a simple template; the process is more complex, and the data and assumptions vary from hospital to hospital.

I mentioned that for some hospital Lean Six Sigma pioneers, the level of waste and non-value-added work was estimated to be 20¢ to 30¢ of every revenue dollar collected. Others have estimated hidden waste to be as much as 25% to 30% of a hospital's total capacity. In a previous chapter, I also used a demonstrated improvement benchmark of 3% to 10% of revenues. From a Lean Six Sigma perspective, this represents an aggregate performance level of 2σ to 2.25σ. Consider a hospital with $300 million in revenues running at a 5% reserve rate as our fictitious example. Also consider that the improvements are based on real Lean Six Sigma implementations. Think about the implications for improvement:

- The potential incremental revenue opportunities are an additional $75 million to $90 million by improving throughput and capacity utilization.
- Realistic cost reduction opportunities are in the neighborhood of $9 million to $30 million annually.
- The $15 million reserve can be increased by at least $12 million to $25 million by the combination of incremental revenues and cost reduction; this covers much of the shrinking reimbursement ground.

Plug your own numbers into these assumptions. Is this not enough interest to look under the hood, conduct a formal and impartial business diagnostic, and quantify the specific opportunities and entitled benefits? It is not as far-fetched as it seems to generate a 10X, 50X, or 100X annualized return on a well-structured and well-executed improvement initiative. One of the humbling moments prior to enlightened leadership is the fact that organizations cannot do everything on their own. Strategic improvement is a legitimate core competency that is missing in most organizations. Otherwise, more of these 10X, 50X, or 100X Lean Six Sigma initiatives would be well under way, generating the actual benefits and solving the new challenges of the healthcare industry. There is a demonstrated return on investment (ROI) for acquiring the right core competency of improvement that leads to a well-planned and well-executed Lean Six Sigma initiative.

Is a 10X, 50X, or 100X Annualized ROI Compelling Enough?

Unlike private industry, hospitals have been somewhat immune from the need for continuous improvement. Again this is not meant to be a criticism: Patient demand combined with reimbursements and other funding have always covered investments and rising costs. As we mentioned earlier, the return on investment (ROI) from Lean Six Sigma and other hospital-wide improvement initiatives is off the charts.

Hospitals have so much in their favor when it comes to implementing Lean Six Sigma. First, they have decades of experiences from private industry about what works well and what does not work. This is an opportunity either to leverage off these experiences or to be talked into creating the same mistakes. In Deming's original book, *Out of the Crisis*, he provides advice about hiring a consultant based on a slick story and lowest cost by saying, "Anyone that engages teaching by hacks deserves to be rooked." There is a repeating theme about a "tools-based" implementation throughout the book. Although it appears to be a safer and simpler beginning, the tools-based Lean Six Sigma implementation does not stick and create a sustainable culture for improvement.

Second, when one looks at the talent pool in hospitals, there are many more high-caliber resources than in other industries. People who routinely treat patients with the highest quality of care or save people's lives will have no trouble at all at adapting the technical concepts of Lean Six Sigma to a hospital environment. Hospital leadership must provide the successful environment for Lean Six Sigma and engage these talented resources. One should recognize that intelligent leaders and managers can be individualistic, think that they know what is right, and put up a higher resistance to change without a solid compelling "show me" business case. This is fair game and underscores the importance of formal sustaining infrastructure: Strategic Leadership and Vision, Deployment Planning, and Execution. This is the largest challenge for hospitals: engaging the voice of X as shown in Figure 10.3. In this diagram, the voice of the patient is assumed. Lean Six Sigma is not about walking into a hospital and creating the typical consultant punch list of idealistic changes for management and the clinical staff. It is about developing, energizing, mentoring internal talent to understand wastes and discover their own improvement opportunities. The success of Lean Six Sigma and any other strategic improvement is highly dependent on engaging and empowering the people who are involved in their own work. This means engaging the diverse network of hospital administration, clinicians and nurses, pharmacy, supply chain and purchasing, quality and compliance, labs, medical records, support

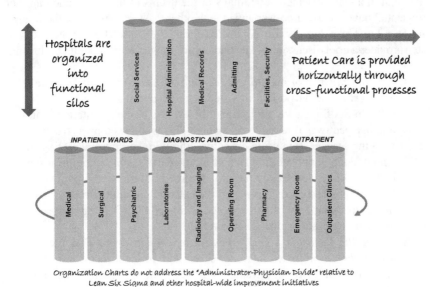

Organization Charts do not address the "Administrator-Physician Divide" relative to Lean Six Sigma and other hospital-wide improvement initiatives

FIGURE 10.3 The process of patient care. (Copyright 2011 by The Center for Excellence in Operations, Inc. [CEO].)

staff, information technology, accounting and billing, facilities and maintenance, patients, and many other groups.

Lean Six Sigma is not about improvement in one silo at the expense of another silo. It is about improving the entire systematic process of patient-centered care so everyone benefits from the changes.

Third, there is a tremendous breakaway opportunity in terms of incremental revenue and market share for hospitals that act now and improve with a bold Lean Six Sigma implementation. There is no option to improvement: The present challenges in the healthcare industry will drive enormous positive changes to patient-centered care and the hospitals' operational and financial success. Watching doom approach or implementing a slow-and-easy/high-risk Lean Six Sigma initiative is not a winning strategy. Hospitals are slowly evaluating and integrating Lean Sigma, and if everyone remains on this path, there will be little differentiation in results. Worse yet, the necessary changes will not occur in time. A very small number of hospitals are on the fast track of Lean Six Sigma and are leaving the rest of the industry in their dust. The big news in this section is that a well-structured and fact-based accelerated approach to Lean Six Sigma is the least-risk/highest-gain course of action for hospitals.

A LEAN SIX SIGMA IMPLEMENTATION PLAN FOR HOSPITALS

This section provides a work plan for beginning a large-scale strategic improvement initiative such as Lean Six Sigma. This is not a full-blown implementation but a realistic work plan for the first 90 days of the Lean Six Sigma journey. Also note that in a real implementation, many of the details of implementation are not sequential but concurrent or overlapped with other tasks. For example, the following Step 1 and Step 2 are usually completed during the elapsed time of Step 3. Each step provides a brief discussion of key underlying points and includes the following:

1. *Educate and mentor executive leadership on the basic essentials of Lean Six Sigma.* The purpose of this step is to create a shared understanding of Lean Six Sigma and understand the executive implementation issues and perspectives of large-scale change. This is followed by a structured working session, mentoring executives through their normal feelings of denial, doubt, applicability, lack of all the details, conflicting priorities, or how to fit Lean Six Sigma into an already-overloaded organization. It is acceptable for executives and the external consultant to have many questions about how best to proceed at this point; it is a big mistake to leave these questions unanswered.

2. *Create the Lean Six Sigma executive leadership team.* This includes a representative, cross-functional subset (six to eight members) of the executive administrator-physician staff, and other designated champions of strategic improvement. The external improvement practitioner is also a member of the leadership team. The overarching purpose of the executive leadership team is to create the formal sustaining infrastructure of

Lean Six Sigma. This team is responsible for the planning, deployment, and overall success of Lean Six Sigma. A secondary objective is to keep the chief executive officer (CEO) and executive team up to date on the progress and detractors of Lean Six Sigma. Initially, the team is involved extensively in the business diagnostic, Improvement Strategy and Vision, and detailed Deployment Planning activities. Further into the deployment, the team is actively involved in Execution and Sustainability.

3. *Conduct the formal business diagnostic.* The outline and specific details of the diagnostic were provided in Chapter 4. The purpose of the diagnostic is to understand the hospital's strategic challenges and adapt Lean Six Sigma to the uniqueness and complexities of a particular hospital environment. The results answer many of the open questions in Step 1 and reduce the risks of implementation. There is a distinct difference between the traditional consultant diagnostic and this process. The diagnostic is conducted collaboratively by the external improvement practitioner and internal resources. The quick diagnostic is more of a tailored implementation planning process because it engages people from the get-go. This process is also not an imposition on people but an invigorator and energizer of people. The people involved in the diagnostic and needs assessment flow through to become members of improvement teams. They provide critical inputs into the improvement strategy and vision, and their ownership of ideas and stewardship of the approach accelerates widespread acceptance.

4. *Develop the Lean Six Sigma Improvement Strategy and Vision.* The business diagnostic provides a snapshot of the as-is situation in both qualitative and quantitative terms. The Improvement Strategy and Vision (Chapter 4) provides an initial image of the "to-be" state. This is the point at which the why, what, where, when, and how of Lean Six Sigma are developed for the organization. This adaptive process continues the shared understanding of improvement in general and replaces risk with the positive emotions of employee involvement. The Improvement Strategy and Vision establishes the urgency and recognition of the need to change and creates a shared commitment and direction for improvement. The Improvement Strategy and Vision is a living process that continuously identifies new opportunities and provides answers to new questions.

5. *Develop the detailed Lean Six Sigma Deployment Plan.* The purpose of Deployment Planning (Chapter 5) is to further define, scope, and prioritize the higher-level strategy and vision of improvement down into very specifically defined, prioritized, and assignable improvement activities. Deployment Planning also includes communication and the design and delivery of customized and more detailed Lean Six Sigma education to the executive leadership team, improvement team participants, executive sponsors, process owners, and other key improvement individuals. The Deployment Plan is an evolving process and eventually

becomes the reservoir of newly identified improvement opportunities. The Deployment Plan includes the key program management instruments of Lean Six Sigma. It provides a detailed and prioritized list of well-defined improvement opportunities at a charter level of detail. This includes a problem statement, project objectives and scope, baseline performance and costs, improvement goals, quantified entitled benefits, improvement team leader and participants, fixed team meeting schedules, a detailed work plan, timetable, and defined milestone deliverables. As a starting point, it is recommended to limit this chartering activity to the initial six to twelve improvement opportunities and fill in the details of the remaining opportunities at a later date based on priorities and needs. Successful completion of these first six to twelve projects will result in valuable lessons learned and add even greater detail to Deployment, Execution, and Sustainability activities.

6. *Launch and mentor improvement teams to a rapid and successful conclusion.* This is the first accelerator of Execution (Chapter 6). The first six to twelve improvement projects provide the momentum and demonstrate the applicability of Lean Six Sigma through the initial results. Effective communication focuses all organizational eyes on these initial projects. Leveraged mentoring (Chapter 6) is critical to this rapid and low-risk success. It is critical to achieve 100% success and validated results because success attracts and breeds more success. For the undecided and doubtful, it is difficult to debate fact-based and data-driven success. These first six to twelve activities should be chosen carefully so they represent meaningful examples of improvement. It is important to avoid trivial improvement activities for which the response to success might be "So what?" Finally, it is important to showcase, publicize, and recognize the successes of the initial improvement teams.

7. *Integrate lessons learned and scale up Lean Six Sigma.* This includes working with the Lean Six Sigma executive leadership team and all other improvement teams to summarize the "what worked well" and "needs improvement" elements of the initial efforts. By this time, the Deployment Plan should also include queued up, ready-to-go improvement opportunities. This step involves a wider and bolder migration of Lean Six Sigma based on strategic needs and aligned to the operating plan. Every organization has a different threshold and capacity for improvement. Larger organizations have plentiful resources to devote full time to Lean Six Sigma. This is not necessarily an advantage. When too many people become involved in Lean Six Sigma, it often takes on a life of its own and drifts off track. Smaller organizations tend to run more lean and mean and may have a more limited capacity to improve. When the improvement level is too low, it affects the rate and magnitude of improvement and is perceived as unimportant. With the help of the outside improvement expert, the executive leadership team can make the necessary

changes in priorities and workloads and find their own sweet spot level of improvement.

8. *Implement the remaining elements of formal sustaining infrastructure.* As executives migrate Lean Six Sigma across the organization, they must build the formal infrastructure to support their efforts. Infrastructure keeps the process of improvement in control and performing at a superior level. A large part of this task involves implementing the Ten Accelerators of Lean Six Sigma. This proven methodology helps the executive leadership team manage the entire Lean Six Sigma initiative, including strategy, deployment, execution, barriers to change, talent development, and other unforeseen implementation glitches.

This is a simplified Lean Six Sigma work plan to get hospitals started on the right track. In a live consulting engagement, there is much more detail because the business diagnostic reveals much more information about the client's leadership, challenges, organization, and performance data. Conducting the diagnostic and developing the improvement strategy and vision are complicated core competencies in themselves. Most organizations do not have the internal skills, objectivity, or time to do justice to these efforts. Instead, they gloss over these important elements with an attitude of "I know what to do" or "We don't need to do this" and get their Lean Six Sigma initiatives launched down a path of high risks, low results, and questionable value. The detailed infrastructure discussions in Chapters 4, 5, and 6 provide the proven leadership, implementation planning, structure, discipline, and follow-through guidance for a successful, off-the-charts Lean Six Sigma initiative.

IMPROVEMENT IS PREVENTIVE MEDICINE, NOT LIFE SUPPORT

As the title of this section infers, Lean Six Sigma and continuous improvement in general will prevent many of the catastrophic events that lie ahead for hospitals that are currently in a "choose to wait and see" or "do nothing" mode. If these passive organizations wait until crisis arrives, they will end up attempting to implement improvement in life support mode . . . and will fail miserably at any notion of continuous and sustainable improvement . . .

Hospitals are at a disparaging crossroad with their business model. No longer is it sufficient to compare oneself to national averages as a basis for doing business. The performance of the entire industry is no longer sufficient, so being on par with the rest of the industry is unacceptable. The formula for success in healthcare has changed overnight, and the revenue sources are now in decline as these organizations attempt to cut their own costs. Hospitals are now faced with transforming themselves into lean and nimble NASCAR pit crews of patient-centered care. At the same time, they must strive for the perfect patient experience. The business model needs to shift from volume to value.

Hospitals have been hit by a tumultuous set of forces: declining revenue from reimbursements, rising double-digit costs, consolidations, and more patient choices.

The executive teams in many hospitals are at an uncomfortable leadership impasse with strategic improvement and Lean Six Sigma. Based on our experiences and benchmarking data, only a relatively few hospitals are proactively implementing Lean Six Sigma and achieving breakthrough results. These are the great hospitals of the future. Most of the industry is looking at, evaluating, learning more about, casually wetting their feet with, or postponing Lean Six Sigma due to budgetary constraints. The real facts are that most hospitals have not made a serious commitment to Lean Six Sigma or improvement in general based on their actions and progress. Refer to the enlightened leadership model: The phases include *insanity, hyperinsanity, reckoning, renewal,* and *enlightenment.* Many executives remain in the early stages of this model for too long, and this reflects the present situation with many hospital CEOs and their executive teams.

Waiting and hoping for change are not improvement strategies. Postponing improvement is like postponing a medical treatment: The longer one waits, the larger the problem grows, and the greater the sense of urgency, pain, risk, and cost to turn things around. If one waits long enough, the person might find him- or herself on life support. In hospital terms, Lean Six Sigma is preventive medicine. Strategic improvement is the leadership wellness policy that protects their organizations from the full negative forces of unpredictable events like the meltdown and slow recovery.

Recognize that the present leadership impasse is an executive choice. In tough times, executives in all industries can choose to wait or prevail, crumble or thrive on turmoil, remain stuck in the past or create the future, destroy culture or build great organizations that endure chaos, become victims of change or lead and benefit from change. Executives across many industries must find their way to the enlightened leadership stage. This is the first major milestone and the turning point at which Lean Six Sigma is destined to become a critical enabler of achieving new results beyond what everyone thought possible. With strong enlightened leadership, the rest of the journey falls logically into place.

Note: This chapter was co-authored by Terence T. Burton and Robert A. DeNoble, who has been working as an advisor to The Center for Excellence in Operations, Inc.'s (CEO's) healthcare Lean Six Sigma and continuous improvement practice. Bob DeNoble is an experienced senior healthcare executive, management consultant, and healthcare thought leader. He was one of the founding Directors of the Harvard Business School Health Industry Alumni Association and was President from 2005 to 2008.

BIBLIOGRAPHY

Arthur, J. 2011. *Lean Six Sigma for Hospitals.* McGraw-Hill, New York.
Caldwell, C., Brexler, J., and Gillem, T. 2011. *Lean Six Sigma for Healthcare: A Senior Leader Guide to Improving Cost and Throughput.* Quality Press, Milwaukee, WI.
Deming, W. Edwards. 1982. *Out of the Crisis.* MIT Center for Advanced Engineering Study. Cambridge, MA.

Graban, M. 2011. *Lean Hospitals: Improving Quality, Patient Safety, and Employee Engagement.* 2nd edition. CRC Press, Taylor & Francis Group, Boca Raton, FL.

The 2010 findings commissioned by the Commonwealth Fund on American Healthcare Competitiveness can be found at the Harvard Business School, Health Industry Alumni Association, http://www.hbshealthal umni.org/article. html?aid=508.

11 Strategic Improvement in Government

INTRODUCTION

Since the 1950s and 1960s, anyone who went to work for IBM, General Motors, Polaroid, Motorola, Xerox, General Electric, Kodak, U.S. Steel, DuPont, and many other flagship organizations was provided with, and expected, lifelong employment. The same held true in federal and state governments. Generations of families worked in these organizations. The emergence of global competition changed that scenario in private industry forever, and every organization needed to redefine and reinvent its business models to survive and remain competitive. Today, government is in a similar situation. Well-intentioned social programs that began with Franklin D. Roosevelt, Lyndon Johnson, Jimmy Carter, and other administrations have evolved and helped many recipients, but globalization is also creating the need to rethink strategic intent, adjust priorities, question continued feasibility, and reinvent the process of government and service delivery at a more affordable cost. The model of government for the past half century was to solve every problem with more programs, more funding, and more resources. Today, this model is on the brink of bankrupting generations of Americans and jeopardizing their basic freedoms if we continue on the same course. Private industry evolved by learning how to focus on core competencies and how to do more with less, and there is a dire need for government to evolve in a similar manner. Governments and other not-for-profit organizations have enjoyed the luxury of avoiding formal improvement initiatives because funding sources were always available.

Many argue the position that government is not a business, and the strategic improvement initiatives in the private sector are therefore inapplicable. Nothing could be farther from the truth. Government is a business consisting of suppliers, inputs, processes, outputs, and customers. The end product is a service, not a widget (it could be a product in the Department of Defense). When any professional leader peels back the onion of government, the leader finds customers (many different people in many different personal situations), customer and market needs, sales and marketing, advertising, physical and transactional operations, planning and budgeting, financial analysis, service delivery execution processes, physical operations, supply chains, customer service and customer satisfaction, and many other identical functions of a typical business. The problem is that in the absence of strategic improvement based on a sensible strategic vision, these functions become clogged with waste, inefficiencies, duplication of efforts, conflicting priorities and actions, entitlements, and spiraling out-of-control deficit spending.

Caveat: The contents, examples, and data provided in this chapter do not represent or promote the political values of Democrats, Republicans, the Tea Party, or any other political group. Government waste is not a partisan issue: Waste has been created by political leaders in all parties and across all agencies and functions since the 1930s, and that trend continues today. The purpose is to raise awareness and demonstrate how strategic improvement can turn our present economic situation around.

WASTE IS EVERYWHERE AND GROWING EXPONENTIALLY

Let us take a business view of government. Cash flow and net worth are negative, profits or surpluses are a rare occurrence, every agency is in the red, and the off balance sheet liabilities are so far out there that they would be disallowable by the Internal Revenue Service (IRS). In spite of the rampant spending binge, government has underinvested in human capital, technology, education, and many other basics necessary to compete in a global economy. Government is running with a net worth of "minus $44 trillion," or about "minus $143,000 per capita." Spending and net worth continue to grow in opposite directions with no end in sight. Present leadership is compounding the problem with a continued top-line *tax-and-spend* strategy. President Obama and every presidential candidate have not acknowledged a true understanding of the magnitude of this problem or committed to reduce government spending by 25% or more—enough to make an initial difference and begin turning the sinking ship around. The administration of 2012 believes that it is government's role to provide jobs and solve every other problem in our sick economy. Congress is stuck in a churn of doing nothing: all participants and all parties. Rome is burning while politicians continue to blame each other for igniting the match or debate the color of the matchbox. Congressional approval is at an all time low. No one in his or her right mind would invest in this business.

There is so much waste in government in the form of wasted costs, wasted time, and a never-ending list of non-value-adding activities that all of us tolerate on a daily basis. Waste is not a partisan issue; it is a function of poor leadership, lack of strategy, inefficient processes, no accountability, and dysfunctional performance and reward systems. Over time, these factors weave the bureaucratic, entitlement culture. The largest *waste factories* in the world are outside private industry in the public sector, and their inefficiencies touch our personal lives in a much larger sense. Here are a few examples:

- The U.S. Postal Service is bankrupt to the tune of $6 billion. For two decades, e-mail has been replacing hard-copy mail. Furthermore, it has paid billions in overpayment to pension plans. Does it not see that it will never compete with UPS and FedEx? What is it doing about its problem? Does it really think that dropping Saturday delivery or selling advertising space on the side of its trucks will solve the problem? Who is going to bail it out, and what do you think a first-class stamp will cost 10 years from now? Obama's solution is a deficit reduction package (more spending on a wasteful organization).

- The IRS spends 7.6 billion hours and $335 billion dollars on IRS compliance. There are almost 500 different tax forms and over 3 million words of instructions; the easiest form (1040EZ) has a 33-page instruction manual. All of this cost of enforcement and the wealthiest individuals and corporations pay nothing in taxes. What is the return on investment for this activity? Washington has become a megacampus of agencies with no unified purpose or strategy, working against each other, and trying to one-up, outdo, or undermine each other.

- The federal government alone employs over 2.7 million workers and hires hundreds of thousands each year to replace civil service workers who transfer to other federal government jobs, retire, or leave for other reasons. Federal government jobs can be found in every state and large metropolitan area and overseas in over 200 countries. The average annual federal worker's compensation in 2008, including pay plus benefits, was $119,982, compared to just $59,909 for the private sector according to the U.S. Bureau of Economic Analysis. It is no wonder that it costs over $425 million per hour to run the federal government.

- Buried in the Department of the Treasury's *2003 Financial Report of the United States Government* is a short section, "Unreconciled Transactions Affecting the Change in Net Position," which explains that these unreconciled transactions totaled $24.5 billion in 2003. The unreconciled transactions are funds for which auditors cannot account: The government knows that $25 billion was spent by someone, somewhere, on something, but auditors do not know *who* spent it, *where* it was spent, or on *what* it was spent. Blaming these unreconciled transactions on the failure of federal agencies to report their expenditures adequately, the report concludes that locating the money is "a priority." The unreconciled $25 billion could have funded the Department of Justice for an entire year. The unreconciled transaction problem continues.

- Prior to the midterm elections in 2011, members of Congress decided to create a super-committee to identify budget cuts. They reportedly invited hundreds of members of their entourage to the Ritz-Carlton Hotel and Resort in Phoenix, Arizona, and spent millions to begin studying the problem. Were there no conference facilities in Washington? Wonder if they were also served $16 muffins? This was another perception-creating boondoggle with no results to date. Then, the government tasked a twelve-member supercommittee, the Joint Select Committee on Deficit Reduction, to come up with $1.5 trillion in cuts while the other 523 senators and representatives sit around for several months procrastinating or working on their next election. The super-committee deadlocked on how much and where the cuts should be made, and failed miserably. This is another clear indication of failed leadership in government.

- Since 2006, the federal government has paid out more than $600 million in benefit payments to dead people. In one case, the son of a beneficiary continued receiving payments for 37 years after his father's death in 1971. The payments—totaling more than $515,000—were only discovered when the son died in 2008. The government has been aware of the problem since a 2005 inspector general's report revealed defects in the Civil Service Retirement and Disability Fund. Yet the improper payments continue because the government is unable to develop a system that can figure out which beneficiaries are still alive and which are dead.
- A recent audit revealed that between 1997 and 2003, the Defense Department purchased and then left unused approximately 270,000 commercial airline tickets at a total cost of $100 million. Even worse, the Pentagon never bothered to get a refund for these *fully refundable* tickets. The General Accountability Office (GAO) blamed a system that relied on department personnel to notify the travel office when purchased tickets went unused. Auditors also found 27,000 transactions between 2001 and 2002 in which the Pentagon paid twice for the same ticket. The department would purchase the ticket directly and then inexplicably reimburse the employee for the cost of the ticket. (In one case, an employee who allegedly made seven false claims for airline tickets professed not to have noticed that $9,700 was deposited into his or her account). These additional transactions cost taxpayers $8 million, and unfortunately the root cause path is "ice." This $108 million could have purchased seven Blackhawk helicopters, seventeen M1 Abrams tanks, or a large supply of additional body armor for U.S. troops in Afghanistan and Iraq.
- The Justice Department has filed lawsuits challenging the immigration policies of several southern border states, claiming that their state laws interfere with federal immigration responsibilities. The states have acted due to lack of federal action. How many decades have politicians allowed this problem to manifest itself with billions of dollars of spending on rhetoric but inaction? In these states, there are thousands of new crimes being committed by illegal aliens, including domestic violence, armed robberies, drug dealing, rapes, and murders. At the time of this writing, one border town was holding over 1,000 illegal aliens in jail for felony criminal behavior. Next, the American people find out by accident that our government has been providing arms to Mexico drug cartels in hopes of tracking down and eliminating their activities in the United States. What are we doing?
- Another recent fiasco was the government's handling of the BP oil spill in the Gulf of Mexico. There were 2,000 available skimmers around the world, but by day 85 of the spill, only 1% of them were working on the cleanup; the remainder were moored to the bulkhead of bureaucratic inefficiency. The Netherlands offered up their ships, but the superior European technology failed to meet U.S. Environmental Protection Agency (EPA) and environmental requirements. These vessels suck up

vast quantities of oily water, extract most of the oil, and then spit over-
board vast quantities of nearly oil-free water—a shade above the 15 PPM
EPA standard. Was 99.9985% oil-free water necessary in the middle of
this catastrophic event? Did anyone consider that deploying many vessels
would have provided the capacity to skim the same areas several times.
It gets even better. Obama and company eventually took the Dutch up on
their offer, but only partly. Because the United States did not want Dutch
ships working the Gulf, the United States airlifted the Dutch equipment
from their ships to the Gulf and then retrofitted it to U.S. vessels. And,
rather than have experienced Dutch crews immediately operate the oil-
skimming equipment, the United States postponed the cleanup operation
to allow U.S. crews to be trained to appease labor unions. Much of the
catastrophe and cleanup time could have been averted if it were not for
the usual bureaucracy, rhetoric, politics, and waste.

- Government's layering of new programs on top of old ones inherently
  creates sickening levels of duplication and waste. Some overlap is inevitable because some agencies are defined by *whom* they serve (e.g., vet-
  erans, Native Americans, urbanites, and rural families), while others are
  defined by *what* they provide (e.g., housing, education, healthcare, and
  economic development). When these agencies' constituencies overlap,
  each relevant agency will often have its own program. With 342 separate
  economic development programs, the federal government needs to make
  consolidation a priority. Consolidating duplicative programs would save
  trillions and improve government service. Based on our research, here
  are a few places to begin:
  - **342** economic development programs;
  - **130** programs serving the disabled;
  - **130** programs serving at-risk youth;
  - **90** early childhood development programs;
  - **75** programs funding international education, cultural, and training
    exchange activities;
  - **72** federal programs dedicated to ensuring safe water;
  - **50** homeless assistance programs;
  - **45** federal agencies conducting federal criminal investigations;
  - **40** separate employment and training programs;
  - **28** rural development programs;
  - **27** teen pregnancy programs;
  - **26** small, extraneous K-12 school grant programs;
  - **23** agencies providing aid to the former Soviet republics;
  - **19** programs fighting substance abuse;
  - **17** rural water and wastewater programs in eight agencies;
  - **17** trade agencies monitoring 400 international trade agreements;
  - **12** food safety agencies;
  - **11** principal statistics agencies; and
  - **4** overlapping land management agencies.

And the list of inefficiencies and waste goes on and on and on. I may be showing my private industry bias, but I do not believe that a competent executive team from a public company could mess things up this badly if it was deliberately instructed to do so. Do you think our founding fathers had this in mind when they were framing the Constitution in 1789?

The U.S. Government is clearly broken with no end to the uncontrollable spending in sight. Government spending has been on a track of 15% of gross domestic product (GDP). The current administration has kicked this spending rate up to 25% of GDP, which in the long term, fundamentally changes the role of government toward more control and micromanagement. Let's face it—everything our government attempts to control ends up deep in red ink. During the past 50 years, Congress has transformed subsistence for the unfortunate into lucrative careers for the unmotivated. Our leaders are interested in creating an entitlement-based economy for special interest groups, rather than an opportunity and merit-based economy for the majority of Americans. The more government subsidizes entitlement programs, the less incentive there is on the part of recipients to contribute real value to society.

Our present economy resembles the Reagan years. Back then it was Russia and the invasion and dominance of the Japanese automotive, consumer electronics, machine tool, and several other industries. We are in the midst of a new cold war – an economic cold war with external and internal enemies. Externally, China and other third world nations are taking advantage of our wasteful political system. The wall is unfair trade and regulatory policies that feed offshoring decisions. The weapons of choice are currency manipulations, technology espionage, trade imbalances, intellectual property hijacking, and foreign investment reserves that have increased American dependency and changed the structure of the business economy. Internally, the wall is our incompetent politicians and their continuous

catering to special interests. They have created a sub-society of bottom feeders that contribute to the debt because they feel entitled to the same standard of living as people that work. How is it that a family on welfare can afford a nicer subsidized home, a larger flat screen TV, a newer automobile, top-of-the-line Nike sneakers, and designer clothing for the entire family, iPhones and other handheld electronic devices, and many other luxuries that are unaffordable to people who work? Almost everyone in America knows at least a few people that could legitimately work or are not legitimately disabled, but instead choose to scam our generous government giveaway programs.

Federal, state, and most local government agencies are still in the traditional mindset of more revenue via tax and spend—passing the cost and effect of their inefficiencies on to taxpayers. The problem with government is that it does not know how to turn this situation around. These types of enlightened leadership and strategic improvement competencies and skills do not exist within leadership in government. Improvement in government is viewed as more programs, more resources, more spending, more rights for those incarcerated or on subsistence programs, or more regulations. Are all these programs worth borrowing money from China, Saudi Arabia, and other countries? Our government has been on an uncontrollable spending binge, and the number of government employees has grown by almost 150,000 in the past 3 years. The only options considered are to cut entitlement programs or raise taxes, and no one considers changing the business model of business as usual. "Process thinking" and therefore "process improvement" (e.g., the notion of doing more with less) are missing in government.

Strategic improvement is a foreign concept because it aims to reverse the only model known to a threatening model of accountability and doing more with less. Many do not want things to change because improvement exposes problems with real facts, it promotes structured and standardized processes with metrics, and it provides accountability for results. What government leaders fail to recognize is that voters do not want them to cut programs, but the waste in programs. Strategic improvement makes it possible to reduce "non-value-added" spending while increasing the level of service. Why has no one considered this very doable option? Voters have lost confidence in the Obama administration and Congress to turn things around, and voters have lost confidence in government as a whole: all parties and all promises. Our government has lost total credibility and has become the laughing stock of the rest of the world. A significant injection of new talent is needed in Washington to turn things around.

Government waste is so obvious and so easy to identify but nearly impossible to eliminate with the mindsets of senior members of Congress causing them to endorse "how things work in Washington" by their actions and the processes of the traditional government model to remain unchanged. There are a number of factors that work against the pursuit of improvement in government improvement. Many of these factors are identical to other industries in transition but on a much more grandiose scale. The next section outlines the major detractors from improvement in government.

THE ENTRENCHED ROOTS OF INEFFICIENCY

Many authors have written dozens of books on the topic of the entrenched roots of inefficiency. In terms of strategic improvement, there are also enough details to produce a separate book on this topic. In the interest of keeping things simple, the following section provides a few nonpartisan "showstoppers" of improvement.

THE OBSOLETE GOVERNMENT MODEL

The model of federal, state, and local governments provides no incentive for improvement because from the perspective of government, taxes and spending are represented by an endless source of funding. Agencies make sure that they spend their entire current budget so they can ask for more next year. Their belief system is, "If people want things better, it's going to cost more money." Throwing money and people at problems does not work and will never work. Within government, all it achieves is the manipulation of the true unemployment figures and the creation of more waste. The performance and reward systems in government are also foreign to improvement. No one gets rewarded for saving money in the government, and there is criticism for not spending the entire budget. Government will never be an enterprise motivated by profit and loss (P&L) and earnings per share (EPS), but all leaders in government need to adopt private industry thinking at least to quantify and measure the supposed costs versus value of their services. They also need to learn to "pull the plug" when an agency or program is producing more waste than value. America cannot afford to continue this rampant spending in the interest of socializing our country. When individuals are feeling the personal budget pinch, the last thing they do is apply for more credit cards and then max them out. But, this is exactly what our governments have been doing to us through this recent meltdown with the stimulus package and other spending strategies. The largest Ponzi scheme in history was not that of Bernie Madoff; it was that of the oval office and congressional participants of the meltdown, bailout, stimulus, and healthcare reform packages.

There are no real solutions in sight, no believable plans, just the usual rhetoric. We are being led by an elitist, idealistic group of individuals, many who have held their positions for 25–40 years or more. Most of them have never held a real job and are totally out of touch with America, particularly the people they are supposed to represent. Teetering politicians filter their messages through the *New York Times* and *Washington Post* in hopes of creating the right perception of who they are trying to be. People are presented with several concealed and *spun* versions of the truth. Every politician promises to cut spending and reduce government waste, but they always seem to get swallowed up by the bureaucratic monster. The majority of federal agencies in the national budget are running in a deficit position. Visualize government as a "megacharity." The goal of any charity is to flow as much of the funding possible to the needed source. With government, the more funding that is pumped in, the higher the ratio of waste vs. true value-added services that is provided to the source. Too much of the funding is being digested and turned into waste in the middle. Pumping in more money results in even more waste and less affordable services. It is a vicious cycle and a losing strategy. The bottom line is a total loss of trust and faith in the government's ability to turn things around. Government is grossly inefficient and wasteful. Many taxpayers might support additional taxes on the wealthy individuals and corporations if there was more assurance of spending cuts and controls were put into place. Today, government has a $15 trillion problem; if it is allowed to remain on a spending spree with the inefficient infrastructure, then what are we to do when the deficit reaches $50 trillion or higher? Doing more (better) with less is the answer, and this is called improvement.

Politicians are reactionary by nature because they want to keep their perceived popularity high and seize the moment. Strategy is a process of sticking one's finger in the air to see what direction the breeze is blowing. Government is literally clueless about improvement and root cause problem solving and instead attempts to improve outcomes (e.g., balance the budget, reduce spending, create jobs, secure our borders, improve relations with other nations, etc.). These are outcomes, not root causes of waste. Besides, root cause problem solving would reveal the real facts, and nobody in Washington is interested in the real facts—just their own facts. There are so many versions of the facts that it seems impossible to navigate through the chaos, but that is driven by the combination of the standard attorney mindset and individual political interests. Government employees are supported by powerful unions. God help all of us if they go on strike. It would save $435 million per hour, reduce waste significantly, and maybe balance the budget! We could go on a never ending 5-Why analysis here and construct the largest fishbone in history, but government waste has become so obvious with the availability of technology that it isn't necessary to figure out this mess.

Government has the opportunity to set new benchmarks with improvement if it adopts a common structure and language of improvement (like the Lean Six Sigma Define-Measure-Analyze-Improve-Control or DMAIC) focused on the tall Pareto poles of spending, implements true root cause problem solving, and makes more data-driven, fact-based decisions. However, government is missing the leadership, strategy, motivation, sense of urgency, and core competencies to improve. It is the challenge of everyone to see that these missing components are transplanted in Washington and in our state and local government activities, but not in the traditional Washington way. A few Republican candidates have mentioned Lean Six Sigma in their campaign platforms.

My greatest fear is that the traditional train-the-masses approach and widespread overlaying of improvement initiatives such as Lean Six Sigma on the present government infrastructure and culture might end up as another agency with thousands of people and their associated pension obligations trying to perform an impossible role while creating yet more churn and waste in government. Besides, there is already the GAO, which brings to the surface many significant improvement opportunities that are not acted on. Many of their findings get politicians to look the other way or hide behind the shield of guilt by association. Nevertheless, there is an urgent need for improvement, and the best way to introduce improvement to government is by a more surgical approach, focusing, for example, on Medicare, the Postal Service, or Homeland Security (with a clear expectation of a 100% nonexemption from improvement). However, enlightened and committed leadership is still the prerequisite for success. Introducing formal improvement to government is not a partisan or special interest problem. It is a serious leadership and talent management problem and a matter of injecting new thinking and new talent in government.

LAWYER-UP LEADERSHIP

Another built-in inefficiency is the *lawyering up* of government. Attorneys with conflicting and special interest agendas also bring with them a very different decision-making perspective that is adversarial in nature, which multiplies the significant waste of resources and inefficiencies in the process of government. The basic virtues that go with *doing the right things right the first time* are compromised in favor of popularity and political power. This attorney mindset culture promotes the negotiating away of our tax dollars on earmarks and other pork spending, all in the interest of striking up a deal—a deal that most voters do not want in the first place. This is also the point at which the voice of the customer is replaced with the voice of self-interests. By the way, this leadership style is prevalent at the other end of the legal services spectrum in divorce settlements, malpractice suits, and insurance claims. But, it is insane to litigate what is right or wrong in business.

This is not a personal criticism of attorneys, but of politicians with legal backgrounds with their continued inefficient practices that continue to proliferate bureaucratic government culture, their inattention to taxpayer-centered needs, and their incompetent leadership inability to turn things around. This is undisputable, and everyone watches the knavery every day through a variety of electronic media. Government culture and norms continue to perpetrate waste, questionable ethics, lack of accountability, and financial irresponsibility. Private industry embraces simplification and improvement while attorneys embrace litigation and complexity. Attorneys by nature look at all the reasons why something cannot be done. Private industry is more fact based and fact conscious. In Washington, people fabricate many versions of the facts, and decisions are based on negotiation, not facts. When politicians arrive in Washington, they quickly forget about the people who they are supposed to be representing. Instead, it becomes a political game of give and take, lobbyist politics, and trying to outnegotiate and outlitigate the opponent. The environment is not team based; it is more I win, you lose. Politicians tell everyone everything they want to hear and then pursue their own motives.

The problem with this litigation mindset is that it is irrelevant to a deliberate and structured, fact-based process of improvement to eliminate waste in government. The typical politician approaches to improvement are analogous to negotiating the sale of 50% of an automobile, performing 66% of a triple bypass surgery, or eliminating clothing!

At the end of the day, many politicians do not really stand for much except their own greed and self-interests. In short, there is a severe shortage of true leadership, ethics, formal processes, accountability and controls, and value-added or achievement-based results in government—just billions on billions of shenanigans, personal agendas, greed, and waste paid for by the next generations. There is no doubt that government needs more enlightened leadership and less bureaucratic activity. It is time to attract and inject this new talent from private industry and begin changing the model.

TALENT NEUTRALIZATION

A second factor of the governmental model is the powerful labor unions, which are very effective at preserving the status quo and promoting a lifelong civil service career, leading to talent neutralization. Between the government infrastructure and the labor unions, the environment is nonconducive to improvement. If a new employee comes with too much motivation, the employee is corralled by coworkers until hid or her behaviors are shaped into the expected norm. These people are encouraged not to think and take risks but to *follow the recipe*—the established bureaucratic policies and procedures, whether they are right, wrong, redundant, or inefficient. The performance and reward systems run counter to an improvement-oriented culture and thinking beyond the box. People are rewarded and promoted for acting and thinking myopically and for not making mistakes (i.e., not taking risks). They become molded into their work spaces each day for the next 20 years for the security and benefits of government compensation and pensions. With seniority comes the rigid entitlement practices and "not my job" or "I'm not changing" mindsets, backed by strong union support. Even in the case of justifiable terminations of fraudulent overtime and other criminal offences, employees and their unions usually win out, which reinforces the entitlement even more.

In my experience and that of many others during workshops and education sessions, this is most prevalent in visiting the state motor vehicle offices, where employees are procedure, form, and right-line Nazis, and customers are treated like goats. No thought is given to scheduling during breaks or lunch; employees walk off, uncaring about customers and lines. Most agree that the customer experience is dreaded and horrible. It is somewhere between difficult and impossible to develop any leadership, strategic improvement, teaming, or motivational skills in this environment. There is a huge disconnect between doing one's job and performance.

Many of these agencies are missing basic internal controls, and expenses begin to run out of control. This results in reports of frivolous expenditures for anything from scuba and ski equipment, Ozzy Ozbourne tickets, designer clothing expenditures, automobiles, boats and fishing equipment, exotic vacations, and other unknown expenditures. Government agencies are overstaffed by an estimated 25% to 50%, so why is overtime necessary? Many government employees routinely work overtime not based on need, but as an entitlement to their total earnings. As government adds more employees, it increases the organizational churn and creates agencies that conflict and undermine each other, increase process variation and waste, and accomplish little for their efforts. There is a great opportunity to reduce costs and create jobs by privatization—outsourcing many activities of government to more efficient and less-costly private industry "for-profit" contractors.

THE ECONOMIC MELTDOWN: A ROOT CAUSE ANALYSIS

The purpose of this section is to illustrate the applicability of improvement in government. The recent economic meltdown and slow recovery are the result of events unfolding over decades by both parties.

BACKGROUND

The true root causes of the recent economic meltdown are directly connected to the founding, function, and fate of the U.S. government-sponsored enterprises (GSEs): Fannie Mae and Freddie Mac. The current system of financing home mortgages has its roots in history dating to the Great Depression. As part of the massive economic programs of the Franklin Roosevelt New Deal in 1938, Congress created the original version of Fannie Mae to restore the mortgage credit markets destroyed during the Great Depression. The Federal National Mortgage Association (FNMA) was established in 1938 but privatized in 1968—acting as the guarantor for mortgages issued by other federal agencies and those it purchased in the secondary market.

The Federal Home Loan Mortgage Corporation (FHLMC), more commonly known as Freddie Mac, was established in 1970 as a secondary market conduit for mortgages. Then, the Financial Institutions Reform Recovery and Enforcement Act of 1989 (FIRREA) was passed in the wake of the savings and loan crisis. FIRREA restructured Freddie Mac as a quasi-public corporation with a board selected by shareholders and president. Post–Great Society Freddie Mac was created to compete with Fannie Mae as both were pushed off federal books and into the public sector.

Here is how Fannie Mae and Freddie Mac work: The function and mandate for both GSEs are to create and maintain a secondary market in which illiquid assets, namely, mortgages, can be traded by converting the assets in asset-backed securities that people can then trade in the financial markets. By creating a more liquid market for mortgages, these GSEs are able to make more capital available for housing finance in the United States—GSEs buy loans from banks, depository institutions, and mortgage companies, repackaging them as mortgage-backed securities (bonds), and selling those securities to investment firms (like Lehman Bros. and AIG), which can then be traded by investors in financial markets. By creating a more liquid market for mortgages, these GSEs are able to make more capital available for housing finance in the United States. Both GSEs receive special terms because of the implicit backing they carry from the federal government and are able to borrow money directly from the Federal Reserve as AAA-rated creditors. The mortgages they hold on their books alone totaled about $2.4 trillion as of 2008. This amounts to 20% of the U.S. national debt before 2008.

The original intent was to help people experience the American dream by providing them with the opportunity to own their own home. People who worked hard and saved up the down payment and then paid their bills on time could become recipients of this American dream. In addition, government passed tax legislation that allowed people to take an interest deduction to help pay for their homes. The problem with this logic is that it did not address the concerns of some liberal thinkers out to social engineer society. They argued the following: What about people who do not work hard (or work at all), cannot save up a down payment, do not pay their bills on time, or make other choices about their personal lifestyle and finances? Shouldn't these people also have the right to experience the American dream? This led to the Community Reinvestment Act (CRA) of 1977 under the Carter administration. CRA was pitched as proconsumer, cleansing of racial overtones, and billed as a way to revitalize neighborhoods. The basic purpose of this legislation was to require banks to make credit and mortgages available to more groups of people formerly excluded from traditional financing options with stricter qualification requirements and controls. In effect, banks were required to provide loans to people with poor credit; these loans were in the form of affordable mortgages (i.e., mortgages with low variable interest rates that required that the borrower need not put money down, just pay the interest for a set number of years, and then sell their real estate at a profit).

In 1992, President Clinton said, "I think every major urban area and every poor area ought to have access to a bank that operates on the idea that they ought to make loans to people who deposit in their bank." In 1995, the Clinton administration made radical changes to the original CRA legislation that increased access to credit by inner-city and distressed communities—in short, it provided public underwriting of subprime mortgages. It forced banks to issue over $1 trillion in risky mortgages to questionable recipients (many of whom were not qualified) or face penalties and legal action. This legislation and the Fed maintaining low interest rates expanded lending and created a housing boom. From 1995 to 2005, the number of subprime mortgages skyrocketed and so did the market value of homes. But, the lending mandates of the Democratic Congress were the equivalent of hedge funding all of these subprime mortgages. The whole social engineering effort was a big risky bubble waiting to burst.

In 2003, the Bush administration saw the obvious handwriting on the wall in the form of millions of unqualified adjustable rate mortgages (ARMs) originated without proper documentation and validation of the loan in a period of artificially low interest rates. As interest rates rose, the notion of "everyone deserves to own a home" would quickly turn into a house of cards. Bush recommended a major regulatory overhaul in the housing finance industry, but the Democratic Congress stymied the legislation, claiming that it would seriously limit access to credit for low-income families, and it was not necessary since Fannie Mae and Freddie Mac were both in great financial shape.

The cracks in the dike that led to the meltdown came in 2005 and again in 2007, when John McCain cosponsored the Federal Housing Enterprise Regulatory Reform Act, which recommended tighter controls and more oversight over Fannie Mae and Freddie Mac. Two prominent and powerful Democrats were right in the middle of these actions: chairman of the Senate Banking Committee, Chris Dodd, Democratic senator from Connecticut; and chairman of the Financial Services Committee, Barney Frank, Democratic congressman from Massachusetts.

Chris Dodd and other powerful Democrats, including Barack Obama, opposed this legislation recommended by John McCain and instead introduced legislation to help subprime lenders in financial trouble rather than fix the problem at the source. In July 2008, Dodd said, "What's important are facts—and the facts are that Fannie and Freddie are in sound situation. They have more than adequate capital. They're in good shape." As an interesting side note, our research also revealed that Chris Dodd received money from Fannie Mae and favorable treatment in personal loans from Countrywide Financial. He also received $165,400 in Fannie Mae and Freddie Mac campaign contributions, including contributions from political action committee (PAC) and individuals.

As chairman of the Financial Services Committee, Congressman Barney Frank sits at the center of power in the mortgage industry. In 2003, Frank and his constituents opposed the Bush administration and congressional Republican efforts and the Federal Housing Enterprise Regulatory Reform Act. At the time, Frank was the ranking Democrat on this committee. In July 2008, Barney Frank commented, "The more people exaggerate these problems, the more pressure is put on these companies, the less we will see in affordable housing." How could Dodd and Frank be so incorrect just 2 months away from the September 2008 meltdown?

Our research also revealed that President George Bush had persistently asked the Democratic-controlled Congress seventeen times for more regulation of Fannie Mae in 2007 and 2008, to no avail. By September 2008, Congress declared Fannie Mae and Freddy Mac bankrupt. The Housing and Economic Recovery Act of 2008, signed by Bush July 30, gave the Treasury authority to purchase the assets of the two GSEs should they fail and to create a new agency to regulate them, the Federal Housing Finance Agency (FHFA). However, their conditions quickly worsened, such that they verged on insolvency, leading the FHFA to place them into conservatorship in early September after much prodding from the Treasury and the Fed.

Interest rates rose as everyone predicted, including the ARM interest rates, which increased mortgage payments and reduced the ability of people to pay their mortgages. This in turn increased the number of defaults and foreclosures, which created a bust in the housing market and lower market values of homes (less than the outstanding mortgage in many cases). Also, having put little or no money down, some people found it more worthwhile and easier to just abandon their properties and leave them with their lenders. This in turn reduced the availability of money, which increased interest rates further and rapidly pulled more homeowners with ARMs into bankruptcy, causing stock values of corporations to fall: bingo, the economic collapse of 2008.

Analyzing Root Causes of Failure

The real Five Why root cause analysis of failure is more complicated, but the legislative process could have been improved to prevent or at least minimize and contain the problem. The meltdown was not a partisan problem but a leadership, strategy, and accountability problem. The causes and effects and the decisions in the absence of facts and analysis are so obvious and so predictable. The root causes of the recent meltdown can be traced to Jimmy Carter. Since that time, both parties failed to do anything about this problem. So, are former President Bush's economic policies to blame? The truth is no. Bush's failure was in not effectively persuading Congress to act on this problem. However, the legacies of powerful Congressmen Dodd and Frank should be that they and their faithful followers passed the legislative changes that caused the greatest economic collapse since the Great Depression.

Although it was not Bush's policies that got us into this mess, the meltdown occurred during his presidency, and therefore he is definitely responsible as well.

To give credit where due, Bush did finally manage to sign into law the Troubled Asset Relief Program, commonly referred to as TARP, to purchase assets and equity from financial institutions to strengthen the financial sector and to address the subprime mortgage crisis. Originally expected to cost the federal government (taxpayers) $356 billion, the most recent final net estimate of the cost, as of October 5, 2010, was significantly less, at around $30 billion, including expected returns from interest in AIG. While it was once feared the government would be holding companies like GM, AIG, and Citigroup for several years, those companies are preparing to buy back the Treasury's stake and emerge from TARP within a year. Of the $245 billion invested in U.S. banks, over $169 billion has been paid back, including $13.7 billion in dividends, interest, and other income, along with $4 billion in warrant proceeds as of April 2010. AIG is considered "on track" to pay back $51 billion from divestitures of two units and another $32 billion in securities. In March 2010, GM repaid more than $2 billion to the U.S. and Canadian governments.

Another important goal of TARP was to encourage banks to resume lending again at levels seen before the crisis, both to each other and to consumers and businesses. TARP was set up as a revolving form of credit of up to $350 billion dollars. As money is paid back, it goes into a pool and then is approved by Congress to be used to fix other issues related to the meltdown and mortgage crisis. This appears to have worked thus far. However, TARP and other bailout programs are temporary improvements in response to a large problem that should have been avoided in the first place. Therefore bailouts are basically bad and a last resort action.

Figure 11.1 provides the Ishikawa or cause-and-effect diagram (CED) for the recent economic collapse. CED analysis combined with the Five Whys (e.g., ask why five times to deep dive into root causes) is used widely in private industry for root cause problem solving. The CED displays the effect (recent economic collapse), the primary root causes (main branches of the diagram), and the next-level root causes. This simple analysis reveals significant information and demonstrates the power of root cause thinking and problem solving in government. Root cause analysis after the fact is helpful in preventing similar problems in the future. Root cause analysis in the design and evaluation of legislative plans and risk mitigation might have avoided a meltdown if politicians were inclined to listen to logic instead of their own self-interests. There are a multitude of root causes for the meltdown, all of which could have been avoided by a long-term strategy, competent leadership, a focus on service quality, adequate legislation and controls, and accountability for results. The CED includes the following root causes and subcauses:

- **The Federal Reserve and Easy Money:** For years, the Federal Reserve (which controls the money supply) set interest rates that were exceedingly low, especially from the period after September 11, 2001, until 2005. These low interest rates made it easy for individuals and businesses to borrow money, even those with sketchy credit histories or little income. This helped to create an enormous bubble in home prices

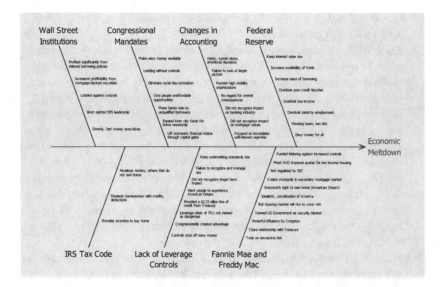

FIGURE 11.1 The economic collapse of 2008. (Copyright 2011 by The Center for Excellence in Operations, Inc. [CEO].)

that we have seen burst in stunning fashion recently. There was much debate during this time and the 1990s about using the Fed to prick asset bubbles, but Greenspan and his supporters adamantly refused, believing the Fed and its operators were not in the position to determine whether assets were overvalued.

- **Fannie Mae and Freddie Mac:** Fannie Mae and Freddie Mac were, until recently, government-sponsored enterprises that operated as private companies with the implicit backing of the American taxpayer. Because of their cozy relationship with the Treasury and their patrons in Congress, Fannie and Freddie took on much more risk than any truly private company could and were overleveraged. That paid off when the housing market was on the rise, but declining housing prices led to the collapse of many of their investments and an eventual takeover by the federal government.

- **Hastily Designed Accounting Rules:** After the Enron accounting scandal, members of Congress acted with extraordinary speed to create a huge new web of regulations. One of these regulations, called mark-to-market accounting, forces institutions to record the market value of their assets rather than the income they produce. This is fine in many instances, but depressed housing prices mean that some assets based on mortgages have a much lower value on paper than in reality. These governance practices drive banks and other investors to "write down" their value, in some cases to the point of insolvency. These practices played a role on the savings and loan crisis of the 1980s. In the recent economic meltdown, the impact of these continued practices creates a serious multiplier effect.

- **Lack of Regulations on Leverage:** Basel II is the revised accord that aims to improve the consistency of capital regulations internationally, make regulatory capital more risk sensitive, and promote enhanced risk management practices among large, internationally active banking organizations. Basel II introduced different weights and corresponding capital requirements depending on the type of assets. The problem with Basel II was due largely to its flawed design, which contributed to the problem of "regulatory arbitrage." A large part of the issue here is a poorly designed risk-weighting system as mortgages were considered riskier than mortgage-backed securities, thereby necessitating higher levels of capital. The other part of this issue was the strategy of hope (hoping that the housing market would continue to rise) and a total lack of action to the warning signals of the collapse.

- **Harmful Lending Mandates from Congress:** The CRA, enacted in 1977 and revised in the 1990s, requires banks to "meet the needs" of all types of borrowers in their communities. It was originally meant to combat racial discrimination but quickly turned into a vehicle for the "affordable housing" goals of many in Congress. In plain English, that means that the federal government effectively strong-arms banks to extend loans to low- and moderate-income individuals, some of whom are unable to repay them.

- **IRS Tax Code:** Our income tax code is filled with hundreds of credits, exemptions, and deductions, some of which are directly aimed at promoting home ownership and lowering its costs. Some of these provide powerful selling points on behalf of home ownership for individuals who might not otherwise be in the market.

The CED analysis summarizes how powerful Democrats in Congress insisted that government-subsidized housing be geared to serve the purposes of social justice at the expense of sound lending practices. With an implicit subsidy to American homeowners in the form of reduced mortgage rates, Fannie Mae and its sister government-sponsored enterprise, Freddie Mac, squeezed out their competition and cornered the secondary mortgage market. They took advantage of a $2.25 billion line of credit from the U.S. Treasury. Congress, by statute, allowed them to operate with much lower capital requirements than private-sector competitors. They used their congressionally granted advantages to leverage themselves in excess of 70:1. This is suicidal for anyone who knows anything about lending.

WOULD IMPROVEMENT HAVE SAVED THE DAY?

Root cause analysis in this particular example is an effective methodology to conduct process postmortems and implement corrective actions and controls. We could continue to drill down into the whys and really understand the problems and what needs to change, but the meltdown and its effects are irreversible. However, root cause analysis is best when used proactively on the front end to evaluate the design of proposed processes and policies to flush out potential risks and consequences or to validate proposed strategic actions and policies. So, a good question to ask is, "Could the meltdown have been prevented?" Best improvement practices presented throughout this book proactively seek potential problems and risks and prevent them from occurring in the first place. When leadership embraces strategic improvement as the cultural standard of excellence, it works. When one looks at the facts leading up to the meltdown, there were many obvious facts and not many unknowns; politicians chose to ignore them because the facts were out of step with their own self-interests. This is the cultural norm in government. Think about this analogy: How many Fortune 100 companies have gone bankrupt by a single bad policy decision? Best improvement practices are backed by strong, unwavering leadership with the ethics and moral compass to do what is right for the enterprise as a whole, regardless of the personal consequences. In business, doing what is strategically and morally correct is not arrived at by litigation. Logically, the answer to this question is yes, but the leadership, culture, and actions of government are not logical like a private corporation accountable to make payroll and stakeholder returns. This model of government is clearly broken and needs to change.

Lessons Learned

The two GSEs were the only publicly traded corporations exempt from Securities and Exchange Commission (SEC) oversight. All their securities carried an implicit AAA rating regardless of the quality and state of the mortgages. The Department of Housing and Urban Development set quotas for GSE investment in affordable housing. Reduced underwriting standards spread into the entire U.S. mortgage market to those at all income levels. A complete decoupling of home prices from Americans' income fed the growth of the housing bubble as borrowers made smaller down payments and took on higher debt.

Wall Street firms that specialized in packaging and investing in the lowest-quality tranches of mortgage-backed securities profited hugely from the increased volume that government affordable lending policies sparked. Wall Street firms, homebuilders, and the GSEs used money, power, and influence to block attempts at reform. Between 1998 and 2008, Fannie and Freddie spent over $176 million on lobbyists. In 2006, Freddie paid the largest fine in Federal Election Commission history for improperly using corporate resources to hold eighty-five fundraisers for those in Congress, raising a total of $1.7 million. In short, our U.S. government manipulated the U.S housing market in an attempt to achieve its idealistic socialization of America. Why was everyone shocked when Fed chairman Ben Bernanke warned the President and Congress just 48 hours earlier than October 6, 2008 (the actual beginning of the meltdown) about a potential economic collapse (just weeks after Dodd and Frank reported that things were fine)? How could a president and his administration, 100 Senators, 425 Representatives, and all of the intelligent resources available to them over several administrations allow this to happen? The meltdown and all other waste are not partisan issues; they are leadership, strategy, infrastructure, and performance issues across many administrations. The ideologies of politicians are great objectives, but the devil is always in the details of implementation. In the interest of being all things to all people, government gets itself too involved with too many areas where it lacks the knowledge and technical expertise and where it should not be anyway. It will take years to recover from this government-sponsored Ponzi scheme. In private industry, leaders would face criminal charges and incarceration for their sickening ethics, underhandedness, lack of accountability and controls, and financial irresponsibility. All of the leaders and decision makers behind the root causes of the meltdown just walked away, leaving the rest of taxpayers holding the bag. This compelling case study demonstrates why there is an urgent need for improvement in Washington and in every state capitol. In the absence of strategic improvement, there are thousands of silent process meltdowns and rampant waste that continue to occur in every government agency.

URGENT NEED: THE INDUSTRIALIZATION OF GOVERNMENT

It is no secret that government spending and government operations are totally out of control with no end in sight. The deficit has risen more since 2008 than in the entire time between George Washington's and George H. W. Bush's administrations. People are so disgusted and "fed up" that it is beginning to feel like a repeat of 1773 when the colonists refused to submit to Parliament's taxation without representation in the famous Boston Tea Party incident. The answer is not "let's throw out the Democrats and replace them with Republicans" or vice versa. What is needed in federal, state, and local governments is the discovery and execution of their own industrial revolution—a major paradigm shift that focuses on the true needs of voting citizens. There are simply too many bottom-feeders in the present government model, more than people who work and make an honest living can afford.

Washington uses the political machine to discredit anyone who speaks out against these wasteful and underhanded policies. People need to open their eyes and brains, get on the Internet, and seek the real truth from nonpartisan sources and avoid listening to the politically motivated popular media. They need to stop placing too much emphasis on the physical appearance or quality of a politician's speaking skills and look at their records. When Thomas Jefferson was elected to the presidency in 1801, there was a high degree of honesty and integrity in the overall government infrastructure and process. People could see the candidates for who they really were and could vote accordingly. Today, government has evolved into a universe of unnecessary complexity, dishonest processes, snake oil marketing, and spin doctors who play with voters' minds and conceal the real facts. Regardless of what is promised in the primaries, candidates go off to Washington and continue the complex legal and political maneuvering games of give and take—and the ultimate outcome is the same: Government *takes* more, voters *give* more, and the waste continues to grow. This will only change if people rise up and express their disappointment with the present infrastructure, process, and decisions of those who are part of this mess.

The first place to trim runaway federal spending is in known waste, fraud, and abuse. Congress, however, has largely abandoned its constitutional duty of overseeing the executive branch and has steadfastly refused to address the waste littered across government programs. In 2003, an attempt by House Budget Committee chairman Congressman Jim Nussle (R-IA) to address wasteful spending was rejected by the House of Representatives, and similar calls in 2004 by Senate Budget Committee chairman at that time Don Nickles (R-OK) were rejected by the Senate. A small group of House lawmakers has formed the Washington Waste Watchers, but their agenda has not been embraced by the whole House.

There is certainly no shortage of information about government waste, and we encourage everyone to investigate these sources as well. Today, government waste investigations and recommendations can be found in hundreds of reports, such as

- Studies published by the U.S. GAO,
- The Congressional Budget Office's *Budget Options* book,
- Inspector General reports of each agency,
- Government Performance and Results Act reports of each agency,
- The White House's Program Assessment Rating Tool (PART) program reviews, and
- The Senate Governmental Affairs Committee's 2001 *Government at the Brink* reports.

The organizations mentioned do a thorough job of identifying and reporting government waste. The problem is that there are few formal corrective actions against government waste.

Powerful politicians suppress these reports because they do not want any affiliation and corrective action—because it will expose their corruption and plug up

the gravy train for others. This practice of inaction promotes even more waste because it will not be acted on, and there are no consequences. Enough is enough.

THE MOST IMPORTANT ACTION: VOTING OUT WASTE

The real issue here is a government culture that promotes leadership incompetence, lack of talent development, and fantasy-based decision making. This culture is promoted the strongest by those who have been in Congress the longest, with very few exceptions in either the Democratic or Republican parties. Washington, like any other infested organization, needs new people with new ideas. In a normal turnaround, replacing leadership that created the problem is the usual first step. However, citizens do not have this luxury with elected officials. For the appointed officials in leadership positions, this is possible with a strong enlightened leader at the top. It would probably do the country good to replace every long-term incumbent in Washington with new blood. If politicians are not representing the best interests of the country and your vote, they need to go—vote them the hell out in future elections and send a strong message of change.

This is the only viable option that effective executives have when their organizations are infested with old thinking and lack of talent.

I like Warren Buffet's recent post floating around the Internet:

> "Pass a law that says that anytime there is a deficit of more than 3% of GDP, all sitting members of Congress are ineligible for re-election." The 26th Amendment (granting the right to vote for 18-year-olds) took only 3 months & 8 days to be ratified! Why? Simple! The people demanded it. That was in 1971 ... before computers, e-mail, cell phones, etc. Of the 27 amendments to the Constitution, seven (7) took 1 year or less to become the law of the land ... all because of public pressure.

The problem is that the people who make up Congress cannot be terminated for poor performance. However, they can be voted out, but this is a longer-term strategy. The situation is not going to change unless the tenured bureaucrats are replaced with new people with new thinking and new ideas. In fact, this situation is a cancer to organizations because people begin to focus more on entitlements than the performance of their jobs. Those who build a real track record for change and turning things around will be reelected in 2 years. Those who fall victim to or continue with the Washington games will be replaced in 2 years. It is hoped this positive trend will continue through the next presidential election because the people are through with the blatant and obvious waste in Washington and in their state and local governments.

A COMPLETE LEADERSHIP OVERHAUL

It is no surprise that leadership in Washington is the underlying root cause of financial failure in government. This is a non-partisan problem that has evolved in a negative direction for the past centuries. In 1824, Thomas Jefferson said, *"I think we have more machinery of government than is necessary, too many parasites living on the labor of the industrious."* Washington has been on the same path but thanks to technology our recent tipping point of financial disaster, it is much more visible. Our American system of government is polarized by the two party system that is more focused on their own party ideologies than compromise around the making of the right decisions. The problems of government are complex, wicked problems that require a strong and seasoned leadership, and balance of different options and viewpoints supported by data and facts. Our system of government is designed around the wrong performance and reward systems, and is also poisoned by lobbyists and special interest groups that literally pay off the decision makers. This removes the motivation and objectivity out of the tough decision making process.

What is the net-net in all of this? Washington is full of weak, lightweight leaders that lack the skills and courage to run anything, never mind the largest corporation in the universe. There is a tremendous vacuum of moral leaders making bad decisions that impact generations of Americans. The Obama Administration is clearly on a mission to create a European-style of socialist democracy while turning a blind eye toward the Constitution and the serious challenges of turning government around. The Administration does not see the need to turn anything around, and views leadership as campaigning for more spending and re-election. Weak leaders procrastinate, point fingers, fabricate, and spin data to support their own ideologies, conveniently explain away poor performance, or blame the prior administration. They hide the truth and avoid the tough decisions that will truly make a difference. They promise everything to everyone because they want to get re-elected and remain on the gravy train. They also make no decisions, or continue to make bad decisions within the context of their special interest pods, with a complete misunderstanding and insensitivity to the longer term big picture of government. Today, too many people view government as a tyranny of political hoagies and liars attempting to socialize America through legislation that caters to special interests at the expense of the true majority. No one can lead when character and the basic core virtues are missing: trust, honesty, vision, integrity, courage, teamwork and empowerment, dignity, respect, commitment, passion, discipline, empathy, listening, and talent expansion of, with, and through others.

So how do we turn this situation around? If we can put all the emotions, excuses, and legalese aside, the answer is through deliberate, tough decision making:

- First, we need to get the best people in Washington. Obviously they are not there now. If you know anything about Lean Six Sigma the data and fact-based evidence of history and where we are heading bear this out. Washington needs a major talent overhaul and now! Congress is clueless about formal and disciplined improvement; they view improvement as a pure win-lose negotiating game.
- Next, we need to install metrics and accountability into this complex system of government. This includes metrics that measure the overall cost and effectiveness of programs, and the individual performance of

key Congress people and other key decision makers. I can envision a visible internet-based scorecard where voters can obtain an up to the minute pulse of the performance of government. Envision a balanced scorecard where Congress and its individual members are rated on a scale of -100 (waste or non value-adding to goals) to +100 (value-adding to goals). Then people can vote based on the facts. Performance-based government that measures the things that really matter is desperately needed. Weak leadership can continue to be weak because metrics, accountability, and consequences for poor performance are virtually non-existent in government. For example, look at the attendance records of politicians; most people in the real world would be terminated immediately for such poor attendance records. The extended infrastructure of unions and special interests assure that decision making remains weak and poor.

- Enough of the namby pamby political leadership games. Obama's super-committee was supposed to place a limit on the debt ceiling and force tough decisions, but the politicians found a way to circumvent what we all pay them to do. Candidly, Obama's super-committee was a deliberate act of indecision while appearing to do something constructive. It was a planned failure from the start to postpone the tough decisions until after the 2012 elections. Government has become the land of make-believe in terms of leadership. Term limits would provide a continuous injection of new talent in government. A firm, balanced budget amendment is a given, but it must also call for new elections to replace incompetent elected officials if they fail to make the tough decisions on a balanced budget.

Historically, organizations in major transition have reached out to expertise outside of their industry to turn things around. Government has been given plenty of time to demonstrate that it is capable of turning things around. It's time for a serious, large scale voter intervention through the election process, and major injections of new business talent from private industry. It's also time to start running government with more of the enlightened leadership, disciplines, controls, and accountability of public corporations. When you think about it, there is no difference: Public corporations are accountable to the stock market, and government should be much more accountable to the American people. The problem is that politicians make sure all of the special interests vote while the voice of the silent majority goes unheard. Hopelessness is not an effective strategy for change, but your voice, involvement, and vote can make a big difference in turning government around.

THE GOVERNMENT TURNAROUND PLAN

Most seasoned executives will openly agree that the best way to deal with complexity is through rationalization and common sense. The first swags at improvement are based on strong enlightened leadership and common sense. Some of the actions may contradict what I referred to as shortsighted attempts at improvement. However, since many of these tactics have never been done in government, they are warranted to begin the transformation process.

The following paragraphs outline a practical approach for eliminating waste and inefficiencies in government. This is a hypothetical improvement plan based on how a strong executive team might turn a sinking ship around. It is based on the typical four stages of a business turnaround but adapted to government. Resuscitating the U.S. economy and global competitive position is a business turnaround situation, and it cannot take 10–20 years. The most successful turnarounds happen as quickly as possible. Stage 1 requires more leadership action than detailed analysis, and the remaining stages pull together a successful government turnaround with a more formal and surgical approach to improvement.

As one reads through the turnaround plan, many activities may appear to contradict the deliberate and structured process of Improvement Excellence™, Lean Six Sigma, root cause analysis, and formal improvement protocol in general. A seasoned, enlightened leader always follows the moral compass, which in the case of government, is our Constitution. This leader also recognizes the need to make the obvious tough decisions without compromising the virtues of this higher, moral compass. Think about these activities in terms of the Six Sigma philosophy. First, processes (i.e., the larger process of government) must be brought under some degree of predictable control before improvement is effective. Otherwise, improvement is like hitting a moving and ever-changing target. Second, the type of activities included in Stage 1 and 2 are of a containment nature, focused on immediate improvements and a cultural wake-up call. Many of these activities are directed to an organization that, as a whole, is operating at less than 1 sigma level of performance! Rocket science is not necessary to begin improvement in these environments because the opportunities are "low hanging fruit" and "fruit on the ground."

The following discussions are not meant to be an all-inclusive and all-encompassing government turnaround plan but to demonstrate the power of improvement thinking and I hope provoke additional value-added discussions with government leaders.

Stage 1: Basic Leadership Containment and Controls

Stage 1 represents the first stage of a typical turnaround situation. The purpose of stage 1 is to stop the bleeding and contain the problem. Government is no different from any other organization that is on a road to disaster and needs to change quickly.

The first step in any turnaround is containment, and this requires enlightened leadership and common sense more than it does Lean Six Sigma. This is not a Democratic, Republican, Tea Party, or other political interest action. The level of nonpartisan waste and spending has not only become disgusting but also become obvious through technology and real-time information. Containment might include the following:

1. Freeze on large-scale stimulus spending, entitlement programs, wage and benefit increases, unused budgets, and discretionary spending. Containment could also include a temporary freeze on the billions of dollars in aid paid to countries and governments that clearly are not sincere friends and allies of America until we fix our own economy and reevaluate their worthiness to receive aid in the future.

2. Replace key appointed officials in government with new blood and new thinking. Even though some of these people will insist on being part of the turnaround, they are the ones who created the problems and are usually less objective in their willingness to change. A good place to begin is in the office of the presidency and the executive branch.

3. Repeal Obama Care, regulatory tax incentives, offshore trade agreements, and other legislation that is counterintuitive to American business investment and job creation. Provide businesses with a positive light at the end of the tunnel so they begin investing in their futures.

4. Initiate a mandatory balanced budget amendment to prevent similar spending disasters in the future. Implement an annual zero-base operating philosophy for government programs and services as part of the budgeting process. Government can no longer freewheel and be all things to all people. The idea behind zero base is that every business, activity, or service provided by the government needs to be justified by a purpose. By this we mean, What is the objective and purpose, and what major societal problem are we trying to solve? Why is this service absolutely necessary? What are the consequences of no action? How does this need stack up against every other priority and need? How does this need fit into the overall purpose and strategic intent? Is the expenditure really necessary, or can it be an add-on to an existing organization? In short, it means legitimate societal and financial justification for existence.

5. Create a small Office of Government Transformation, reporting directly to the president. The objective of this organization is to plan, organize, deploy, execute, and measure strategic improvement in high-impact areas of government. Engage these resources initially on improving the largest known problems as outlined in reports by the GAO, inspector generals, Congressional Budget Office, and other reliable sources. The objective is to focus on no more than five to ten mission-critical areas and not spread resources thin. This will establish improvement traction. Also, the people who participated in creating or allowing the problem to occur should be part of these improvement initiatives. There are many serious process problems reported but left unfixed, and the problems are most likely still occurring. The potential for even larger problems is also possible if these areas are not formally improved at the root cause level.

6. Make the performance of each member of Congress more visible to the voting public. Expose the unethical members of Congress for their contributions to the current economic situation and inform voters of the facts

so they can make the right choices in the next elections. Provide citizens with an ongoing scorecard on how individual members of Congress voted on certain issues or attendance and participation. Members of Congress are usually absent from their job a few days per week while off visiting with special interest groups and rallying support for future votes. They do not even vote on many issues. They were elected to do a job, and most of them are not doing it. What would happen to the regular working person if he or she disappeared for 2–3 days per week?

Stage 2: Immediate Analysis and Corrective Actions

Stage 2 is the next logical activity in a typical turnaround situation. This is an immediate quick diagnostic of the present situation to identify high-impact corrective actions that can be implemented quickly. These might include the following:

1. Downsize government by at least 10 to 15% immediately across the board. This might seem like a contradiction to previous discussions in the book, but this action is feasible in organizations that have been insulated from improvement. This level of cuts will not cause the government to skip a beat because it is so grossly overstaffed. This is a major reason for the inefficiencies and variation in government processes: too much elapsed time and too many handoffs and touch points. Organizations that go through this process find new ways of handling workloads or stopping wasted activities very quickly.
2. Plan to reduce government spending in the next 12–18 months by 25% by more surgical and analytical means. This should be accompanied by an evaluation and cost/benefit analysis of services, value of services, and risks—all quantified and based on data and facts, not emotions. This step is a logical reduction to improve service quality at less cost, not arbitrary cuts to create emotions around key programs. This level of reduction would be literally transparent to citizens and taxpayers. The turnaround is a mission to do more with less. Like General Motors and the rest of private industry, it would be fair to ask for wage and benefit concessions since they are far above the national average. This should also incorporate activity outside Washington, such as national and global staffing (and associated assets) related to war, diplomacy, or continuing to serve as global police, nation builders, and peacekeepers. A mandatory reduction will get people thinking about how to do more with less, which is always feasible and possible.
3. Consolidate all obvious redundant programs and implement basic measurements and controls. As mentioned, some overlap is inevitable, but 80% to 90% of the overlaps can be, and should be, consolidated. Again, this a major root cause of process inefficiencies and variation: too many different processes and too many handoffs and touch points. There are too many bureaucratic fiefdoms and right-hand agencies

running around not knowing what the left-hand agencies are doing. Another objective is to purge many of the bottom-feeder organizations and capable individuals of society who should not be receiving government subsidies or are receiving illegal subsidies.

4. Reorganize government based on purpose and strategic intent. This refers to agencies that may not appear to be redundant but are either working at cross-purposes or not sharing critical processes and information. The objective of this step is to restructure government away from its silos and more toward key government services and cross-functional processes.

5. Implement a balanced scorecard performance measurement process across all agencies and budget responsibility centers. Define the right cascading metrics and begin measuring performance visually through electronic dashboards. Implement more real-time, event-driven metrics for critical government activities.

6. Implement a formal talent management process similar to the GE model. Limit terms for members of Congress. Define talent requirements and acquire new talent from private industry with a for-profit mindset and an appreciation of basic improvement techniques such as Kaizen, Lean, and Six Sigma. Provide opportunities to develop talent and career growth. Establish clear personal performance objectives and reward high achievers. Identify the low performers (e.g., the lowest 5% of performers) and replace these people with new talent annually.

7. Eliminate or significantly limit lobbying as it exists today. This may be an area for increased regulation and legal consequences for unethical practices. No government agency or politician can be independent and objective when being paid off by some special interest group. Maybe it is time for a new bill placing all lobbying funds in a general pool to be used specifically for improving government. Government needs to focus on the moral compass of doing the right things right the first time, not what they are being influenced to do by lobbyists.

Stage 3: Formal Improvement (Lean Six Sigma, Outsourcing, Enabling Technology, etc.)

The federal government doubled in size in just the past few years. The direction of out-of-control government spending cannot continue without severe fiscal and human consequences down the road. Government has been trying to become all things to all people and in the process has continued to spend money for programs on top of programs. Stage 3 is the rationalization of government through strategic improvement. The purpose of stage 3 is to target government's role on the social contracts that deliver the most value to society as a whole and then deliver these services with best-in-class practices. Stage 3 is where government is stablized enough to introduce deliberate and structured improvement such as

Lean Six Sigma, outsourcing, technology-enabled improvement, and other formal initiatives. Activities in Stage 3 might include the following:

1. Rationalize the government's mission, role, and services from a strategic social contract perspective. Government does not exist to solve every problem or be all things to all people—and it should not be. Recognize that social contracts with positive-value propositions are much different from socialization. This is the refocusing of government based on a match of core competencies to specific society needs. Many of the roles of government would be delivered more effectively through state and local agencies or through privatization and third-party providers.

2. Engage in proactive business process improvement across all agencies so that services are not compromised by the 25% spend reduction. At this point, government has less funding and resources, so the only option is to learn how to do more with less—like every other organization has done in response to the meltdown and slow recovery.

3. Conduct a detailed and quantified cost/benefit analysis of government services. This is the basis for implementing an ongoing zero-base philosophy of government based on hard, evidence-based justification. Controls need to be in place to keep government lean and on point. Government does not possess all of the competencies internally for success. Part of this step should include consideration of strategic alliances, contracting, or more efficient and less-costly third-party service providers. There should be a process for sourcing government services to keep costs in line with outside suppliers. Since the budgeting process is zero based, offer incentives to agency executives who do not spend their entire budget.

4. Implement a governmentwide continuous improvement philosophy. This includes creating the environment, leadership, formal infrastructure, motivation, and rewards for superior performance. This step will require the implementation of fundamental changes with government unions, much like private industry has done with its continuous improvement initiatives. The purpose is to drill down and evaluate the productivity and effectiveness of various government agencies and their respective processes, practices. wastes, and costs. Many of these improvement initiatives should produce incredible savings in processes and practices that are now capable of identifying and weeding out fraudulent, unnecessary, and legitimate recipients of services.

5. Redefine performance criteria across all government agencies. Implement digital performance dashboards to monitor activities, elevate process problems, and track resolutions. Eliminate the entitlement pay grades based on seniority and implement a pay-for-performance system.

6. Reengineer the model of government. This goes beyond continuous improvement or business process improvement, beyond another amendment or additional enhancements to existing programs. The objective here is to get people motivated and thinking about how to deliver services directly, by totally different means, and in near real time. This is the integration of improvement and technology across larger-scale transactional and knowledge networks, with much larger opportunities for improvement. The defense segment is well on its way to reengineering weapons systems; they just need to reduce the life cycle costs of these programs.

7. Implement a visible and widely followed and publicized balanced scorecard for every member of Congress. Imagine the voter and nightly news peer pressure of viewing an individual senator's or representative's track record in near real time (e.g., where they stand on issues, what they are leading and involved in, how they voted, attendance, sources of lobbying funds, and other metrics), evaluated into an aggregate score that directly relates to whether their actions are value-added or non value-added to the budget deficit.

Stage 4: Keeping Government Healthy and Trustworthy

When executives allow the "continuous" to escape from continuous improvement, waste finds its way back into the business. The same is true in government. Stage 4 is to ensure that the sustaining infrastructure to identify and improve problem situations quickly is alive and functioning well. Some of the more familiar approaches to maintaining improvement and keeping government healthy and trustworthy include

- Maintaining a formal improvement executive core team comprised of leaders from different areas who discuss in-area and cross-area process issues.

- Having regularly scheduled reviews of key process metrics and performance, open discussions about process issues, and plans for continued improvement.
- Using skip-level diagnostics and audits of key processes to ensure capability and superior performance.
- Exhibiting leadership by walking around, encouraging people to be open about problems without consequences, continuously looking and mining for new improvement opportunities.
- Sponsoring "skunk works" initiatives by which an autonomous team looks for totally different ways of doing things.
- Continuously reporting on improvement projects in queue, in process, and completed. Along with this is usually reporting of benefits achieved by executive responsibility area, by function, by type of improvement, and by other criteria that provide additional intelligence and positive peer pressure.
- Integrating improvement into the formal performance review process as one of the expected criteria for compensation and promotional opportunities.

Government faces a serious dual challenge of turning around its fiscal problems while turning around its loss of trust and respect on the part of the American people. Open and well-communicated strategic improvement is the best way for government leaders to restore the lost virtues and values of honesty, integrity, dignity, respect, trust, and commitment to change with the American people. Strategic and sustainable improvement is also the best way of keeping government and the American people on the right track to a better future.

THE CALL TO ACTION

Our government continues to add $3 billion/day to the deficit, and this is not only an unsustainable model but also a path to economic collapse. While the rest of the world is figuring out how to do more with less, our government continues on an opposite direction of *doing less with more*. Improvement Excellence™— the mastery of developing and implementing successful strategic and continuous improvement initiatives, transforming culture, and enabling organizations to *improve how they improve*—is a philosophy adaptable to all types of organizations. Manufacturing companies, financial institutions, hospitals, government agencies, and other organizations all have processes, wastes, and the opportunity to improve. When it comes to strategic improvement, government is clearly far behind all other organizations. We cannot rewind how we landed in this predicament, but there is a silver lining in the cloud. Government has the opportunity to set an all-time record with improvement—to the tune of trillions of dollars over the next few years.

Although improvement has been around since Frederick Taylor in the 1920s, we are now approaching a new apex of improvement opportunities. Technology is evolving faster than organizations can learn and assimilate it. The new economy is full of new opportunities and new problems—*everywhere*—and more opportunities than ever before. No one is and should be exempt from improvement, including government. Not only are there trillions of improvement opportunities available but also many higher-purpose opportunities, such as restoring American manufacturing and competitiveness and providing an even better environment for our children and their children to flourish economically in the future.

BIBLIOGRAPHY

Carney, Timothy P. 2009. *Obamanomics: How Barack Obama Is Bankrupting You and Enriching His Wall Street Friends, Corporate Lobbyists, and Union Bosses.* Regnery, Washington, DC.

Cho, David, Jia Lyann Yang, and Brady, Dennis. June 26, 2010. Lawmakers guide Dodd-Frank bill for Wall Street reform into homestretch. *Washington Post* A1.

Congressional Budget Office. 2005. "Budget Options." Washington, DC.

Dodd-Frank Wall Street Reform and Consumer Protection Act, Public Law 111-203, U.S. Statutes at Large 124 (2010): 1376.

Gasparino, Charles. 2010. *Bought and Paid For: The Unholy Alliance between Barack Obama and Wall Street.* Penguin Group, New York.

Kleiner Perkins Caufield Byers (KPCB). Figures provided. Mary Meeker, Investment Partner, USA Inc. video, http://www.kpcb.com/usainc.

The Heritage Foundation. http://www.heritage.org/research/reports/2005/04/top-10-examples-of-government-waste, accessed July 25, 2011.

Immergluck, Dan. 2004. *Credit to the Community: Community Reinvestment and Fair Lending Policy in the United States.* Sharpe, Armonk, NY.

Lewis, Michael. 1989. *Liar's Poker: Rising through the Wreckage on Wall Street.* Penguin Books, New York.

Schweizer, Peter. 2009. *Architects of Ruin: How Big Government Liberals Wrecked the Global Economy—And How They Will Do It Again If No One Stops Them.* Harper Collins, New York.

The Fred Thompson Report, 2007. Government at the Brink: *The Root Causes of Government Waste and Mismanagement.* Townhall Press, Arlington, VA.

U.S. Bureau of Economic Analysis. http://www.bea.gov/, accessed July 25, 2011.

12 Epilogue

This is the end of the book, but the beginning of a renewed journey of strategic improvement in the new economy. The aim of this book is to rock the soul and emotions of improvement in everyone, and provide the renewed direction and inspiration for improvement in this challenging economy. Now it's time to "improve how we improve." Executives that follow the guidance and lessons learned throughout the book will rediscover their own new journey of strategic improvement, and create a positive, long term impact on hundreds or thousands of people in their organizations.

Improvement is not optional: The need for improvement never goes away. The longer one postpones improvement, the higher the urgency, pain, risk, and cost of change. Many leaders have lost sight of the most obvious fundamental of business: The only way to get better is to improve current conditions. Executives have traded in their true commitment to Lean Six Sigma for many *improvement dysfunctional* behaviors that are driving culture backwards, all in the interest of illusive short term results. They are too preoccupied with immediate reason leadership and do not know how to improve, or are waiting and hoping for things to change. Consequently, too many organizations are in "improvement-neutral" while their people ask, *"What will the next improvement program be after Lean and Six Sigma runs their course?"* This is clearly symptomatic of the improvement experiences these people have lived through in the absence of strategic leadership and vision, and a formal sustaining infrastructure. Organizations that continue to skip or skim over these critical success factors have no chance to achieve continuous improvement success in the new economy.

Although many organizations are in the midst of recovering from the largest recession since the Great Depression, it is not the end of the world. However, it needs to be the end of excuses for freezing, postponing, or abandoning true structured and disciplined improvement. In the cloud of the 2008 meltdown and slow recovery is a new beginning for organizations. Instability, chaos, turmoil, and uncertainty are the historical norms in business and in life. These attributes are not necessarily bad; they just appear in different cycles and at different levels of disruption. They are just there like electricity, freeway traffic, airline delays, weather, and gravity. There is no need to fear both sets of characteristics because they are uncontrollable events. However, the response to these events is a controllable set of choices. Following this thinking, the past is what it is, but enlightened leadership can create the future by building talent-rich organizations that learn to thrive on uncertainty. Leaders who continue to run around with their hair on fire, change direction by the minute, place a freeze on improvement, wait and do nothing, jettison their people, and destroy culture are on a collision course to failure.

It is time to shift gears and get really disgusted with our current economy and the mediocre responses to it by all industries—especially our government. It is time to reach deep down in the soul and pull out the talent, the burning desire, and the determination to change. The potential to improve is all in there waiting for a different perspective, a different motive, and a different choice—and the ball is in your court. In the book, I used two terms to that relate to this wake-up call: behavioral alignment and enlightened leadership. It is in this face of adversity and devastation that great leaders become enlightened and rise to the occasion. Great leaders do this over and over again and thrive on the challenges that frazzle and cripple other organizations.

Continuous improvement is not achieved through mass training, executive mandates, or a fanatical focus on improvement tools. For most Western Hemisphere organizations, the greatest missing link since the 1980s is that continuous improvement is first and foremost a cultural standard of excellence that is created and sustained by leadership. This cultural standard is backed up by a larger moral purpose of improvement and a greater philosophical reasoning for *improving how we improve.* This larger purpose goes way beyond financial success and way beyond the self in the bold pursuit of workplace security and longevity, best places to work, community relationships, or regaining "Made in U.S.A." global competitiveness. Organizations accomplish this cultural transformation through the right improvement vision and strategy, best practices leadership behaviors, and a formal sustaining infrastructure. Leadership's role is constancy of purpose and to create the successful environment for continuous improvement by the right behaviors, decisions, and actions.

The book has provided the next generation of improvement in the new economy called Improvement Excellence™: the mastery of developing and implementing successful strategic and continuous business improvement initiatives, transforming culture, and enabling organizations to *improve how they improve.* Improvement Excellence™ is based on a combined strategy of Deming back-to-basics, innovation, integration of enabling technology, and adaptive improvement. This framework of Improvement Excellence™ includes three distinct and very important components:

1. The *Formal Sustaining Infrastructure* of Strategic Leadership and Vision, Deployment Planning, and Execution. Embedded in each of these infrastructure elements is what is referred to as the proven "accelerators" of strategic improvement.
2. The *Integration of Improvement Methodologies,* which ensures that the right improvement methodologies and tools are applied to the highest-impact opportunities correctly, creating breakthroughs in systematic performance followed by continuous improvement best practices; and
3. The *Rapid Deployment and Rapid Results Improvement Model* is called Scalable Lean Six Sigma™. The model is based on the simple Pareto principle: Target the largest opportunities and focus limited resources

on these opportunities with the necessary limited set of improvement methodologies. The idea is to focus on the right-big things that keep everyone awake every night.

Enlightened leadership is the engine of Improvement Excellence™. Enlightened leadership is a definable process of continuous personal discovery in the relentless pursuit of excellence and superior business performance. This definable process includes the leadership stages of *insanity, hyperinsanity*, reckoning, and renewal. These stages often create a humbling and sometimes brutal cleansing of current assumptions and beliefs. The true greatness in leadership arises when organizational success depends on innovation and doing something that has not been done before. Enlightened leaders internalize this noble new end in mind with the utmost courage and confidence of their convictions, even though they may have not worked out all of the details. Yet they strive for and lead others down a renewed path of success while unfolding this new strategic destination—much of what appears at first to be impossible to achieve. Enlightened leaders recognize the need to make these proactive adjustments or bolder course correction decisions immediately while time is on everyone's side. Enlightened leadership is a continuous cycle of innovative leadership improvement.

A crucial take-away from the book is that no organization is exempt from improvement. As mentioned, the need for improvement never goes away. The only way to get better is to improve current conditions. Every organization has hidden waste and non-value-added activity. However, there is a larger barrier to improvement, especially in industries outside manufacturing that have been insulated from the need to improve. Underlying the history of public and private corporations is a long presence of productivity improvement by their industrial and systems engineering functions. Although it is true that manufacturing organizations have nearly 100 years of experience with improvement, the discipline has evolved significantly in these organizations—particularly into the professional, knowledge, and transactional process space. Public and private corporations possess the deepest knowledge and experiences about improvement because of their history. Much of their professional, knowledge, and transactional process activities are converging with the requirements of industries such as healthcare, financial services, not-for-profit agencies, and federal, state, and local governments. These industries can and must adapt Lean Six Sigma and other strategic improvement initiatives because they all have a tremendous opportunity and urgent need to improve. Many of these organizations are at the tipping point at which they can no longer rely on an endless supply of revenue funding or pass the cost of inefficiencies on to customers. Lean Six Sigma is very adaptable to the uniqueness and complexities of all industries. When organizations fail at this adaption process, it creates many questions, unknowns, and risks. When they fail to achieve success, it is not the fault of Lean Six Sigma. Most of the time, organizations make much quicker and impressive progress when a seasoned improvement consultant helps them through this adaptation process. Lean Six Sigma must also be approached as an investment with an entitled return on investment (ROI), not a cost or another high-risk program. Remember: When improvement is approached and managed as an investment, there is also an ROI in the cost of external help. Relatively few organizations are successful on their own; the most successful Lean Six Sigma organizations reached out for external help on their journeys. The cost of a poor start or a failed initiative is considerably more than the cost of external help. A handful of hospitals and state agencies have made significant strides with Lean Six Sigma and have achieved remarkable results. It is time to get the rest of the industries on board. We need to make U.S. healthcare more accessible and affordable, and we definitely need to reduce the country's $15 trillion deficit.

Two other facts about Lean Six Sigma and strategic improvement have been mentioned over and over in the book with different selections of words. Below are additional words of wisdom and encouragement to reinforce the renewed journey of improvement in the new economy:

1. First, improvement is not revolutionary; the successes only appear that way. Some readers may be intimidated or overwhelmed by what it takes to achieve continuous and sustainable improvement. Others may view it as a challenge of starting a revolution or introducing major disruptions in their organizations.
2. Second, improvement invigorates organizations and creates strong positive cultures. Improvement is often viewed negatively as if people are losing something. This loss is perceived loss, and successful improvement initiatives generate much more gain than loss – especially for the workforce. The cultural climate in high performance improvement organizations is much more positive and upbeat than in improvement dysfunctional organizations.

Let's elaborate on the first point. When one looks at the benefits in a high performance improvement organization, it is both impressive and threatening. How will we reduce warranty and returns by $35 million? How will we reduce patient length of stay by 50% or boost revenues to an equivalent of a $210 million addition? How will we reduce cost of claims by $28 million? How will we reduce time to market for new products by 80%? How could we possibly reduce operating costs by $300 million? How will we increase revenues by $280 million? It requires a revolution and lots of disruptions, right? Wrong, dead wrong!

Those who treat improvement as a revolution, a "copy and paste" initiative, a frantic masquerade, or emergency response to new problems fail miserably. High performance improvement organizations live and breathe improvement every minute of every day. Leadership is committed for the long haul by their consistent behaviors, decisions, and actions. The organization begins their journey with a well thought out and shared vision and implementation plan, and the risks are reduced to zero. At a high level, improvement is a philosophy and cultural standard of excellence with a higher purpose, and is weaved into the daily thoughtware of how people work. At a tactical level, improvement is a structured, controlled, deliberate, and continuous process of making things better; the specific methodologies and tools are the means, not the ends. When people inside these organizations look at where they began and where they are now, their perspective of the journey has been much more of a controlled evolution, not a revolution. When an organization improves every day the benefits of their evolutions quickly add up to revolutionary proportions.

Let's now elaborate on the second point. In high performance improvement organizations, the values of honesty, integrity, candor, courage, teamwork and empowerment, dignity, respect, commitment, passion, discipline, empathy, listening, a clear vision and expectations, and talent expansion (of, with, and through others) are practiced like a faith.

- People are engaged and empowered, and lead and influence change. They joke about their old archaic ways of doing things. They have a cross-functional process and teaming view of the business and make improvements that benefit the larger process.
- They have a stronger view of relationships and collaborating directly with others than they do of a formal organization chart. They proactively seek out opportunities and prevent problems before they occur. When problems occur, they deep dive into root causes and eliminate problems so they and others do not have to deal with the same issues over and over again.
- They are constantly tapped by management and others for their knowledge and experience.
- They are data-driven and fact-based, and expect the same conduct from others (and have a low tolerance for those who are winging it). They thrive on change because they have the skills to deal with and benefit from change.
- These are high spirited teaming organizations where people look forward to coming to work and making positive contributions every day.

Talent is the key to evolving an organization's basic values, competencies, and fundamentals of improvement—continuously! Great organizations also stick to their basic values and fundamentals of improvement before, through, and after the chaos cycles. These high performance improvement organizations will also achieve the greatest benefits from improvement in the future.

Welcome to the second decade of the 21st Century and beyond - the greatest improvement renaissance in history. In the next decades, every industry can and must improve, especially the new entrants to Lean Six Sigma and strategic improvement. Here we all sit looking at literally trillions of dollars of new opportunities across all industries. Personally, I become very irritated when I listen to claims by educators, politicians, newscasters . . . and several executives that "America can no longer compete." Come on, we can do better than this! The executives of all industries are both capable of implementing improvement, and compensated for their moral obligation to reel in these opportunities. Collectively, we have the opportunity to accomplish great things or sit passively while other countries show us the way. Beyond mapping the renewed journey, my hope is that this article and my forthcoming book energizes the masses and restores America's global competitiveness and excellence across all industries. Through this book I solicit your passion, commitment, and help in this challenging but achievable improvement renaissance.

Index

A

Abbot and Costello example, 102
accelerating continuous improvement
  acceptance, 43–46
  building, 36–37
  deployment planning, 38–39
  diminishing value and waste, relationship, 28
  DMAIC, 33–35
  essentials, 23–30
  execution, 39–41
  framework, 32–33
  fundamentals, 23
  implementation infrastructure, 35–41
  improvement bathtub curve, 26–27
  improvement excellence, 30–33
  individual project paths, 40
  next generation of improvement, 30
  payoffs through layoffs, 28–29
  Scalable Lean Six Sigma™, 41–43
  strategic leadership and vision, 37–38
acceleration entrapment, 7
acceptance, 43–46
accessibility, 66
accounting rules, 235
achievement-based education, 104
acknowledgment, 59
acquisition, 114, 172
adaptability, 143
adaptive and innovative improvement, 101
addition to work vs. part of work, 25, 144
adjustable rate mortgages (ARMs), 232–233
admissive characteristic, 66
A3 document, 86
advertising effectiveness, 186–187
airline tickets example, 222
aligning organizational behaviors, 56–60
Amazon, 75, 158, 159
analysis, 34, *see also* DMAIC (Define-
          Measure-Analyze-Improve-Control)
answers for why, what, how, where, when, 62
Apple, 75, 155, 158
applications, hospital
  benefits, defining and quantifying, 209–210
  cost issues, 197–199
  fundamentals, 197
  implementation plan, 212–215
  improvement expectations, 215–216

  improvement opportunities, 203–205
  leadership enlightenment, 201–203
  Lean Six Sigma, 199–215
  return on investment, 210–212
  thinking process vs. silos, 205–208
  value proposition, 208–212
assessment, current performance, 78–79
assumptions, unrealistic planning, 178
AT&T, 158
attentiveness, best practice leadership, 65
attraction relationship, success/culture, 153–154
authenticity, 65
automated dashboard format, 196
automation, 157

B

background, economic meltdown, 230–233
balance, best practice leadership, 65
balanced performance management systems, 193–196
Bank of America, 158
bank transaction tax, 48
basic essentials, 23–30
bathtub curve, 26–27
behavioral alignment, leadership, 56–60
Belichick, Bill, 113
"below-the-line" improvement activities, 99
benchmarking, *xix*, 1, 79
benefits
  business diagnostic, 79–80
  cumulative mapping, 152
  hospital application, 209–210
benefits package value analysis, 192
Benny (shop steward), 12–15
Bernanke, Ben, 237
best practices
  change management, 108
  conscience, 65–67
  discipline, 64–65
  fundamentals, 60
  knowledge, 62, 118
  leveraged mentoring, 118
  passion, 62–63
  project management, 133
  vision, 60–61
bill HR 4646, 48